*For Bi, a free [...]
(I helped make th...
— Jordan.*

About the Author

Maya Thorn is a traveller, a feminist, and a seeker of peace. She believes in magic. *Psychonaut* begins with her as a teenager, discontent with society. She is now in her early thirties and still in awe of this heartbreaking, beautiful, world. She loves to write, and this is her first book. She writes about what she knows best: Her experience as a human, thus far. Please have patience with her teenage self, she does mature, in tandem with the prose.

For Bianca,
a free spirit
(I helped make this)
— Jordan

Psychonaut

Maya Thorn

Psychonaut

Olympia Publishers
London

www.olympiapublishers.com
OLYMPIA PAPERBACK EDITION

Copyright © Maya Thorn 2021

The right of Maya Thorn to be identified as author of this work has been asserted in accordance with sections 77 and 78 of the Copyright, Designs and Patents Act 1988.

All Rights Reserved

No reproduction, copy or transmission of this publication may be made without written permission.
No paragraph of this publication may be reproduced, copied or transmitted save with the written permission of the publisher, or in accordance with the provisions of the Copyright Act 1956 (as amended).

Any person who commits any unauthorised act in relation to this publication may be liable to criminal prosecution and civil claims for damage.

A CIP catalogue record for this title is available from the British Library.

ISBN: 978-1-80074-034-1

First Published in 2021

**Olympia Publishers
Tallis House
2 Tallis Street
London
EC4Y 0AB**

Printed in Great Britain

Dedication

This book is dedicated to Lynx. I am so grateful for your love and for you believing in this book.

Acknowledgements

I would like to thank the friends that I made throughout my journeys, and even the ones I've lost. Thank you for making the world less lonely. Also, a special thank you to Jordan Mowat for your help editing the manuscript in the early days of bringing *Psychonaut* to life.

Run

This story begins with an ending.

    My heart pounds violently in my chest. I sprint as fast as I can. I need to get to the other side of town without being recognized; caught. My leg muscles sting, but my goal is more than enough fuel. Bookbag on back, I awkwardly lug my heavy guitar case, switch it from right arm to left arm, mostly succeeding to not bash my legs with it. Dropping it is unthinkable. It's stuffed with everything that could fit, with everything that I will need.

    It's a school day, making me even more conspicuous than I already am in this bleak, xenophobic-ridden hole called Greenwood. Everyone I've met in the couple of months of living here have been racist morons, hillbilly self-proclaimed "fag beaters," brainwashed military patriots, or religious zealots. I don't belong here. I never could.

    I make it to Sally's, the small diner at the edge of the dull, decaying, main drag. Here the asphalt turns from road to highway. It's the only place in town that sells bus tickets: my portal to freedom. I dart up the steps and a gust of wind slams the door shut behind me. Eyes glance up at me, but everyone is too polite to let their eyes linger. Most of the dozen or so small tables are taken. The diner's full, but lifeless. Identical plastic tablecloths host people that also match; tired, weathered, conservative. There isn't anything original or cheery in here. It suits the town perfectly. I go to the counter and ask if they sell tickets for Greyhound buses going to Halifax.

"Twenty-three dollars, please," replies the short, plump, middle-aged woman behind the counter. Relief cascades over me as she dusts flour off her hands onto her apron and sells me the pass. This escape attempt might actually work. This attempt *has* to work.

I try to slow my breath as I take a seat at an empty table by the window. Eyes vigilant, I'm ready to duck if someone that would recognize me were to enter the restaurant. My classmate Jory is the only one with information on my whereabouts. I'm pretty sure I can trust her with my secret or, at very least, to be apathetic. I take my journal from my backpack, hide my head in it and start to draw. If I look busy no one will try to strike up conversation. My presence is already peculiar enough. Surely, Sally's is full of regulars. People that are all already familiar with each other.

Regulars, doing, eating, saying what they regularly do, day after day; killing time in their boring lives.

I glance at the gaudy wooden cuckoo clock on the wall, again. The minute hand has barely budged. Every second feels like ten too many. The clock hand crosses nine thirty and a nervous drip of sweat slides down my brow. My heart thuds in my chest, as if also wanting to flee. The bus should have arrived minutes ago. Nervousness escalates with every inhalation, and each exhalation.

Finally.

A rundown Greyhound bus trundles into the parking lot. I slip my sunglasses over my eyes to disguise myself as best as I am able, then go outside and hand the driver my ticket. Bored and barely looking at me, he hands me a tag for my guitar case.

I hastily toss the heavy case in the luggage compartment and rush onto the bus. Sitting down is glorious. Even the stained, tattered cushion seems magnificent in its own way. I've pined for and planned all the details of this moment for months. And suddenly it's not a futuristic fantasy: It's literally happening. The engine revs to life, and I watch the town and the people that had me trapped slip away.

The bus takes the slow route. We pull into all the miserable, backwater towns along the way to Nova Scotia's capital. They're all the same. A smattering of small ramshackle houses with a general store advertising a post office and liquor sales. Nothing more. The only thing we pass that remotely stands out is a sign that directs to a *"Zoo! Exotic Animals from All Over the World!"* I'm boggled. The people here aren't in captivity like the zoo animals... yet they're here. How did so many people wind up in these destitute places? But what really baffles me: Why do they stay?

The bus weaves through the orange and yellow trees that line the highway. The *only* beautiful thing here is autumn's effect on the leaves. Each day the colour of the foliage would change vividly enough that, for a moment, I could pretend that I was somewhere different than the day before. Suddenly, it occurs to me that my dream has become my present reality. My long-buried smile surfaces and shocks me as I catch it reflecting back at me through the windowpane.

We pull into *another* dismal little town. There's a couple outside that are having a hard time saying bye to one another. They share a hug and a kiss, then the girl joins the queue coming onto the bus. Seconds after, she turns around and goes back to her guy for another goodbye smooch. They repeat this a few times. It's adorable and refreshing to see people in love.

The girl finally peels herself off of her sweetie and steps up onto the bus. Her long colourful patchwork skirt gently sways against the seats lining the narrow aisle. We make eye contact, and smile, and she takes the seat next to mine. Her big hazel eyes pierce mine and, beaming confidence, she gets conversation started.

"What's your name?"

"Sarah," I say, with my usual air of dissatisfaction. "What's yours?"

"Tara Nova." The word blows over me like a gust of wind.

"Nice name!"

She grins. "The only good thing my father ever did for me was give me this name." I laugh.

"What are you doing?" she asks.

"Running away," I admit, knowing I can trust her.

Now she laughs, and says, "Me too."

Assuming I was speaking metaphorically, she goes on to talk about the problems she's avoiding.

Problems that are still going to be there when she gets back. Student loans, behind on rent, an ex, that's stopped paying child support… I guess this is one of the few times in my life where someone mistakes me for being older than I am. She asks me what I'm running away from.

"Home."

"What! How old are you?"

"Sixteen."

She closes her eyes for a moment and relaxes into her seat with a sigh. "All right, sister, tell me your story."

It all spills out. How I've been devising my escape since before my parents forced me to move to Nova Scotia a couple of months back. To leave, I needed money. After school, I spent my afternoons picking juice apples. Every crate of apples brought me eleven dollars closer to my seat on this bus. On average, a crate would take three hours to fill. Those frigid orchards were as vast as they were eerie. Only a couple of old, drifting drunks were as desperate as I to work the orchards for a fraction of minimum wage.

I had to shake the trees with a giant metal rod then duck as the apples rained down, often pelting me in the head. Next was the crawl. Down on all fours on soggy ground, picking up and tossing the apples into huge wooden crates. Often it would be raining and I'd be shivering in the dampness. Some of the apples were rotten, and I'd slide my bare thumb through nasty, wormy sludge. My back and legs would ache after the afternoons and evenings hunched under the trees. It was absolutely worth it though. I had a purpose — a plan — the one that's unfurling right now.

Tara Nova has her arms stretched around my shoulder and is in a deep squeeze by the time I finish describing how this moment came to be.

I unzip my knapsack and show her the nut bar stockpile. Every morning, going to school, I'd take two from the pantry. Every night, I'd stash both bars. Nut bars galore... in the pockets of pants, toes of shoes, or simply just wrapped in clothes, at the back of my closet.

"If I eat minimally, I've got enough food to sustain myself for a few months."

She arches her eyebrow, visibly impressed.

"I'm heading to BC. I used to live there. My best friend Chantelle and her grandma Macy, say I can stay with them when I make it back."

Like many others that I've met in the east, when I talk

about the West Coast, their eyes ignite with sparkles of wonder. It's different there. Way different than this side of the country. The land's more beautiful, vast mountains, oceans, and rainforests. The weather's more forgiving, too. It's as if it influences the folk in the west to also be more warm, open, and content.

We chat and laugh the whole ride to Halifax. She tells me that, in spite of being a new mother, she supports what I'm doing. Tara Nova takes a worn notebook from her bag, rips out a square of paper and scribbles her address onto it.

"Send me a letter. Let me know how things turn out for you!"

The Greyhound pulls into the station and we follow the slow file off the bus. We hug goodbye — this time, one is enough — and wish each other good lives. I grab my guitar case and locate the ticket booth.

Determined to sound and look as adult as possible, I puff out my chest as I approach the counter. With the deepest tone I can manage, I ask for a ticket to Vancouver. The vendor looks me in the eyes, then narrows his. The beginning of a question seems to dance on his lips. In my head I telepathically encourage him to just sell me the ticket. He drops what seemed to be the urge to inquire where my guardian is and returns to his monotony. A ticket prints out and he hands it over, no questions asked. I do my best to stay calm and act as if this bus ride will be nothing more than a boring hassle. Joy is totally out of place in the clusters of grumpy budget commuters. But, once a bit of distance is gained from the ticket booth, I can't help but smile from ear to ear. It takes all I can muster to not skip my way across the terminal. Head in the clouds, I nearly stumble over the bulging luggage and crossed legs of a fed-up looking traveller. He looks at me, annoyed and spiritless — does he not realize that this is where destiny takes root?

There are several hours and several stops before my next bus reaches its destination: Montreal, Quebec. There I'm to connect with a bus going to and through the gargantuan province of Ontario that hosts the Great Lakes, vast coniferous forests, and endless expanses of snow in its north. Night comes and I toss and turn sleeplessly among the dim, sporadic lights. Somehow I manage to refrain from the urge to sprawl my legs across the lap of the stubbled old man sleeping next to me. At around six a.m. we pull into the Montreal bus depot. The driver calls, "Last stop! Dernier arrêt!" and corrals us out into the terminal.

Half awake, but fully alive, I find the gate where my next ride is scheduled to depart from. I've got about an hour to wait. The station is ghostly. All the restaurants, shops, and cafes are closed. I sit down and people-watch from the sparse selection. Most sit and rub their tired eyes. Some stroll in idle circles. Despite the sleepless night passage, I effortlessly stay alert. There is no way I'm missing my chariot.

Two

A vaguely familiar man enters the station and my world quakes. I'm almost certain he's Gregoire, an uncle that I've met on a couple occasions. He's fervently pacing up and down the platforms, doing a scan of each gate. His eyes bulge wild and wide beneath his receding brown hairline. I turn my face away, praying that he'll rush past me. A tense minute passes and I discreetly peek back, hoping he's gone, only to lock eyes with him. What went wrong? At this point my mom was still supposed to think that I'm sleeping over at Jory's house....

He clears his throat and, in aggressive French, states, "Hi, Sarah. You have to come with me."

"Non!" I refuse.

Gregoire grabs my arm. I yank myself from his grip and, with a hard, determined stare I proclaim, "I'm getting on the bus. This isn't your decision. This isn't your life!"

Flustered, he tries again, this time with a whisper of weakness cracking through his voice. "Come with me, *please*."

"Leave me alone!"

He rests a heavy hand on my shoulder. As I try to wriggle out of his grip he declares, "If you don't come with me, I'll phone the police."

The air thickens. I hold my ground in silent desperation. He takes his phone from his pants pocket and dials the three threatened digits: neuf-un-un. I try to maintain composure, desperately hoping that my bus will board and leave the station before the cops arrive. I'm stupefied by the threatened authority of the police. Would they chase me if I ran? I bet I could outrun them.

After several tense minutes, my bus's engine starts to rev. The driver steps out and starts taking tickets and loading passengers. I move towards the lineup. Gregoire tries to pull me away from the queue, and the chauffeur turns to us and asks what all of the commotion is about. My uncle starts explaining to him that I'm in the midst of running away from home. That I'm supposed to be in my parents' custody, two provinces away. It's obvious from my uncle's tone of voice that he expects the bus driver to agree that what I'm doing is unacceptable. Gregoire yammers on with an air of keeping the conversation between the adults, while maintaining a casual grip on my upper arm. The driver cuts him off, turns to me and asks me how old I am.

"Sixteen."

The driver laughs and tells my uncle that, when he was sixteen, he left home, too. "I turned out fine. Let her go!"

I almost burst into tears of laughter at this small miracle. What are the odds that this driver would be here, driving this bus from this station? It's as if it's more magic than coincidence. Synchronicity... is that what this phenomenon would be called? I've heard of such a thing, but have never experienced it. Or at least, have never noticed synchronicities happen to me.

My bamboozled uncle is at a loss for words. My new pal, the bus driver, has bested him. Gregoire releases my arm. The driver takes my ticket and warmly waves me onto the bus. As I take my first step, two stern policemen strut over. A colder, stronger hand is placed on my shoulder. I tremble as it pulls me backwards. My heart sinks. I ask the driver if he can wait a few minutes. He winks and says he can stall the departure, a little. I turn back to negotiate with my uncle and the oinks.

They tell me that since I'm under eighteen years of age, I am not legally able to decide where I live. Until one turns eighteen, they aren't allowed to leave home without parental consent. I've done my research. I waited until I turned sixteen. I inform the police that the laws vary from province to province, carefully reciting the spiel I've memorized in the event that it would be needed. In Nova Scotia, the laws differ and one's able to decide for themselves where they live when they're sixteen. In stilted French I explain to them that sending me back would be futile, because the law in Nova Scotia would simply permit me to leave again. Internally, I notice myself praying to a God that I hold much doubt in, begging that I wont be forced to return Nova Scotia. I would not be able to afford another bus ticket if sent back. Apple season is over.

The cops make a phone call to verify if the law in Nova Scotia is different than it is in Quebecs. It is.

"All right then!" the bus driver ushers them on, apparently having listened in. "Let her get on the bus!"

"Oui!" I whoop.

The policemen don't relent. We continue to debate as the station starts to come alive with people pretending not to stare. Passengers on what should be my bus are starting to complain. "We're late! I've got a connection to make!" The bus driver gazes at me compassionately for a held moment, then looks at his watch and apologizes, he can wait no longer. My heart sinks and physically aches as I thank him for trying to help. He wishes me luck and I have to turn my head so he won't notice the tears welling up in my eyes. The door folds shut, and I watch the bus slip out of the station, carrying my freedom with it as it vanishes.

Gregoire asks me to spend the day with him. The cops say I'm either going with my uncle or to the police station. I choose Gregoire and the police walk away, satisfied. As I follow Gregoire to his car, I state that he owes me money for the bus that he made me miss, and refuse to get into his car until he compensates me for the fare. He promises he'll buy me another ticket tomorrow, if I still want to leave. I smell bullshit and ask for the money upfront. He assures me several times that I can trust him. It sinks in that I don't really have a choice but to give him the benefit of doubt. Maybe all is not lost. Maybe my wings aren't clipped. Maybe. I try to stay optimistic through my desperation.

Gregoire drives me through Montreal towards his home. The city has barely started to stir itself awake. We stop at a red light, though there are no cars passing. I break the long, tense silence, and ask him how he knew that I would be at the bus station. Apparently, at school, Jory gossiped about my whereabouts. Some goody-two shoed, vapid moron, phoned my mother. Jory was the only person I had told about my plan. I thought I could trust her. She had even agreed to drive me to the bus station from school. But, the night before, she phoned me, and said she had crashed her car. I actually believed her at the time. I was a fool for involving someone else in my plan. I didn't even need her. I figured out how to make it to the diner on my own, ran that ridiculous mad dash across town to get my ticket to Halifax. Now here I am, in Greg's minivan. Thanks a lot Jory, you dumb, ignorant, sheep. Are you so boring that you need to gossip and fuck up other peoples' lives to be interesting enough to talk to? Pathetic.

We pull onto a one-way street, and Gregoire parks the van. I'm ushered through the doorway under a spiral staircase of a small brick house. My aunt and three cousins are at the table eating breakfast. Jaws drop at my arrival. All conversation ceases.

"Bonjour," I say, not sure why I'm bothering to concern myself with pleasantries, to act like I'm something other than the elephant in the room.

They finish eating, get dressed, then each leave for their schools and job. Barely two days into trying to take my life into my own hands, these daily routines and destinations already seem undesirable, confusing, even *ridiculous* to me. Gregoire takes the day off work. He joins me on the couch of the family room, mutes the TV that was left on from the morning news, and rekindles our dispute. Continuing with his presumptuous attitude, he tries to point out to me that I don't know how to take care of myself, that I won't be able to. He asks all sorts of questions. Questions like how I will feed myself. So, I show him the mountain of nut bars and insist I could find a job before all the bars are consumed.

"You know, you need identification cards to get a job and to enroll in school!" He says, as if pterodactyls would swoop down and devour me if I were to turn away from conventional school. I show him my SIN card, birth certificate, and a photo I.D from school. His facial expression shifts as he looks over my documentation, fanned out on the table like a royal flush. He tells me he's impressed, and perplexingly proud. It's probably a ruse, a shift in strategy, but he almost seems genuine.

We spend the day hopping on and off the metro and

walking around the interesting parts of the city. Gregoire somehow succeeds in convincing me that Montreal is filled with musicians, artists, vegetarians, all forms of my favourite kinds of people. I've never lived in a city before and find myself being seduced by the seemingly unlimited potential of interesting people to meet, music to dance to, art to participate in, and cultures from all over the world to learn about.

While we're waiting for the lunch bill after a vegan buffet, Gregoire announces he's postponing reimbursing me for my bus ticket: I have to wait three months. He gives me an ultimatum — stay in Montreal and live with his family, or return to my parents' house in Nova Scotia. I'm livid about the betrayal and don't trust our new "deal," but am powerless.

Without a millisecond of hesitation, I choose Montreal. At least I made it out of my home in Nova Scotia. I guess that was really the main goal, I had just never considered going somewhere other than back to Vancouver Island. I still deeply miss my friends back out west. But there is an intrigue to living in this city. So, I'm kind of okay with being here, for a little while. Am I naive to think Gregoire will actually buy me a bus ticket in a few months? Doesn't matter — it's enough time to come up with something lucrative enough to make my way across the country — panhandling maybe?

Living with a different family is revelatory. Every household and upbringing are a unique environment. This one is a drastic and healthy one. My cousins actually get along with each other. They laugh, talk, and share things without fighting. My aunt and uncle are happy and in love. They spend lots of time together, cook, talk, walk the dog. At mealtimes conversation and laughter flow. Everyone is kind to one another. It's shocking and refreshing.

I'm enrolled in the only English school that would accept a new student. It's rated as one of the worst schools in the city. At first, the hard edge seems exciting, admittedly the kind of place I've only experienced vicariously through TV. But it turns out to just be depressing. Because of gangs, we aren't allowed to wear any colours. The teachers record whenever someone leaves the classroom to use the bathroom, like it's some kind of mental hospital. The popular kids are just snobby assholes that make fun of the poor kids, which there are a lot of. I actually find myself missing the school I went to in BC. I used to dis it because it was mostly filled with over-privileged sheeple. Now, I realize how privileged of a complaint that was. At least the atmosphere was relaxed there.

Last year was my first year of high school. I became dear friends with a tribe of special and inspiring people. They were all activists and artists. Each one of them was refreshingly unique, deep, and fun. We shared affinities and passions, and became super close through lots of laughter and adventures. All of me is still set on getting back to BC. I just have to wait a few months.

One of my friends from BC gets me in touch with her older sister that moved out here. She invites me to a potluck at her and her roommate's apartment. Everyone's older than me. It's intimidating. They all have interesting stories of what they've done since finishing high school. Hopping trains to get out east, travelling through Mexico, building wells in Cambodia; some of them are even ultra-talented, semi-successful musicians, but they're actually down to earth about it, not pretentious at all, making them even more intimidating! They all have a clever wit and sense of humor, are informed about global events, and are passionate about making the world a better place. I'm inspired. They're all so cool! They make me realize that I want to go travelling too, more than anything else.

Unfortunately, despite really liking them all, I become paralyzed by shyness. I'm just an ignorant little girl with nothing to offer. I'm too insecure to phone them up or drop by, as they so chilled-outly welcome me to do "anytime". Our friendships dwindle after a few painfully awkward gatherings.

School continues. I attend my classes and do my work, which turns out to be all it really takes to succeed with outstanding results. My English teacher tells me I write at a university level. I tell him it's probably because I write so many letters to my far away friends. Maybe I actually am smart. This is another revelation for me. I've never been interested or applied myself in school or, well, anything for that matter. I just have fewer friends here, so I have a lot of spare time. Not to mention, it's freezing outside, and I'm living with people I like, so I'm actually in the house a lot nowadays, and make time to do homework.

Being in the city has had its perks. I've seen bands at clubs, sketched and journaled while buzzed on espresso in colourful cafes, gone to art shows, and just enjoyed being surrounded by a plethora of cultures. But, for the most part, I'm still lonely and longing to be back on Vancouver Island. The novelty of living in Montreal wears off more and more as its harsh winter sets in. One lonely and cold February evening I phone Chantelle. She isn't home, so I speak with her grandma, and ask her if I'm still welcome to live with them. Without hesitation, Macy says, "Sure! When should we be expecting you?"

"Is a few weeks from now, ok?"

She chuckles, "Sure. I look forward to seeing you."

Three

As I climb up the stairs towards the outside deck of the Vancouver Ferry, I pinch myself to make sure that I'm not dreaming. While I cruise over the velvet sea, Quebec begins to thaw from my bones. I rip off my jacket, turn towards the sun, close my eyes, and take a slow deep breath. The slightly salted air smells and feels familiar in my lungs. It starts to sink in: I've made it home.

  I walk off the Ferry in Nanaimo and see Macy waiting for me in the terminal. She's dressed how she always is in my memories, bundled in her favorite thick blue wool sweater. Apparently, she doesn't share my sentiments of finding BC's weather to be gloriously warm. Her kind eyes smile alongside her laugh lines as she says, "Welcome back," and gives me a hug that makes me blush. We get into her old red station wagon — it still has seats as comfortable as a couch — and start the drive north up Vancouver Island, to our town Comox. I ask Macy where Chantelle is.

  "She, ah… she had to get ready for choir practice tonight."

  I shrug it off, a little disappointed that I have to wait a bit longer to see my best friend. Macy and I share forced conversation with a lot of pauses as we make our way north. "What a beautiful day. What's Montreal like? How are the cats?" By the end of the first thirty minutes our banter has become more silence than sound. Macy turns up the volume on the radio to dampen the emptiness. Clouds start to creep into the sky.

By the time we pull off the highway and drive into Comox, the sky shifts to dark grey. I look up at Queneesh, the glacier, peeking from behind the grey clouds. As I take in the glaciers' beauty, I sigh a confused sigh, it's half overjoyed, and half melancholic. This is what I've wanted for so long. Why doesn't this feel blissfully triumphant? It's as if I can sense something bad coming. Maybe it's just leftover nerves from the awkward silences of the car ride.

We pull into the driveway just as rain starts to pour. I grab my bags and fall back into familiar habits. Without even thinking, I lead the way into the house. Macy tells me Chantelle's in her room. "Oh," I say, faintly, as I realize that she could have come to meet me at the ferry. Surely Chantelle heard us come in, but she doesn't come out to greet us. I go to her bedroom door and knock.

"Come in." I open the door. She's sitting on her bed, petting one of the cats. She gives me a weak smile and says, "Hi." Nothing more. "Hi."

In the past, we've been inseparable. It's been too long; the gap is felt. I implode. It's already clear she isn't excited to have me here as a constant in her home. I try to get the conversation flowing out of excruciating silence.

I notice her guitar and ask her to play me a song. Her face lights up a little as she picks up the instrument. The ice starts to melt. She sings me a few of her new songs, pausing between each one to hear my feedback. I don't dare to stray from comments like, "the line about 'how even the most inspiring people are hypocrites' was so deep," or, "I missed your beautiful voice." Despite my comments being genuine, I'm wearing a serious poker face, hiding that I'm deeply hurt that she hasn't even asked me how I'm doing or said anything along the line of "nice to see you." Soon, she has to leave for choir practice — in Macy's car... so... uh... why didn't she come to the ferry to meet me? It's horrible to be shown that I desperately want to be here, so much more than I'm wanted here. If I even am wanted here at all.

I sit in the empty living room, dumbstruck. Rain pelts onto the ceiling and I curl into the cave at the back of my mind that's filled with dark thoughts and fears, cowering from the sudden reality check. My whole life was uprooted. I physically ached from how much I missed everything and everyone in BC. And for my friends here, well, only one small thing changed: one of their friends moved away. And they all had each other to fill in the gap I left behind, until the bummer wore off. Their lives went on, pretty much the same, ultimately unaffected. I do not matter. I'm an insignificant grain of sand.

Macy returns about twenty minutes later and smiles at me as she shakes off her umbrella in the foyer, my poker face returns her smile. She leads me to the studio that's built into the back of their small house. Macy's a painter. The studio is about the size of a one car garage. There are canvases everywhere, half-finished abstracts, colourful still-lives. It's definitely cluttered, but it's beautiful clutter. Admittedly, it's pretty cool, living in an art studio. An artist being one of the only appealing careers that I can picture myself in once, well, if I ever become old. She hands me a foamy and tells me I can pick a table to set up a bed on. I hear a meow and look at the glass door leading to the backyard. Two of their six cats are pawing at the door: like me, seeking shelter from rain.

Setting up "my" spot in the corner of the studio doesn't take long. I lean my guitar-less case against the wall at the foot of the mattress after I finish taking my clothes and journals out of it. I curl up on my table bed, too timid to go back into the house, not wanting to overwhelm Macy with my presence. After a few minutes of listening to the sky cry, I open my eyes and look to my left. There's a cloth hanging with a quote from the Dalai Lama.

The True Meaning of Life: We are visitors on this planet. We are here for ninety or one hundred years at the very most. During that period, we must try to do something good, something useful, with our lives. If you contribute to other people's happiness, you will find the true goal, the true meaning of life.

I am moved and humbled, kinda grasping the concept — ish. Maybe I'm looking at life from the wrong angle. I guess I really am quite fortunate if I compare myself to what most of the other people on this planet are experiencing. From a place of perspective, I let out a long sigh and whisper to myself that everything is, and will be, okay.

The next morning, as I get dressed for school, I do a little happy dance as I realize no more black and white dress code! This turns out to be bittersweet. I grab my jean skirt that I haven't worn in months. When I step into it, I need to jump to get it up my hips. I suck in my stomach as much as I can and barely succeed in pulling the zipper up. There's an inch of belly and hip hanging over the waistband of the skirt that used to be loose on me. How the hell did I gain so much weight? I've practically fucking doubled! I guess always being bundled in warm layers merely hid the evidence of all of Montreal's croissants, bagels, and cheese. I'm mortified. It's t-shirt weather, so I can't even hide my gut and love handles under my poncho until I have time to work off all the flab. I suck it up and suck it in as Macy drives us to school. We're ten minutes late to homeroom because Chantelle needed to change her clothes four times. I suppose I would have, too, if I had had four outfits to choose from that even fit me.

Seconds after receiving my class schedule, the bell for first period sounds and the halls fill.

"Sarah!"

I turn around and see Kennedy, one of my close friends. She runs over and gives me a big hug. It feels so good to have someone be excited to see me. "I can't wait to hear about Montreal! It's so cool that you're back!" The halls empty as students shuffle around us. She gives me another big hug, and her big green eyes sparkle as she says, "Meet me at the front garden at break time!" As she turns to rush to her class, I wonder how I could have forgotten how adorable and sweet she is. She has such a big personality for someone who's only five feet tall. I skip my way to class, which happens to be French.

I make my way through the emptying halls, late again already. I open the door to French class and familiar faces smile at me in surprise. There's even a few "Woah, it's Sarah!" from visibly excited childhood friends. The French Immersion group is a relatively small and close group of students. We shared the same classmates all throughout junior high, instead of being scattered around into different combinations of pupils like the abundant English students were. The teacher couldn't care less. He barks at everyone to quiet down and focus on the lesson. I take my seat at an empty desk. As I fluently follow along with the lesson, I realize that I learnt more language from a sojourn with a French family than I had in the ten years of prior school.

By the time the school week is over, it's as if being in the east was just some weird dream. Like my clothes, it doesn't fit. I've handed out resumes all over town. Surely, I'll be able to pay rent soon enough. I've been giving Chantelle a lot of space, which seems to have led her to be okay with my living here. I settle back into my family of friends quickly. Many fun, high spirited weeks roll by. I'm where I belong.

I attend school and do my homework regularly and continue to be astonished at how easy it is to get good grades. I had never applied myself before Montreal. Despite the flurry of friendly reunion, I find I can keep up. Macy congratulates me on my good marks and it makes me feel like she genuinely cares about me. I relax a little and try to silence my inner bully that keeps whispering that I'm an annoyance and a burden.

Things with Chantelle have been a bit of a rollercoaster. I'm starting to wonder if she's bipolar. She'll go through friendly and enthusiastic phases where all feels well. Then she'll plummet back into a depressed shut-out-the-world phase, sometimes in bed with the curtains drawn for weeks. When she's like this I feel like she loathes my existence. So lately, I'm out of the house as much as possible, just trying to give her space.

I've been hanging out with Kennedy a lot. Most afternoons we smoke weed and philosophize. Our brains are extremely synergetic. We are constantly finishing each other's sentences as we arrive to a fascinating amount of "aha! moments." Revelations that lowly (un-high) minds would be unable to fathom, for they're simply too advanced for un-high minds to comprehend. This brings us to another realization: Pot helps everything. We regularly give ourselves cramps from laughing fits.

Macy hasn't been selling much art lately. Her savings are dwindling just to feed and house me. It turns out that my intention to contribute financially to the household hasn't been as easy to manifest as I had anticipated. I hand out copies of my resume all over town, again. My only work experience is babysitting and apple picking. My one "special skill" is speaking French. But speaking French is redundant here. My sole reference is Macy, my "landlord." Regardless of my inexperience, I'd assumed that, somewhere between convenience stores and burger shacks, someone would get back to me. I was wrong.

Months go by. Macy, alone, is supporting me. I eat her food, use her soap and shampoo, internet, phone, electricity. She hasn't complained about it to me but, as time goes by, I start to feel more and more guilty. It's no longer a private anxiety that I'm a burden — it's a cold, hard fact.

Four

Summer comes, and everyone's spirits rise. Even the tension between Chantelle and I softens. She seems to have magically transformed back into sweet and fun. Chantelle, Kennedy and a few others from our circle of friends invest in a palmful of hash together.

Best investment ever.

Day after day, we wander around the beaches and parks talking and laughing, trying not to get caught smoking. This is the West Coast I ached for — the tribe I had pined for. Most days we meet up at a park that's central but tucked away. At first, it's just because it's a relatively equal walking distance from everyone's home, but it soon becomes so much more to us. We've christened it "The Dome." At nighttime, when you lay on your back at the centre of The Dome, the sky swallows you whole and one finds themselves inside the centre of the sphere of infinity. The longer you stay, looking up at the stars, the deeper you're able to feel the complexity and beauty of the galaxies. We've come to respect The Dome quite a bit, to speak of it with the highest of honour. With our newly found galactic comprehension, we try to find parallel awe in other beautiful spots. But none evoke such expansiveness. The Dome has become our portal to cosmic understanding.

A friend's mom gives a bunch of us a ride to a river one day. She pulls me aside and hands me eighty dollars. Eighty dollars! She says, "Don't spend it all in one place, and let me know when you need more. The weight of the world shouldn't be on a young girl's shoulders."

I say a stunned "thank you," leap out of my shyness, and give her a hug. For a little while I feel like I'm getting a taste of what it probably feels like to be a normal, carefree teenager.

With only a few weeks of summer left, my haze of giddy laughter and hash smoke is interrupted. A Pizza Shop calls me in for an interview. I can hardly remember dropping off the resume. Excited and full of hope, I shower, shave my legs (not a common bother of the patriarch that I normally participate in), put on the jean skirt that fits me again, a preppy looking baby blue tank top, and a bit of Chantelle's mascara. I make my way to the Pizza Shop, purposely five minutes early, projecting interview questions in my head. I'm a bag of nerves. I've got no skills to offer, and I really need this job. I open the door and step into what feels like an oven. It is hotter than the thirty-three degrees Celsius it is outside. The owners, a friendly husband and wife in their fifties interview me on the stools by the counter. "What grade are you in? Would you be willing to work evenings after school? When can you start?" That pretty much sums it up. My first reaction is relief and optimism. Lucky me — they were desperate for employees!

I have my training shift the next day. Macy lends me her old bike. It takes me the better part of an hour to get to work. But it's summer, so biking is totally manageable, even enjoyable, plus it helps to shed more unwanted weight.

The job turns out to be really simple: toppings on bread, bread in oven, bread out of oven, repeat. It's disgusting though. I'm either sweating my ass off working the ovens, or assembling slimy salami and cow pus onto pizzas. It makes me sad to be participating in animal cruelty. But I've mastered the art of numbing myself. I try to distract myself by talking with the other employees. Conversation doesn't come easily. They're all working here so they can buy fancy cars and clothes; we've got no common ground. The owners are always there. It turns out my bosses' friendliness was quite put on. Being married for a long time seems to have brought them to a state of constant passive aggressive bickering. The staff rarely get caught in the crossfire, but the atmosphere is toxic.

It feels good to be able to chip in at home, that I am able to put up with and stay at my shitty job. I start paying rent and buying food. It was painfully apparent that Macy was seriously struggling to support me. The cupboards were barren, the gas tank only got filled up with pocket change, and instead of replacing our broken washing machine, we now wash our clothes by hand. The job absolutely sucks, but I desperately need the money. I'm already in the habit of counting down the days to my paychecks.

Five

Summer quickly comes to an end, as so much of my time is now filled with work. Macy's bike gets stolen one day whilst I make pizzas. My shifts usually end around ten p.m., which is later than the buses run. Now, to get home, I'm stuck waiting for a delivery going in the direction of where I live. On slow nights, I often have to wait around to catch a ride much later than my shift ends. When I do get home, I'm exhausted. I trudge into the studio, drop my bags, and pull out my homework, glance at it, but wind up collapsing into sleep instead. My grades plummet. Whatever, school's totally bogus anyway. It's purpose is just to condition the sheeple to be cogs in the holy economy.

As the days become increasingly short and dark, Chantelle transforms back into a territorial ogre. We find ourselves talking less and less, and as weeks pass our friendship, once again, fizzles out. Shining in the summer, and wilting in the cold. Days go by where we don't even speak. When I'm home I isolate myself, and try to stay out of the way. The atmosphere is awkward. There is nothing I can do or say to remedy the situation. I don't have anywhere else to go. I fall into a heavy depression. I start to envy and even resent my friends. They don't need to work. They're loved and cared for by their families. Their lives are so easy! None of them understand how stressful and degrading my life has become. I start skipping school. At first just a few classes a week, but it snowballs, then it avalanches, into a few classes a day. I just direly need some "me" time, some time, where I can relax. Marijuana is my medicine. I need it to cope, to endure the job that I've come to loathe, to handle how stressful school has become, to tolerate my claustrophobic home life.

In February we're assigned new classes for the second semester of school. There's a boy in my Civilizations class. He catches my eyes with his long, curly red hair. I can't quite turn my gaze as I notice his colourful baggy pants from elsewhere, like some other country elsewhere. How have I not noticed this boy before? He must have felt my stare. He looks over and we lock eyes. We both blush and smile. He walks over and takes the seat next to mine. Civ becomes the only class that I attend regularly. Lynx — the boy — and I sit beside each other daily. He's not just cute, he turns out to be really cool! Like really, really cool. The more I get to know him, the more I like him. He's different. He's really open minded. He's kind to everyone, not concerned about high school hierarchy. He's lived in many different countries where his parents volunteered as medical aid: Belize, Vanuatu, St. Lucia.... He's spent most of his high school life living in other places, that's why we had never met until now. He's grateful, and mature about it all, too, doesn't brag or act superior. When we talk, neither of us can contain our nervous smiles. It's pretty obvious that we're both crushing hard. I can't believe that a boy like this actually likes me! He could easily pick so many of the other girls at our school. When I can't think of anything to talk about, I draw to calm the butterflies in my stomach.

He lives about a five-minute walk from me. Soon we're in the habit of meeting every morning to go to school together. I'm still skipping class a lot, but I wake up on time for the car ride with Lynx, not my courses. He has a little sister that he drops off on the way in the mornings. He's so kind to his little sister. He's just really… quite… very… nice.

I'm always asking him to tell me stories, to paint me pictures of what it's like in far-off lands and other cultures. I express the deep wanderlust I've had inside of me for as long as I can remember, tell him my grandest dreams are those of travel. He suggests a trip to Whistler for the weekend. His sister lives there, so we'd have a place to stay.

"I know it's not super exotic, but it could be fun…" There's a trace of insecurity in his voice. This is crazy! How can a boy like this be doubting himself?

"Really?! That sounds amazing! Anywhere but here!" I say, with a humongous smile.

Friday, after school, Lynx drops me off to pack my bag for the trip. I scurry around the house to the backyard, slide the studio door open and dump out my school books onto the bed. I grab my cleanest(ish) clothes, my bud, and a half full bottle of wine, then zip my bag shut. With a bounce in my step, I make my way to Lynx and we set off for the ferry in his car.

"Floyd or Zeppelin?" he asks. "Let's start with Dark Side of the Moon," I reply. We get to Nanaimo and find a place to park where it seems unlikely that the car would get towed from, then jog to the soon to depart ferry. On the boat, we grab a paper cup from the cafeteria, and find a discreet spot to pour the wine.

Tipsy by the time we dock, I find the courage to grab his hand. He turns beet red and firmly grips back. Neither of us are brave enough to make eye contact. At Horseshoe Bay, his sister's boyfriend is waiting for us with a couple of his buddies. We say hi and all introduce ourselves, then pile into

Aiden's truck. They're all really trendy and normal, clad in pretentious, slave labour, brand name clothes. About ten minutes into the drive, I decide that they're morons. They keep calling things "retarded" and "gay," then laughing as if that was a clever and insightful thing to say. I feel out of place. They seem like the kind of people that usually avoid weirdos like me, and vice versa. We find some common ground though, the guy in the passenger seat - I've already forgotten his name - pulls a twelve pack of Molson from under his seat and hands us all a beer. We get into Whistler, nicely buzzed, and pull up to the backdoor of the bar where Lynx's sister works.

Aiden sends her a text. A minute later, the big metal door swings open, and a really pretty bubbly girl waves us in. "Quick, quick! she insists as she sneaks us into the bar." We follow her to a crowded row of stools and she gives Lynx a long hug.

"Sarah, Kloe. Kloe, Sarah."

Kloe pours us each a beer, then has to go back to pour drinks for the line up of people at the counter.

We walk to the edge of the dance floor and wait for a good song to play. The music that the DJ is playing is all contrived pop music. We agree to wait out a few more songs before forcing ourselves to dance. I've never seen a large crowd groove to and actually enjoy top forty songs. It's actually a little shocking to see so many people get enthusiastic about such mediocre music. I'm used to open mics, folk shows, punk shows, and raves. But here, in my first pretentious bar, the songs just feel so hollow and annoying.

Several tequila shots later we find ourselves dancing to the horrible music whilst laughing at ourselves. We lock eyes and our lips stumble towards each other and we start to kiss. Our tongues aren't synchronizing at first, but we keep going. After about ten seconds it feels a bit more natural. "We Belong Together," by Mariah Carey, starts to play. Our lips part as we burst into laughter and mock the song, too insecure to continue kissing through the love song.

"Do you want to go for a walk?" he asks.

I nod enthusiastically. We find Kloe, thank her, and make plans to hang out in the morning. The Tequila keeps us warm while we sway around town. We pass a hotel with a hot tub on the other side of a four foot high fence, and Lynx eyes me mischievously. "Nice fence, huh?"

"Uh... I guess so..." I reply, confused.

He looks up and down the street, then swiftly scales the wooden wall. Laughing, I follow his lead. All of a sudden, we're stripped down to our underwear, immersed in the hot tub. Ten minutes pass before a security guard comes and demands that we leave. Soaking wet, we find a taxi and make our way to Aiden's house. We knock on the door and wait, shivering in the snow. We knock again. No one answers. Turns out the door is unlocked, so we let ourselves in, hoping that this is, in fact, the right house. We find the living room couch, toss aside the clothes, empty pizza boxes, and the bong that were strewn on top of it, then lay down in each other's arms, talking, laughing, and kissing, as we drift to sleep.

In the morning, we're woken early by sunlight coming through the windows. We close the blinds and cuddle. I pretend that I'm drifting in and out of sleep, out of fear of sharing awkward silences, and just wanting to make this moment last. Hours later the people living here stir awake. I recognize Aiden walking down the hall: we have, in fact, slept at the right place. Over toast and coffee in the cluttered kitchen, Kloe asks us if we want to go up the mountain. Lynx and I exchange an awkward glance.

"We don't have gear, or money."

She offers me her skis. Aiden lends Lynx his board, then they instruct us on how to sneak onto the gondola at the base of the hill. You just have to slip through the exit gate when no one is looking. Once you've made it up the base of the hill, you're in the clear as long as you don't go all the way back to the very bottom. There are other lifts halfway up the mountain. An hour later, in a drowsy blur, we are riding up towards the summit. We look at each other, surprised. "Wow, that really was easy."

The whole day is spent careening down powdery slopes under a beaming sun. We laugh and make silly sound effects as we frolic in the snow. As I watch Lynx trudge up the slope to me after a wipe-out, the white-tipped mountains rolling out behind him, I realize how comfortable with each other we've become. Being with him feels as if I'm reuniting with a lost piece of myself.

We have a mellow evening back at the house, tired from not really sleeping the night before and being on the mountain all day. The following morning, we try to sneak onto the gondola again. A worker spots us this time, calls over to the lifty to stop the gondola, then asks us to leave the hill, giving us a "first warning." She goes on to say that if we're caught trying to sneak on again, we will be banned from the mountain. The rest of Sunday goes by all too quickly; it's soon time to return to life in Comox.

We thank Kloe and hop back into Aiden's truck to start the descent down the winding Sea-To-Sky highway. After about twenty minutes we are forced to halt. There's a roadblock due to a crash further down the road. Aiden turns to us and says, "This could take hours to clear, and I gotta get to work. Are you ok with hitchhiking?"

Lynx looks to me, arches his brow to see if that's all right. "No problem!" I say, enthusiastically. Aiden wishes us luck while we hop out, then does a one-eighty to drive back uphill.

"Don't worry, I'm sure we'll be fine." Lynx says, leading the way past the roadblock to where the traffic starts again.

"Worry? I'm not worried, I'm excited! Curious to see who we're going to meet!"

He laughs. "Yeah, me too!"

We walk down the highway, past the collision, then for another half hour with our thumbs up, smiling at the cars passing by. The hitchhiking adventure is a little anticlimactic. An SUV pulls over. A sweet elderly woman inside says, "Oh dear, be careful! Hitchhiking is dangerous!" clearly oblivious to how she's contradicting herself by welcoming two strangers into her backseat. We drive down the stunning mountain road, look down at the ocean, islands, and forests, and make polite small talk, mostly about her grandchildren. She goes out of her way and takes us to the ferry terminal. "I want to make sure you darlings arrive safely."

On the ferry Lynx and I stare out at Vancouver Island as we approach it. He looks at me, "Hey, Sarah?"

"Yeah?"

"Are we like dating now?" Internally I jump for joy.

"I'd like that."

Within mere days we've become inseparable. Within a couple of weeks, we are acknowledging that we're in love.

My depression has dissolved. Living with Chantelle and

Macy is still uncomfortable, but I'm high on love. Life has become way easier to cope with. At home, I keep my distance, mind my manners — nothing more. All of my problems seem small and manageable now.

When I'm not working, or at school, I'm at Lynx's. I don't think I've made a spectacular first impression on his parents. The first time we met came at an unexpected moment. Lynx and I happened to have just smoked a huge doobie. If our red slits of eyes didn't give it away, perhaps us keeling over in uncontainable laughter did. Perhaps. Since then, they've grown quite fond of me, what with Lynx's school attendance mysteriously dropping since we've been dating, and catching me hop out of his bedroom window twice after not giving us permission to have a sleepover. So, yeah, they couldn't be more thrilled with their son's new girlfriend. Despite all this, they still treat me kindly.

On Easter long weekend, we decide to go camping on one of the small islands. Vancouver Island, where we live, is a very large island off the west coast of Canada. Between Vancouver Island and the main continent of Canada there are many smaller islands. We take out a map, I close my eyes, and swirl my finger around the map, stop, and open my eyes to find out which island my finger has landed on. "To Hornby Island!" Lynx proclaims. With high spirits, we pack up Lynx's car and set off in the pouring rain. We disembark the ferry onto the little island and slowly drive through a blinding downpour.

Without warning, the rain stops abruptly and the sky clears. We drive until we come to a funky building with cars parked all around it. There's a sign advertising today's spring farmer's market. We enter the hall and almost immediately an older couple has called Lynx's name from the booth they're selling jewellery at. Turns out they're old friends of Lynx's parents. We all get introduced and start chatting. They laugh at our camping idea, and kindly offer us the option to stay in a trailer they have parked on their property. We gratefully accept Wanda and Henry's offer. Tenting in this rain would have been less than ideal.

Rain pours for most of the weekend. We spend a lot of our time in the trailer making love. We drive around the island and go for a few beach walks, but are more than content to just spend time inside. On Sunday morning, Wanda invites us into the house for coffee. As we take off our shoes in the mudroom, I notice a blue and silver hand painted sign advertising Tarot Card Readings.

"Did you make that sign?" I ask Wanda.

"Yeah, I used to do readings, but I don't like to any more. I just hated it when I'd have to deliver bad news."

"What exactly are Tarot Cards?" I ask.

"They're a medium for oracles to receive information through — I guess you could call it 'fortune telling'."

"Oh wow!" I gasp.

She snickers and says, "You want one, don't you?"

"I would love one! But, of course, only if that's alright with you."

"Sure, honey."

She asks if I'm comfortable with having Lynx present for the reading. I nod. She brings us to a cluttered round table in between their kitchen and an attached hand-built greenhouse filled with colourful flowers and baby fruit trees. She begins to clear space on the table.

"Well, come on! Don't just stand there!" she says in a jovial voice.

We hop in to help, moving the clutter from table to counter. Once the table is cleared, she wets a cloth and gives it a wipe down and tells us to sit down. With a bright pink lighter she sets flame to a cigar-shaped bundle of pale grey leaves, then waves out the flame and, with a feather, spreads the beautiful smoke and aroma around the room. After that, she takes the seat next to mine and unwraps a large deck of cards from a piece of red silk. She hands me the deck of cards and says,

"Just hold them for a little while."

"Should I think about certain things? Should I ask questions? Should I try to keep my mind calm and clear?"

"It's not complicated, honey! Just hold them!" she barks, then lets out a little laugh after. "Oh, right, about that coffee."

Wanda gets up from her seat, throws Lynx a hand powered coffee grinder, and barks again, "Make yourself useful!" As Lynx starts to grind the coffee, Wanda smiles and winks at him. Lynx and I lock eyes, knowing what the other is thinking — is she nuts?

She returns to the seat next to mine. "Are you ready, honey?" I nod excitedly. She gets me to shuffle the deck until I feel like it's been shuffled enough. "Don't overcomplicate it this time!" I follow her next instructions, and part the deck into three piles, then reassemble the piles in whichever order I feel compelled to. Next, I'm told to place my left hand on top of the deck and sweep the cards into a wide arc. I do all this, still nervous I'm not doing it properly, though I'm sure Wanda would have words for me if I weren't.

"Now pick seven cards," she instructs. I pause, not sure how to pick the right ones. Maybe I've over thought this already and ruined my attunement to the cards. Do I just choose randomly? Wanda seems to have picked up on my anxiety.

"Sheesh honey, you've got to learn to relax! What are you, fifteen? Go on! Hop to it! Pick your cards!"

I laugh, trying to pretend that I'm not embarrassed, then pull seven cards from the arc. She takes them and places them in a cross within a cross. Wanda flips them face-up, one by one, each revealing a picture stranger than the last. She pauses with a little comment after each flip.

"Huh."

"Hmmm, I see…"

"Oh crap!"

"Oh, shit!"

"Huh."

"Damn, little girl!"

"So, your home life ain't so peachy? School neither. You've got dreams, ambitious dreams there, little one. You weren't exactly dealt the easiest hand." She pauses and stares at me until I realize she's being puny.

"You know what? Screw the reading! Why don't you two come camp out here once you're done school? We won't charge you rent. You can help out around the yard if you feel like. There're tons of tourists in the summer, so lots of work! You'd be able to put money aside to go travelling.

"Something tells me that, more than anything, you want to see the world. And, honey, it ain't gonna happen if you stay where you are now. Oh and, sorry kiddo: Something unwanted is coming your way, soon. Fucking hell, I hate giving tarot readings!"

Wanda bundles up the cards and returns it to the heap of clutter. "Ugh, I need some time to calm myself. Run along and play, honeys."

I'm in disbelief! It feels like a miracle to have been offered a free place to live, on a beautiful island with kind magical people.

"Oh my God, Lynx, we could be backpacking around the world come fall!"

He smiles, says, "Let's do it!" then, after a pause, says, "Hey Sarah, do you want to go to the trailer and make some coffee?"

After having a long "coffee" in the trailer, we walk through forest trails to a beach, and suddenly it's nearly time to make the last ferry back to the Big Island. We knock on Wanda and Henry's door to thank them and say goodbye. They give us big hugs and say, "Now, don't hesitate if you want to come here for the summer!"

Curiously enough, Wanda was right. A few days after being back in Comox I receive some bleak news from a classmate whose father, is my parents' realtor. She mentions that my parents have been posted back here, assuming that I knew. I want nothing to do with them. I call Wanda and ask if I can move to Hornby now, before summer starts. She doesn't ask any questions, just says, "Sure, honey. I thought I'd be hearing from you." That evening I tell Macy that I've decided to leave town and move to Hornby Island. For the first time in months, we have a conversation that flows, feels warm, and lasts more than a couple minutes.

I drop out of school. I quit my job. It's hard to say which one felt better.

I go to school to collect my things. My hippie, punk and self-proclaimed "anarchist" friends all astound me with uptight reactions to my announcement that I'm dropping out.

"I'll figure it out," I say, with a mixture of naivety and deeper knowing. There has to be more to life than doing what society conditions us for. There has to be some other path than sticking to the cultural conveyor belt. I don't want to be the kind of person that lets fear beat them down into conformity.

"My life's gonna be amazing!" I proclaim, adrenalin dancing through my veins. "Don't let the man get you down!" I wink, twirl, then skip away. Energy and excitement surge through me. I've never felt so alive.

Six

Life on Hornby is very mellow. I'm spending most of my time drawing, taking nature walks, and catching up on sleep. My home is now a hollowed-out van on Wanda and Henry's property. The van is quite private, it's a two-minute walk from their house, and even has its own little yard with an outdoor kitchen, enclosed by blackberry bushes and trees. To me, it's paradise. Finally, and for the first time, I have a nest that's mine, somewhere I can actually relax. A place where I am not a burden and in the way. The stresses from living a life that was spent mostly being somewhere I didn't want to be, doing things that I didn't want to be doing, are now but a memory. I'm literally healing. Not having to endure school and a job that I hate has liberated me from my marijuana dependency. I've simply just lost the desire to smoke all the time. I spend half of my time on the Big Island visiting Lynx and my other friends, but being there is all fun and no stress now. Everything feels different.

On one spring weekend, I'm hanging out with my friends in Comox. For some reason, I'm buzzing with euphoric energy. I skip and dance around them as they stroll, drawing quizzical looks from passers-by.

"I don't like my name!" I declare. "It's time for a change!"
"All right, what's your name then?" they ask.
"Phoenix! Actually, no! November! No! I know… Maya! My name is now Maya! Maya Thorn!"

My friends laugh, smile and accept it. I'm feeling particularly sensitive for some reason, and am deeply heartened from their reaction. I thank them for being open minded and amazing and for how lucky I am to have such wonderful friends.

"The world's going to treat Maya better than it treated Sarah!" As I enthusiastically express my racing thoughts, another one comes dancing in — by changing my name, have I just tapped into a magical method for improving one's circumstance? One of the Universe's keys to magic? I think so!

Lynx moves into the van with me right after he finishes his last exam. Living together is blissful and natural. Henry and Wanda stuck to their offer, and are letting us stay for free. We aren't wasting money on things that the status quo considers necessary. No fancy new clothes, computers, cars, not even cell phones. The less I have the more stress-free and at peace I feel. We're lent old rusty bicycles. They can't even shift gears, but we're content with them. We get around by bike as often as by hitchhiking. On Hornby, hitching is effortless once you're a familiar face, which only takes about a week in such a small place. I'm working as a vegetable farmer, and as a vegetarian cook. Despite those jobs sounding similar to apple picking and cooking pizzas, they are worlds apart. The hours fly by in the warm company of kind bosses and laidback co-workers. I'm getting paid to learn skills that I want to have! Not to mention, the money is going to be spent on actualizing my dreams, not barely scraping by in undesirable circumstances. Both jobs give us free food to live off. Due to our minimalistic lifestyle, our travel fund is manifesting quickly.

When we aren't working, we're at the nude beach. There are almost always interesting people to hang out with. One sunny July day I meet someone who makes a particularly strong impression on me. The familiar face of one of the welcoming locals, waves at us to join a hushed gathering. Crystal's in the midst of reading her poetry to the group. She's fearless and intimate, fiery and wise. She goes on to tell us stories of the adventure she's on. She's been backpacking for the past eight months, solo! She started in Guatemala, then hitch-hiked north through Mexico and the United States. She just got to Canada last week. I ask her for travelling advice.

"Your intuition will never lead you astray. Unless you're a stray, then your intuition will always lead you."

A few days later, Lynx and I bump into her at the beach again. She's heading off the island, "following her wanderlust into her miss story." We give each other hugs, then she squeezes my hand and says, "See you when I see you!"

On my next beach day, I pass a man lying in the sun beside a colourful cardboard sign, "~*Palm Reading * $20*~". As I walk by, staring at the curious doodles of symbols on the sign, his eyes open and meet mine.

"Would you like a reading?"

"Um, I'm not sure. What is a palm reading?" My fingers squirm anxiously.

"Palmistry, also known as chiromancy, is an ancient science of understanding a person's character, their past, and future, by reading the lines, mounts, and fingers on one's hand. Like destinies and snowflakes, no two palms are alike, not even on identical twins"

"Interesting," I say. He takes that as a "yes," sits up and instructs me to sit cross legged facing him. "Why not," I think.

I join him on the sand and show him my right palm. His eyes widen and his jaw drops — I snap my hand back to my chest in alarm.

"Oh, it's nothing bad!" he explains, unfurling my hand again while tracing the seams in my palm as he describes them.

"Usually people have two separate, clear and deep horizontal lines under their finger mounts.

Those two lines are called the "Heart" and the "Head" line. You only have one line. I have only seen this marking once before. It symbolizes the potential to master harmony between head and heart. But the truly astonishing part of your palm is the large triangle taking up most of your hand, with another medium-sized triangle in its centre. This is a sacred and revered symbol and is truly extraordinary. I didn't know souls like yours still walked the Earth. You have been here since the ancient times. You can do whatever you want to in life."

He pauses and looks deeply into my eyes. "Always remember that: *whatever you want*. Believe in yourself."

"Huh. Wow!" I say, but really just taking it with a grain of salt. I take out a twenty-dollar bill.

"No, keep it, I insist. It was an honour to help guide you towards remembering your fate."

"Huh. Well, thank you very much," I say, a little more convinced. Or, at least more convinced that he actually believes what he saw. I walk away, intrigued and determined to learn if this could actually be true, obviously wanting that fate.

I start investigating the palms of all my friends, often to their surprise. They all have two horizontal lines. In the centres, there are no clearly marked triangles within other triangles. I start checking out the palms of acquaintances, too.

The more I look at palms the more mine does in fact stand out, quite a bit. I ask around, seek others who do chiromancy, but can't find anyone. I must be patient. Surely, eventually I'll encounter other palm readers, I hope, eager to discover if they'll also see something so lavishly special scribed in my flesh.

There are frequent concerts and parties, most with really good musicians and DJs. It's hard to say whether the music is genuinely better here, or if I'm just more open to it because of my elevated emotional state. We go out dancing all the time. Without a doubt, this is turning out to be the best summer of my life. Well, to be optimistic, the best summer of my life thus far. Summer comes to a close. I'm pleasantly exhausted. Lynx and I each have a little over four thousand dollars.

"Now's the fun part," says Wanda. "You get to decide where to go."

We pick South America. Lynx wants to go somewhere he's never been, and I want to go somewhere with a noticeably different culture, land and language. Sometimes, I feel this deep, intuitive connection to the Amazon rainforest, coloured by the kind of nostalgia you feel for a home you've left behind. When I was young, I had a recurring dream about running through the jungle in my bare feet, vines and leaves whipping past me. Part of me believes I've lived there in a past life. We buy return plane tickets to Sao Paulo, Brazil. Our flight leaves early in November.

After travel expenses, we're each left with a little under three thousand dollars in spending money for our trip. We're both giddy with mystery for what we're about to embark on. Little do we know that our highest highs will come with the lowest of lows.

Seven

Getting all the way to Sao Paulo from Vancouver takes three transfers. We bought the cheapest tickets available, so each of our flights have looong layovers. The first flight lands in LAX at midnight. We've got twelve hours to wait until our connecting flight to Lima, Peru. We try to nap on the ground, but every ten minutes or so an obnoxious announcement about making sure to not leave your baggage unattended loops and echoes through the sleepy gates. On the long flight to Lima, we toss and turn in the uncomfortable seats, still unable to get any shut eye. By the time we're airborne to Sao Paulo, we're both exhausted and pass out shortly after taking our seats.

    A flight attendant taps me on the shoulder. It's time to straighten my chair and buckle my belt. We're landing. In Brazil. Stunned and half-awake, Lynx and I start to frantically flip through the guidebook we've "borrowed" from the library. As our ears pop through the descent, it just dawns that we have no idea what to do or where to go once we land. The guidebook says Sao Paulo has a downtown worth wandering around, while also warning to steer clear of certain squalid neighbourhoods that are not safe. As we shuffle off the plane, we decide to make our way to the city centre, and from there figure out what to do next.

    We grab our backpacks from the carousel, step out into the warm, pink, early morning, and in horrible portugues try to ask a taxi driver to take us to the city centre. We are let out in a quiet neighborhood and pick streets at random in a jetlagged blur. Soon the smoggy air becomes sweltering. Around every corner are more rows of gates and tall cement walls with shards of broken glass protruding out of the top, guarding what I imagine to be lavish mansions. After several blocks of roaming, we pass another pedestrian, and I realize how strange it is to be the only ones on the street. Are we even downtown? It sure doesn't seem like it. Where are the shops and the bustling crowds? The greater Sao Paulo area has twenty million inhabitants, so really, we could be anywhere. This city is notoriously dangerous, though wherever we are, seems tame enough. We walk some more and still haven't come across anything lively. We've attempted asking people for directions on how to get to a more interesting area of the city, but our Portuguese is pathetic. Spanish, which we learnt a little of in school, we could probably get by on — but not the tongue-tied, lisping, drunken Spanish that is Portuguese.

We have friends of a friend who live in Florianopolis, a large island off the east coast of the country. We weren't planning on giving them a call right away, if at all, but feeling clueless and adrift sparks us to get in touch. We give them a call from a payphone and they invite us to stay with them. Grateful for a destination, we decide to undertake the long migration to Florianopolis. We flag down another cab, and do our best to enunciate where we want to go: Terminal Bandeira.

Once on board the bus, we play a telepathy game. Lynx and I put our heads together, then one of us visualizes a colour. The other has to guess the colour that the other is visualizing. We get it right three times in a row, congratulate ourselves, then stop, not wanting to spoil the magic. Before long, we both drift into much needed sleep, foreheads still together.

In the morning, our bus crosses the bridge to the island and drops us off in its main city. The crowd is a dense flurry of stylish, upper class society. We stand out like grubby white thumbs on a manicured brown hand. My eye catches a fancy pink hat coming our way with a beautiful smiling woman under it, waving at us. By the time we realize it's Beatriz, we're already in her warm hug. We follow her broad brimmed hat and the clack of her designer high heels through the city centre, cutting our way through the maze of crowded streets to their condo. Beatriz, her husband Teodoro, and their three children who are in their twenties, live together on the eighteenth floor in one of the many gigantic modern sky rises. We struggle speaking but succeed in getting most things across in engluease, hand gestures, and exaggerated facial expressions, after the original "nice to meet you" that we got from a phrase book: "Prazer em conhecê-lo," and "Obrigado você também," are basically the only phrases we're able to string together. Their condo is immaculate, yet still there's a maid that's scurrying around us, dusting in silence with her gaze lowered as the rest of us converse. They notice me make eye contact and smile, then go on to explain that having a maid is the norm. There's so many people competing for work, thus hiring help is very affordable. "She'd be in absolute poverty if it weren't for us."

Shortly after, they tell us they have another condo that's on the beach and ask if we'd like to go spend some time there with them. We smile and say, "Obrigado.".

Beggars come up to the car and knock on the window almost every time we stop at a red light. I thought I'd seen people in rough shape back home. But here, there are so many more impoverished folk, and they all look like they're in much deeper misery; scrawny and starving, dirty, many of them shoeless, walking the scorching asphalt with painful looking blisters. Beatriz rolls down her window, barely enough to fit a couple fingers, and gives one of them some coins. As we make our way through the outskirts of the city there are more and more tiny shacks lining the road. The shacks are built from scrap metal and plastic, scattered on the noisy, trash laden roadside. There'd be no safety, privacy, or hygiene living in one of the countless makeshift homes. A part of me starts to judge Teodoro and Josefina for living excessively whilst being surrounded by poverty, until I realize that I'm doing the same thing. Instead of giving my money to those in need I'm choosing to spend it hedonistically, on travel. I'm just projecting my own guilt.

We pull up to a tall gate with a security guard watching surveillance cameras. The guard recognizes Teodoro and Beatriz with a forced grin and opens the gate for us. As we drive up to their other western-style condo, I'm in shock at all the realms people are living in, side by side, with spider webs of boundaries between the economic classes. I try to shake off the shame and enjoy the kindness of our hosts. At least I'm experiencing one side of Brazilian culture, I guess that is sort of purposeful, in the sense that it's educational, right? When I envisioned being in far off lands I had imagined being in unfamiliar and illuminating cultures and traditions — not being a beach bum in a bubble of a first world luxury.

We all head to the shore together. Lynx and I lay out a sarong on the soft sand, and Beatriz unfolds her beach chair and umbrella. I lather myself in coconut oil to get a tan while Beatriz rubs herself with skin whitening cream. Here too, the media has succeeded in disempowering and profiting off the people by selling whatever image of beauty is the hardest to attain.

Back at the condo, Teodoro introduces us to erva mate and how it is drunk here. He has a special cup reserved solely for mate drinking. Hot water is poured into the green powdered leaves, then sipped through the bomba, a special straw with a sieve on its end. Mate has a lot of caffeine and healthy nutrients. It is the ubiquitous drink here, replenishing everyone with the energy drained by the sun's intense heat.

Lynx and I spend the week. We swim, draw, and make a bunch of colourful bracelets with the bag of beads we brought from home. By the end of our week, we're wrestling with boredom. Boredom — how shamefully extravagant is that? Lynx and I had imagined that being in South America would be otherworldly, a series of unprecedented adventures, pulling us along like a river's flow. Seeking something more exotic, we decide that it's time to venture on. On our last lazy day of laying in the sun and swimming, we bring our guidebook along to see what there is to do nearby, and decide on Iguazu Falls, famously exquisite waterfalls on the triple frontier of Brazil, Argentina and Paraguay. Foz do Iguacu has a campground. We invest in a *cheap* tent and a cooking pot, then pack our bags for the journey. We thank Beatriz and Teodoro, say goodbye to their safe and secure microcosm, then board another bus.

The campground is huge! Or maybe it just seems that way because we're the only campers. Maybe it isn't tourist season? I get heat stroke our first afternoon. From the shade of a tree, I watch the workings of nature throughout the rest of the day. Instead of squirrels running around like there would be back home, there are similar sized — even bigger, actually — reptiles scurrying all over the campsite. The curious creatures have spikes down their spines, and slithering, snake like tails.

For a second, I wonder if they'd claw through our tent, then realize how ridiculous that thought is. Probably. Hopefully.

Early the next day, we go for a wander, before the heat becomes debilitating. Lynx spots a sugar cane stalk amongst the foliage lining the road. He cuts the top off with his pocketknife and we suck sugar out of the fibrous stock as we walk barefoot down an empty dirt road.

On the third morning, we pay the toll for the walking trail to the falls. As advertised, the waterfalls are stunning. But there are tourists all over the place, rushing through, cameras out, taking more pictures than time to stop and bask in the beauty of this sublime place. Despite the rush of people, the rush of the falls is still breathtaking. A myriad of rainbows spring from the mists, cascading into the jungle canopy. The cool air from the downpour and shelter of jungle plants tickles our skin with mist — I delight in the majestic massage as it rejuvenates me from the couple of days in the scorching heat of the exposed campground.

Back at camp, Lynx and I get to talking about what to do next. Seeing as we're on the border of Argentina and Paraguay we decide we ought to leave Brazil. Partly because it's the most expensive country in South America, and partly because Brazil is the only country on the continent that speaks Portuguese, rather than Spanish. Because I had taken a Spanish course in high school, I'm confident I will be able to communicate the basics. Being able to have conversations with people would make a world of difference. We decide on Paraguay, our reasoning being that we've never heard anything about it. At the time, jumping into the complete unknown seems like a brilliant idea. What could be more interesting than the unknown?

Eight

We catch a bus to the border then follow the signs to the Paraguayan Customs Office. It's a small building with four sleepy men leaning on a dusty desk, listening to a crackly radio. Upon noticing us their expressions change from boredom to confusion. We smile as we slide our passports onto the desk, figuring that would speak more clearly than our rusty Spanish. The men check our photos, then flip through each page. Conversation erupts between them before turning to respond to us. The man whom I assume is in charge looks Lynx in the eye, as if addressing me would either be futile or inappropriate. He sputters out rapid-fire Spanish. I make out the word "Brazil" several times, but am not able to decipher anything else.

"Por Favor, Podemos entrar Paraguay?" I ask. A bit taken aback to see the female take charge of the conversation, the man looks at me and repeats what seems to be the same, indecipherable, speech.

After a couple more reiterations, he sighs and relents. He darts his eyes from Lynx's to mine and asks, "¿Por que quieren ir a Paraguay?" (Why do you want to go to Paraguay?).

"Viajar" (travelling), I answer. Looking flabbergasted, he raises a finger, as if to say "one minute." The officers form a huddle while Lynx and I wait awkwardly. The men all nod, stop talking, then turn all their eyes onto us.

The leader says, "Forty US Dollars, each."

It's all I can do refrain from blurting "You speak English!" He puts out his open palm, beckoning us to fill it. We hand them the cash. For the first time, they're cheery towards us. They smile and say, "Gracias," then give each of our passports a stamp. "14 Dias En Transito." (Fourteen Days in Transit). Before we've even pocketed our passports, they start waving their arms hastily, urging us out the exit door.

We step through a portal from a calm to a chaotic world. The streets are packed with vehicles of all shapes and sizes, whizzing and swerving around pedestrians. There are horns honking out every note in the octave, sounding out from all directions. A policeman standing in the back of a pickup truck, a rifle out, zooms around a sharp corner. Lynx and I look at each other; we both have giant grins on our faces. Now we're travelling. Excitement flows through my veins. I feel alive. We stroll through the dusty congestion seeking a map of the country, and a Spanish English dictionary.

Finding a map is harder than imagined: we assumed that it'd be a common item in a border town. Some of the stores have armed men standing guard at the entrances, despite the shelves inside being nearly empty. Unfamiliar brands of cheap candy and chips, mate, plastic flip flops, nothing that seems valuable enough to warrant having an armed guard. As we get further into town, the crowd thins. We continue searching the stalls and stores. Rummaging through a pile of second-hand magazines on the back wall of a half-empty shop, we finally come across a map of the country. At the cash register, I notice a slightly worn Spanish English dictionary under the shopkeepers' packet of cigarettes. I point to the dictionary and ask, "¿Podría comprar?" He nods and sells us both of the things we were seeking. We now feel ready for all that will come our way.

The shop owner directs us towards the sleepy, plain bus depot. We pick Yby Yau as our first destination. Our decision is made entirely based on "Yby Yau" being a neat looking name. We've got no idea if it's a city, a town, or a village. We'll find out when we get there. As we wait for our bus, we study our dictionary and see that it's missing the whole "F" and "P" sections and has a baffling and hilarious number of typos. But hey, it's better than nothing! An old bus trundles in and we walk over and ask the driver, "¿Yibee Yo?"

"¿Huh?", he says, with facial expressions.

We show him our map and point to Yby Yau and ask, "¿Bueno autobus?" He nods, and waves us aboard. Everyone's crammed together, sweating on each other as we slowly truck down a bumpy dusty road. It takes several hours to get where we are going. Because this bus is so different from any other ride I've been on, I love every minute of it. Every lurch and jostle are joyous. Come to think of it, I've loved being on busses since the one that cruised me out of Nova Scotia.

"Ibie Ah-ouw," the driver announces, as we pull into a dusty square littered with little shacks selling refreshments. "Ibie Ah-ouw!" the driver repeats, now looking directly at Lynx and I.

"¿Yibee Yo?" we ask. The driver rolls his eyes and nods. Out Lynx and I hop with our backpacks. There are several women selling fried chicken and fluorescent sugary drinks, all trying to make a sale, calling out their goods while going up to the windows of the busses that are coming in and out. After repeatedly saying, "No, gracias," to what they are selling, all eyes remain on us. We smile shyly and are returned with friendly looks of bewilderment. We ask, "Hotel?" A few people point down a road, still looking astonished. We follow their directions and arrive at the one and only hotel in about a minute. Yby Yau is a very small place. The hotel has about ten rooms. When we sign our names in the logbook, I notice that it's been a couple of weeks since anyone else has passed through. The hotel keeper shows us our humble room. We take a nap, a bit out of being intimidated by how much we stand out in this village, but mostly due to fatigue from the scorching heat.

After our snooze, it's time to explore. Before we've even reached the street corner, a group of teenagers calls to us from the front porch of a small house. They've got ice mate to share. We join them under the shade of a tin awning and conversate as best we can. They do most of the talking. My Spanish is unevolved, but I'm able to understand far more than I can express. They tell us how, in the middle of every afternoon, when the day's at its hottest, everyone just hides in the shade and drinks mate. *Everyone*. We share several rounds of mate while talking and laughing about how complicated it is to understand one another. After our bellies are sore from laughter and litres of mate, the afternoon heat fades and Lynx and I decide to go for a wander.

Within minutes, we're nearly at the edge of the village. There's a family sitting in front of the last little house on the road we're on. We smile at them and they wave us over. Again, talking is slow, but enthusiastic. They say that Lynx looks like Jesus and that I look like Princess Diana. They go on to tell us that we are the only foreigners they've ever seen here that aren't missionaries. They walk us to the school to show us the painted mural of Jesus Christ on the front gate. "Mira, pareces Jesús!" the mother insists on Lynx. To me, Lynx looks nothing like the painting, he's just white with long hair. Why is Jesus always depicted as white, anyhow? He's from the Middle East! I wish my Spanish was good enough to articulate my anger and frustrations about the brainwashing the European settlers and the church have influenced. Come dinnertime, they are bewildered to hear we don't eat meat. After kindly insisting that we're "muy loco!" for being vegetarian, they batter and fry up some cheese. It's passed around with heart-warming generosity, and is obscenely delicious. As the sun sets, we're doing more smiling than talking. The crickets speak for us, filling the night with their song.

Back at the hotel, as we review the day, a humbleness settles over Lynx and I. The villagers' excitement to meet us seemed parallel to our own excitement to be backpacking. It dawns on me that hanging out with us might be the closest thing to travelling that some or most of these people will ever get to experience. I'm starting to have a more appropriate emotional understanding of the gift that it is to come from the developed world. It overwhelms me with both gratitude and guilt.

We figure we ought to keep moving. We have less than two weeks to cross this land-locked country. In the morning, we return to the bus square, and buy tickets to another arbitrary place, guided only by our twisting tongues. Our bus is hours late. We spend the morning chilling with the vendors and the many others who just seem to be hanging out in the square. We make some more bracelets: with a bunch leftover from our beach time, we have enough for all the kids. I wonder if they'll still have them if I ever return, years down the line. An elder woman slices a miniature watermelon in two and hands us each a half with a spoon. Delighted, we joyously eat the refreshing gift. I can already feel my Spanish improving, just from a day of chatting and studying our superb dictionary.

The bus drops us off on the highway at an abrupt cluster of stores and restaurants. We seem to be in the commercial centre of a farming county. As we're walking down the street someone runs up to us, smiling widely, he hands us a little flyer that reads "Fiesta Rave." We return enthused smiles and thank him. With a while until the evening comes, we go and have a beer at one of the basic restaurants lining the highway.

Seconds after we sit down in dusty red plastic chairs with faded coca cola logos on them, two middle aged men pull up chairs to our table, uninvited. The copious stench of hard liquor wafts off their words, which quickly turn warlike.

"You two are educated, but we are intelligent. There's a difference, you know?" I make out from their slurring Spanish. We nod awkwardly, not wanting to provoke them. A group of young people, led by the party flyer guy, come to our aid, insisting we join their group.

Once we're safely out of earshot, one of the girls says in accented English, "Those two are danger men. Stay away from them. They are danger!"

"Muchas gracias," we say to our new friends. A Spanglish banter sparks up amongst us as we pile into the back of a pickup truck and make our way to the party. Talking remains difficult, but words aren't necessary when you're dancing. At a farm, somewhere near where we met, we dance until the sunrise. Most of the music is reggaetón, it's "muy popular" here. The fusion genre of Latin rhythms, dancehall, and hip-hop definitely has potential, but most of what was played at the party was choppy and obnoxious.

In the morning, our friends take us back downtown," and

wait with us until a bus comes. We hug goodbye, and climb aboard. This time, there are two empty seats. We take them, smile an "I love you" at each other, then promptly fall asleep. Sometime around mid-afternoon, we are shooed off the bus "Ultima Parada"(Last Stop), into another village.

At its edge there is a general store with about half a dozen men inside. Upon noticing us they all freeze. Conversation ceases. Everyone's staring at us with looks of total incredulousness. I almost burst into laughter — this feels like an exaggerated scene in a comedy film.

"Hola," Lynx says. They all remain silent then, after a few seconds, a couple of them offer faint nods. We try to be casual as we take a look around the barren store. We don't really know what we're looking for, yet feel oddly obliged by our onlookers. For some reason, there's an abundance of bags of olives on the sparse shelves.

"Yum, olives," I say. Lynx giggles tensely, and I narrowly succeed in holding back awkward laughter. Without an ounce of discretion, everyone's still staring at us in loud silence. We purchase the olives then exit stage left, leaving our audience just as paralyzed as when we entered. There doesn't seem to be much to this village either. There isn't even a hotel. We do a U-ie, back to the bus stop and leave.

We continue to pick destinations at random, closing our eyes and pointing, using the same method that had taken us to Hornby. Guess where we end up? Another village that seems to be the commercial hub of yet another farming county. Lynx and I shrug, a little disappointed by our far too mellow day. As we start to take in the surroundings, a man in an immaculate farming sombrero with thick rimmed, good-quality looking glasses walks up to us and surprises us by starting a conversation in impeccable English. We're thrilled to meet someone we can communicate in depth with. Andreas is a mobile veterinarian and invites us to join him tomorrow for his day of work. "Wow! Yes Please!"

At dawn we hop into his truck and start to drive through the endless farmland. Before long, the truck swerves. The three of us look out the passenger-side window to see the smeared remains of an enormous snake.

"Good," he says. "Those ones are poisonous." We pass a huge ranch with "Reinheit Viehzucht" carved into a gigantic wooden archway.

"What language was that?" I ask.

"German," he replies, somberly. His eyes don't leave the road ahead as he speaks. "I am sorry to say but there are a lot of Nazis in the area." Our jaws slowly fall open as this impossible fact sinks in. "They immigrated here after the Second World War, exiled and denied entrance by many other countries because they refused to show remorse about committing the Nazi atrocities. The ones in the area speak German, not Spanish, nor Guarani — the local native dialect. They have German stores and schools that are 100% segregated. And the barbaric bigots are incredibly rude to the Guarani natives. Every time a Guarani is hitchhiking and I stop to give them a ride, they're afraid. Due to the way they've been treated by the Nazis, they are usually more comfortable riding in the back of my pickup truck." He goes on to tell us he's the odd ball here, and that he's grateful to have met some travellers to spend time with.

"Why do you stay here?" we ask. He meekly nudges his glasses up his nose.

"Someone has to."

At the end of visiting farms with ill or injured animals, Andreas brings us back to another tiny commercial area. There are two hotels, directly across the highway from each other. Most highways have traffic. Not this one. The first hotel refuses to let us stay, giving no reason why. To our great relief, the one across the road admits us, albeit at a much higher cost than anywhere else we've yet stayed. We don't have other options and, surely, they realize this. Morning comes, and we leave with zeal.

Between the drunken men, the Nazi rumours, and the hotel rejection, I question if we're being given whispers of a reality check. I question if it's near the degree to which our naivety is in need of one. A clueless roam through the isolated boondocks of one of South America's poorest countries, a country never mentioned in our media, a nation we know nothing about, despite being quite tame, was perhaps charmed. Maybe picking names at random from a map in a place such as this is not the greatest idea. We decide to make a more informed decision for our next destination. As we study our map we learn that we need to get to a place called Concepcion. It's where the road forks and leads to the two Argentinian border crossings.

Concepcion's bus square is by far the largest we've come across in Paraguay. Some of the taxis are horse drawn carriages. Time seems to have wound us backwards. From a shabby carriage ride across dirt roads, and ones of worn, uneven, cobblestone, we are taken to a small hotel downtown. Conception seems big enough to be considered a town proper. Perhaps even a city. The hotel appears to be decaying from what once could have been lavish splendour. There are intricately hand carved railings and beams, colourful patterns painted on worn tiles, walls with chipped paint motifs, and peeling paper. From our small, faded blue room, we can climb onto a little porch that has us sitting above the main road, floating amid all the action.

On our first walk, we find an open-air market. It's a manic bustle compared to the neglected village shops we've grown accustomed to. We recognize the apple-ish scent and yellow of dried chamomile flowers from a woman vending herbs, and buy a few handfuls. I start to thank the vendor then burst into uproarious laughter as she hands me the dried flowers. Seconds later I'm keeled over, on hands and knees. People begin to stare. They probably all think I'm loco. Realizing this just makes my laughter more impossible to quell, and I make even more of a scene. Lynx looks at me, clearly embarrassed and baffled.

"Mefloquine," I manage to gasp.

He pulls me out of the market while saying, "lo siento" (sorry), to everyone that returns his gaze. We've been taking mefloquine, one of western medicines anti-malarials. Alongside vivid dreams, one of the side effects of mefloquine is fits of uncontrollable laughter. I'm horrified by my inability to articulate to the crowd that my laughing fit was completely unrelated to the market.

Back at the hotel we drink our chamomile the way mate is drunk. We fill our cup with chamomile flowers, put our filtered straws in, and down several rounds of tea, parched from the sun. The last thing I remember is putting the cup down on the table. I wake up in a daze, Lynx passed out beside me. I step out to the balcony to get my bearings and realize that night has fallen. We tranquilized ourselves. We hadn't realized the chamomile's strength. A day is spent coming in and out of consciousness. Our waking moments are brief and hazy.

The next morning, we're still groggy. After tons of mate, we finally start to wake up. On a mid-day walk, we wind up in a little store selling inexpensive coconut liqueur. Just being able to buy liquor is a novelty. We're still underage back home. On our way out of the shop, I notice some dark green melons.

"Lynx, check out the funky melons!"

"Those are avocados, sweetie."

"No way! They're perfectly round, the size of an infant's head, and have a thick waxy rind. They have to be melons!" Lynx grabs a couple and pays the shopkeeper for "dos aguacates."

"He's humouring you, they're melons!"

"We'll see about that." Having been out of North America before, he already knew that there are hundreds of strains of fruits and vegetables that never get imported into Canada. I'm learning things that seem like they should be common knowledge. This is just more evidence and conviction that our school system falls so very short. We feast on the decadent creamy "melons" from our balcony, overlooking the timeless town from our tiny balcony portal.

We let ourselves stay in Conception for a few days. It is definitely my favourite place that we've yet been. It feels alive after all the small villages. Yet it isn't totally perfect here. Some of the street corners have guards with rifles. We try to be friendly, smile some "hola's" their way, but they ignore us, Buckingham Palace style. In spite of the militant presence, the atmosphere feels relaxed. We spend a few days sitting on our marvellous balcony, sip coconut liqueur, smoke cheap handmade cigars we found at the market, and pretend we're adults.

With only a few days left until our "Fourteen days In Transit" stamps expire, it's time to hustle. Our map shows one border crossing in the north, and one at Asuncion, Paraguay's capital. I'm drawn towards Asuncion simply because another city will probably have more to do and see than another village or farm county. Another bus delivers us to the capital's downtown late in the afternoon.

The architecture, much like Concepcion, gives the impression that it flourished here at one time. If, and why, remains a mystery to us. The buildings haven't been maintained, and now they rot into the city. It's quiet. The roads are fairly empty, with even fewer pedestrians than cars. There are hardly any shops or restaurants. It's eerie and disappointing. We come to question, *again*, if we are actually downtown.

The ceiling in our hotel room is high, but the paint is chipping. There's a bit of garbage left in the corners, empty bottles and crumpled old newspapers. It feels like being in the ruins of a palace. At night we lay awake, both trying to ignore the tangible invisible bugs hopping all over us. After a restless and icky night, we find the border crossing, and are informed that this is the only open border on Paraguay's west. Big Fiew! We hadn't a day left to spare in our "14 Dias En Transito."

Nine

In Argentina, all of the national parks offer free camping. We head for Parque Nacional Rio Pilcomayo, the park that's nearest our border crossing. We find ourselves in a clearing surrounded by trees and shrubbery, with fire pits dispersed here and there. Like at Foz do Iguacu, we are the only campers. There's a boardwalk that leads us through muggy marsh under brilliant blue sky to a large river. From the little dock at the end of the walkway we can make out the heads of crocodile-like animals waiting patiently for their prey (us?) among the bushes that line the water. There's a sign advising people to swim with their shoes on for protection against the piranhas. Even though it's exasperatingly hot, neither of us are brave enough to jump into the river.

After a few days of having the park to ourselves, a family shows up. As we look on, hesitantly, the kids dash and cannonball into the river, barefoot. Lynx and I laugh at our cowardice yet remain too afraid to go swimming. We decide to carry on while we have a chance to and catch a ride to the highway with the family the next morning. They're heading west. At the highway we hop out, wait for a gap in the high-speed traffic before then darting across to the eastbound side and sticking our thumbs out. For every car that zooms by, the sun rises a little higher, and it becomes more and more hot. With our backs to the traffic, we walk for what feels like eons. We're starting to wonder if hitch-hiking is even a thing here.

The heat becomes scorching. A car finally pulls to the shoulder of the freeway. Hoping it isn't a mirage, we run to catch our ride.

As soon as we get into the car the two in the front ardently lecture us in perfect English. "You should never hitch-hike in Argentina! Sometimes people just disappear!" I wonder if we got lucky, or if they're just being uptight. Either way, I'm very relieved and grateful for the ride and its air conditioning. Our hosts are a brother and sister heading home from a vacation. They're young adults that are still living with their parents, and explain that that's common here. We chat pleasantly for the duration of the ride. When we arrive to Formosa, their city, they invite us to their home. A house hidden from the public eye, behind a towering gate. We spend the afternoon unwinding in their pool, brave enough to enter this water. In the evening they bring us to the bus station. We thank them for everything, then purchase tickets going to Resistencia, the city that our hosts recommended.

We arrive mid-morning. Lynx and I walk cluelessly in an already sweltering heat until a man runs over to us. "Where are you from? What are you doing?" he asks. "Backpackers, marvellous! We don't get many over here!" Fernando's also a traveller. He invites us to come and stay with him, insists that he'd like to return the same hospitality that he receives from strangers whilst on the road. "Besides," he says, "I've been bored lately and it'd be nice to have some company." Elated, we follow him to his home.

Like our friends in Resistencia, Fernando's manor is fully concealed behind a hulking wall. He types in the ten-digit password and the gate opens. There's a terrifying guard dog, as if the giant locked wall with broken glass protruding out its top wouldn't be enough of a deterrent. Fernando calms his hysterical dog and ties him up. He warns us to stay away. "He's as vicious as his bark."

We follow him through beautiful, art-filled halls to the guest room. I sigh as an artificial coolness evaporates the sweat from my skin. From a ceramic thermometer on the wall, we learn that outside it's forty degrees Celsius. Fernando makes sandwiches. As we chat and snack in his gorgeous courtyard filled with resplendent plants, he tells us that he's hosting a New Year's Eve party and we should stay at least until then so that we can join the celebration.

We spend half a week in luxury, drinking, smoking, talking, and laughing. There's a hummingbird that keeps coming around the porch. Every time we all join in child-like awe to watch her. Like the darting hummingbird, Lynx and I are already feeling pulled in many other directions. Hiding behind a gate is frivolous.

New Year's Eve arrives. Quite late into the evening, the guests begin to arrive. Some of them speak English. I practice my Spanish, and they, their English. Again, we drink, smoke, feast, and laugh. We lie to ourselves with resolutions that by tomorrow we shall have reigns on drinking, smoking, and feasting. The clock strikes twelve and we all flutter around giving kisses on cheeks and big jolly hugs. Around four a.m., most of Fernando's guests leave. Before the door is even closed from wishing the last couple well on their way, he turns to us and asks if we have the energy to keep celebrating. The rest of the "night" is spent at a dance club. By 10 a.m. we stumble our way back to Fernando's.

Through our hangover, we decide that the time to continue on our journey has come. Fernando suggests Salta as a destination. The hummingbird reappears as a good omen.

A night bus chariots us into the Andean mountain range. As the sun peeks over the mountains, we step off the bus, into a crowded station. There's a plethora of other backpackers. I suppose we're on the beaten path now. We haven't seen any other travellers since Foz Do Iguacu.

As Lynx and I rub our eyes awake, a tall, Western European-looking dude with a backpack on walks over to us and says, "Everything OK? You two look lost."

"Just sleepy and surprised," Lynx replies.

"All right, cool." says the friendly snow giant.

"Do you have any recommendations of somewhere interesting to go?" I ask.

"Start at Jujuy, then keep going to the other villages on the hippie trail. Trust me, you'll like it."

Jujuy is small, yet there is an abundance of hostels and cheap hotels. Indeed, we are on the well-worn trail. We ditch our bags at a humble guesthouse then go outside to discover where we are.

Most of the houses and stores are small and constructed out of adobe: handmade, sun dried clay bricks from the mountain side. When a building gets too old it returns back to the Earth without causing any harm. The ancient and futuristic adobe structures are completely eco harmonious and comfortable too. They naturally stay cool inside during the heat of the day and hold warmth during the chilly nights.

Walking through the small streets, our gazes are up, marvelling at the spectacular hills. From the ground, someone whistles at us. A small man, crouching on the ground extends his hands full of leaves upwards to us and asks "¿Quieren Coca?" We look at each other, to ask, not really needing to.

Pure coca leaves are ubiquitous here. They are used by many and considered to be sacred, a divine gift from la Pachamama, the Mother of Earth and Time. Coca leaves are used to make cocaine. Unfortunately, this association often gives coca a bad reputation. Cocaine is a drastically different substance than coca leaves when used in their traditional manner — dried and chewed. Cocaine is toxic and ruins lives; coca does the opposite. Coca, when used in it's pure and traditional form, is a miracle medicine, and a superfood.

When used the way la Pachamama presents them, coca leaves are a healthy and essential part of life in this region. They help one cope with the harsh realities of living high in the mountains, as they remedy altitude sickness. Due to their dense nutrient content, they are a healthy stimulant. They combat malnutrition, something direly needed as most of the people living in this area are living in poverty. Coca leaves contain more protein than meat and more calcium than milk.

Also, Riboflavin, Vitamins A, C, E, B1, B2, Magnesium and Phosphorus. Coca can cure chronic anemia, depression, osteoporosis, and leukemia. The list goes on.

If coca leaves were to be banned here it would result in the people suffering from weakness, malnutrition, and respiratory difficulties. Help with altitude and an extra bounce in one's step is a necessity of life for coping with the physically demanding, underpaid, laborious lives that are the reality of a lot of the local people's day to day life.

We pass a man sitting on the street selling a beautiful handmade guitar. Lynx picks it up and starts strumming. It's a little twangy, but definitely special!

"¿Cuanta cuesta?"

"1000 pesos." The three of us smile, all feeling like we're

getting a good deal. I'm sure we could talk the price down — probably quite a lot — but it would feel greedy and hurt our hearts. We make our way out of the village and go sing-hiking up a mountain trail.

We chew coca leaves as we ignore the advice given to us by our last hitch, and walk with our thumbs out towards Purmamarca, the next village along the "hippie trail." The winding mountain road is hushed and nearly devoid of traffic. As we start to wonder if we should turn around, a sleek black car appears from around a bend and pulls over. Inside are four dudes that look about our age. We squish into the backseat with two others and the guy in the passenger seat sparks up a doobie. We roll up the windows and laugh our way through the serpentine road. Around a sharp corner, we see a police roadblock ahead. Caught off guard, we roll down the windows and smoke billows out. There is no time to discreetly turn around. Half a minute later we are parked at the two awaiting cops. Rapid conversation ensues between the two guys in front and the policemen. I can't quite make out what is being said. The two guys in the front switch seats and miraculously, the cops smile and wave us on. We calm our racing hearts and ask our buddies what just happened. It turns out our original chauffeur doesn't have a license. But, seeing as these boys are locals, the cops decided to go easy on them. They tell us that we got *really* lucky, that police here are often corrupt and it is not uncommon for them to commit horrendous acts. We have a good laugh about it all while I shrug off the sentiment that it might be wise to travel a bit more cautiously.

We drop our packs in a humble guesthouse in the next village and go for a hike up into the surrounding mountains. On the trail we meet a friendly group of travellers from Buenos

Aires. Our legs dangle off a ledge, overlooking the mountain range, and together we awe at our planet below. They also share a joint with us and we sit on the edge of the sky together, mesmerized by the vast and stunning landscape.

Deep red hills, crisp blue sky, snow-white fluffy clouds. We hike to Tilcara together and have street empanadas with a few bottles of cheap, yet delicious, local wine. Afterwards, we all head to a lively folk concert.

While I sway to a song, I am hit with a burst of awesome gratitude. I'm in disbelief of how good it feels to be here, to be me. Am I still in the same life that "Sarah" would have lived? Everything feels almost too good. I'm free. I'm loved. I'm in love. I'm happy. Soulfully, humbly, happy. I believe in a future filled with walking all of my dreams. I have liberated myself from the overworked, mundane lifestyle that my culture sold me as the only realistic way to live. The life I marvelled at wondrously, but rarely believed was available to me, has become my reality. Life is in my hands now. I haven't bought into the path of student loans, a mortgage, two point three kids, and one and a half dogs, secured behind a white picket fence. I am not a victim to the mirage of a "good life" that has so many people fooled and trapped.

We hang out with the crew from Buenos Aires for a few days, easily finding common ground in wine-hiking. They teach us more about Argentina. Buenos Aires is a modern anomaly, an international city with a considerable amount of affluence and diversity. They all belong to the middle class and understand that they've lucked out on that one. They all went to university which enabled them to secure careers. Despite that they are beyond overqualified for their jobs, they are still fortunate to have them. Going to university doesn't guarantee a job here. Decent housing is expensive; most of them still live with their parents. They're all on their yearly two-week vacation now. None of them have more than a couple weeks. They hope that with the passing years they'll be granted the ability to take time off and travel more. The Buenos Aires boys proudly tell us how Argentinians are great musicians. From the little we've seen, this may actually be true, somehow. They go on to tell us that the police here are incredibly corrupt, and can get away with practically anything. That we should avoid the cops at all costs. And, if we're ever in another situation where we have to deal with them, we should be completely polite and compliant, to avoid giving them an excuse to take advantage of their nefarious power.

Lynx and I trundle to the next town on a rickety old bus. After another wander in the mountains, we make our way back into the village and see a crowd huddled in the central plaza. Everyone's laughing. Curious, we join the onlookers. A man is holding a cloth bag. Seconds later I notice a tail hanging out, waving in the wind. I squint to see further, questioning my eyesight. The guys' mate lifts a baseball bat in the air and comes down on the bag with full force. There is a deadening horrible shriek, a cat in absolute agony. The crowd erupts into laughter again, egging the guys on. Lynx and I are flabbergasted and horrified. But, we are outnumbered. Devastated, we hurry our way back to our guesthouse. The cat's holler loops in my brain as I shiver. Before we reach our guesthouse, we cross another group. They have a cooler, and a bat. We hear another howl, this time, it is coming from the cooler. They lift the lid and inch or so, and shake it, bashing a different cat around. Lynx bursts into tears and tells them to stop. They explode into menacing laughter. I pull Lynx away as he looks ready to punch someone, lost in the cats' terror, too distraught to realize he could become the cat. Back in our room, we are both in tears. What could possibly motivate people to do this?

    These villages don't feel like a utopic fairy tale land any more. So, we decide to leave, and purchase tickets for a bus headed to the Bolivian border. Our bags are heavier, we've been collecting rocks. But we are also stronger than we were at the beginning of our trip. We're getting accustomed to carrying our packs. We fall asleep on the bus ride and arrive at the border crossing as dusk is melting into darkness.

Ten

There's a line of folk at the door of the customs office, far different than the deserted Paraguayan border. After a long, nervous wait in line we get to the desk and a worker instantly stamps our passports and waves us through the gateway. "Bienvenidos a Bolivia." We walk into a town called Villazon. There's not much traffic. The food merchants are all packing up their stalls for the day. We walk uphill, under dim, flickering street lights, wanting nothing more than shelter for the night. The crowd thins as we move deeper into town. I start to wonder if the lack of pedestrians is due to nightfall, or if we're in a rough part of Villazon. A man approaches Lynx and I and queries if we're looking for a hotel. He knows of a "good and cheap" one and offers to show us the way. Lynx thanks the man, who proceeds to lead us up the road. The two of them banter and I find myself losing pace with them. My gut goes cold and, suddenly, I am filled with anxiety. Something inside me is screaming and urging me to turn around. The crowd thins even more as I follow the man and Lynx's swift, strong steps. I want to interrupt and tell Lynx that I don't trust our guide. My throat feels dry, as if there's a lump of paste clogged in it. I stay silent. The fear of being rude overrides obeying my intuition. Their pace becomes more brisk, until I am panting to keep up. Our guide swerves right, onto a narrow, even darker, side street. I grab Lynx's shoulder to pull him back onto the main road. I'm ready to voice my illogical terror. I open my mouth and am struck silent as a large man in a puffy green jacket emerges from the shadows.

He pushes off of the wall, towers over the three of us, and commands us to stop walking as he takes a badge out of the chest pocket of his coat. He's a narcotics enforcement officer. Curtly, he demands us to show him our passports. We immediately comply and hand our identification over. He barely glances at them before pocketing them with his badge. In rapid Spanish, he proclaims something about drogas, blancas, and la frontera.

He commands that we follow him.

"¿Que?" feebly fumbles from my lips. We look around, seeking onlookers to encourage us to not play along. There is no one else sharing the side street.

He gets right up into my face and yells, "Drogas!" Spit spatters on my cheeks. I want to turn away, but we are already trapped under his outrageous demands. He's shown us his badge; we don't want to see his gun. What else are we to do? The two men shove Lynx to move and start a fast strut. The man who offered to lead us to a hotel is now obviously the narcotic officer's sidekick. We're jogging now, tethered to our pocketed passports. We are led farther and farther from the main road. Farther and farther from the safety that a crowd brings.

Finally, in pitch blackness, they come to a halt. There are no streetlights. The officer's accomplice turns on a weak flashlight and I make out a cement wall with rocks and trash scattered on the ground. They rip our bags from our backs and throw them on the ground. The narcotics officer starts rummaging through our backpacks while the other man holds the flashlight. Stupefied, it is now evident that this isn't a lawful search. We weren't brought to a police station, but to the filthy outskirts of town. In the strongest tone I've ever heard come out of my throat I demand our passports back. The man looks over his shoulder and levels a hard stare at me. I am stunned as he miraculously throws them at Lynx's feet.

    Seconds later, they finish scouring our bags. The cop demands that we face and put our hands on the tall rock wall. I see my silhouette appear on the cold concrete as the flashlight becomes trained on me. The man in the thick green jacket starts frisking me, aggressively. Pats quickly turns to gropes. Breasts, ass, crotch. The narcotics officer grabs my arm and pins me into the wall. He shoves his dry, cracked, filthy, fat fingers up my cunt and starts feeling around. Petrified, I hover above my body and watch for a few seconds, as if this is not happening to me. Then, seconds later, it is. I return to my body and start screaming. We come out of our paralyzed idiocy. Lynx grabs a large jagged stone and threatens it in the air. They are flustered and back off for a second. We grab our bags and run. Run like gazelles being chased by lions. Eyes forward, not daring to look back. Never has my body moved anywhere near as fast as it is now. We come to a street and turn, thoughtless, following the far-off street lamps. Finally, we are back on the main drag where there are still some stragglers from the day. I never knew how much solace the presence of a few strangers could provide. At last, we can stop running.

    We spot an unambitious sign in front of a metal gate that reads "Hotel." We ask the guard if there are any vacant rooms. He shakes his head, unconcerned with our dilemma. "¿Por favor? Tomaremos cualquier cosa." We're literally begging for anything. Only when my voice begins to crack with emotion does he reluctantly agree to rent us a space for the night. For a brief moment, I'm relieved.

We're given a key and pointed across an unadorned courtyard towards our room. We open the door, a dull light bulb rocks back and forth above the filth. This room is clearly reserved for paupers and vagrants. There is a cement floor, a small dirty mattress — nothing more. There's an even filthier shared bathroom across the courtyard. Everything is disgusting. Our revolting surroundings perfectly embody how I feel inside.

In the room, I try to explain to Lynx how the sensation of the man's fingers are lingering inside of me. His dry cracked hands have left a haunting presence. I start to tremble. Lynx goes to the pump outside and fills our cooking pot with water. Rain starts to pour. I burst into tears and cry as I crouch over our cooking pot and try to cleanse myself of the invasion with ice cold water. I feel sick. So sick. I feel stupid. So fucking stupid. No matter how long I wash myself, I can't shake the feeling of disgust that lingers.

Lynx takes my hand and helps me to the bed where he laid out our sarong over the filth. I lay in his arms and sob. Slowly I begin to relax and sleep begins to take hold. Lynx turns out the light and, suddenly, I see and feel ghosts in the room. They whisper. They drift over to me, tangibly shifting the texture of the air. In a panic, I turn the light back on and the spirits disappear. We leave the light on all night. Lynx holds me, and eventually I drift into sleep, but into more nightmares.

Disenchanted, deflated, and drained, we hoist what remains of our bags and leave to find the bus station. Walking through Villazon, we see puffy green Policia jackets everywhere we turn. There are clusters of men sporting them. I wonder if the men from last night are among them. I'm having a hard time breathing. This isn't fun any more. I'm filled with fear.

We splurge for a nicer bus. The kind of bus where everyone is guaranteed a seat and the route is more direct. It's really not expensive at all. It turns out Bolivia's the poorest country in South America. The driver takes his seat and blasts the volume on the radio; the sub-par, obnoxious, headache-causing reggaetón that is impossible to tune out. Now that our bubble of bliss has been broken, Lynx and I realize how sick we are of constantly being forced to listen to reggaetón.

Our tickets are for La Paz, the capital city. As dawn's light has barely begun, we are shaken awake and shooed off the bus. The driver tells us that the miners are protesting, *again*. They've blocked every single road entrance in and out of La Paz. I ask him why they're protesting. "Their working conditions are extremely dangerous, deaths are common, and the pay is basically slave wage." Once the driver finishes dumping the passengers and all of their stuff onto the side of the road, he turns around and drives away, utterly apathetic about tossing us out into the sprawling outskirts of La Paz.

At first, I'm nervous to be walking through the protests. But, to our surprise, we're mostly ignored. We walk all morning to the rhythm of turmoil. The miners in protest have set scattered tire-fires on the road. Pillars of smoke join the layer of smog that hangs low in the sky. Hours pass where we see no violence, and through the exhaustion we become calm. As we near the city, the shacks and buildings thicken. Around midday we start the steep descent into the valley towards the city centre, and reach streets within the barricade. A taxi driver spots us and rolls down his window "¿Distrito turístico?" We climb in.

The tourist district is a small section of steep and narrow streets in the downtown vicinity. The larger roads are packed with mini vans, cabs, busses, and bicycles that pulse in and out of each other. The air is thick and grey. It's the most polluted air that I've ever seen or inhaled. The sidewalks are as busy as the roads and aren't really separate from one another. They're laden with vendors selling various wares. We push our way through the steep crowd. There's a lot of young boys competing over polishing the shoes of the more well-off men, in exchange for meagre coins. It's dirty. It's loud. My rose-coloured glasses have been shattered. The city is sad. It's just a myriad of people trapped in poverty and pollution. What an ignorant asshole I was to see this sort of environment as exciting, before.

We find a cheap hotel. This time the receptionist is welcoming. He shows us to our basic room, making sure that it's to our liking. As I'm dropping my bag onto the bed, I see a sign on the wall, and my jaw drops and I start to cry. There is a warning poster that reads:

Oficiales de narcóticos encubiertos no están autorizados a tratar con los turistas. Si se acercan a usted, alertar a las autoridades.

Undercover narcotics officers are not allowed to deal with tourists. If they approach you, alert the authorities.

How could I have been so stupid? Why didn't I bother to research where we were going? Dejection and frustration cling to me like the pollution in the air.

After a few days of wandering the congested metropolis, we both miss being in nature. A shop owner convinces us to sign up for a bike tour. "Death Road," internationally labelled as the world's most dangerous road, is a narrow, winding road carved into the hillside that connects La Paz with the Amazon Rainforest. It got its name because, every year, several vehicles topple over the edge. However, Death Road is also acclaimed for its magnificent beauty. On the tour, there's about a dozen other backpackers. Lynx and I feel embarrassed for being in a guided group of tourists. We criticize ourselves for conforming to what typical tourists do, not what, in our minds, travellers do. Far away, and high above the city, the van parks and we are each given a bicycle. The others drop away down the road and around the cliffside one by one. It's nice to be on a bike again. I haven't been on one since summer on Hornby. We hop on our bikes and fall into a speedy glide down the steep and narrow road. One side is lined with lush jungle, waterfalls and vivid vegetation. On the other side there is a sheer, deadly drop, overlooking vibrant hills bellow. As I cruise downhill, riding the edge of danger, my spirits lift. I'm reacquainted with the feeling of awe and enthusiasm to be travelling, blessed to have the life that I have. We get to the bottom, barely having peddled, and Lynx and I leave the group and make our way back into La Paz, both feeling more open to take part in typical tourist stuff.

We arrange a four-day jeep tour. There are no roads where we are going, so the driver has loaded enough gas and water for the next four days onto his jeep. We're brought to spectacular rock formations in the desert, hot springs, geysers, borax fields, colourful lagoons, salt flats, all far from human civilization. At moments, the geography makes us feel like we're on a different planet. It's an uplifting reminder of how magical Earth can be, and of how tiny we are in the cosmos. The Dome pales in comparison to Bolivia. We are in absolute awe of this spectacular jeep journey, and unsure whether we should celebrate or lament it only costing twenty-five dollars a day. For the first time in my li

We decide to continue on the recommended path for a little while, a little out of fear of getting into other jeopardy situations, and a little out of realizing that touristy things are popular for a reason. Onward — to Cuzco, Peru!

Eleven

Cuzco is the city that's nearest to Machu Picchu, the ruins of a fortified ancient Inca city high in the mountains, and considered to be one of the seven wonders of the world. Cuzco swarms around us, hordes of wealthy travellers from all over the world. Many of whom carry the hurried and stressed energy of their normal lives, as they take a brief vacation. There's an abundance of spiffy-looking hotels, restaurants, massage parlours, and tour agencies lining the city centre. We walk towards the edge of town, where the bustle of commerce begins to thin out, and duck into a random guesthouse. It's less than five dollars a night. Our room is cold and contains nothing more than a bed with oodles of thick, worn, dusty blankets. Cuzco is at an altitude of three thousand, three hundred and ninety-nine metres. The nights are going to be quite cold, drastically contrasting from the warm, sunny days. It's beautiful, but there are so many tourists that it feels like we're back in the culture we come from.

One afternoon, Lynx goes for a stroll while I take a nap. When he returns to our room, he tells me that he was offered cocaine. I chuckle and ask him what he said. He laughs, puts his hand in his pants pocket and pulls out a white wad wrapped in plastic and tosses it onto the foot of the bed.

His eyes are alight with curiosity. I don't know much about cocaine, but it seems like he was sold quite a lot. Like... a lot, a lot. We're lucky that cocaine came to us in Peru, otherwise we could be in a Bolivian prison! That thought is too awful to connect with emotionally. I just shrug it off, detached. We crush some of the condensed powder into fine lines, guessing what size of line is normal, then roll a ten soles (about three dollars) bank note into a straw. I plug my right nostril as I inhale the line of powder with my left. I guess television taught me something useful after all. I can taste it dripping in the back of my throat, chalky and strange. We talk passionately about this and that while we build little sculptures with the rocks we haven't crushed yet. After some minutes, the high starts to wear off. We do another line and I feel clear headed and awake. Lynx picks up the guitar. I dance while he strums. After our next line, I sit down with my journal and start to scribe poetry. Poetry that in the moment seems like it isn't complete crap. "…these words are composed from rocks and songs. Blow my mind. I'm wide awake whilst I weave through this dream. Woven alpaca wool warming my whole while we watch stars where the sun was weaning just moments ago. I blink with the stars. In another blink, this will be nothing more than mere memory…"

  The next afternoon, we find ourselves in a shop near downtown. While I browse the seducing clothes, Lynx strikes up a conversation with a man. After a little while, I join them. Inti tells us he's a shaman, comes from a lineage of shamans. His family has been passing down wisdom and inherent powers, from father to son, for generations. He tells us his friend and fellow shaman has just arrived from the jungle with a sacred and mighty visionary substance.

  Ayahuasca is an Amazonian vine that is combined with various other plants, then brewed into a hallucinogenic potion. The elixir is revered as a wise teacher, unlocking cosmic wisdom in those who drink it. It's intended use is for healing purposes. Healing of illnesses, addictions, as well as emotional wounds. Eyes shining, Inti goes on to praise the vine concoction and all its powers, before finally asking if we'd like to take part in an Ayahuasca ceremony. "The Moon is full; the timing is most auspicious now."

Not only because Inti is asking for a gargantuan sum of money to take part in his private ceremony, I'm hesitant. I'm not feeling one hundred percent comfortable with doing hallucinogens. Since my assault in Villazon, I've been experiencing random waves of panic. It seems like a bad idea to enter psychedelia with a negative emotional foundation. Inti claims that Ayahuasca would be perfect medicine for what I'm going through. I'm still a little nervous about the idea but Lynx really wants to do it, so, I decide to be brave and agree to take part.

We barter Inti from one hundred and fifty down to one hundred US dollars, citing posters we've seen around town which advertise Ayahuasca ceremonies for a fraction of what he's asking. He counters by telling us he is offering an authentic life-changing odyssey, that the cheap ceremonies only have one shaman for about twenty people, and they water down the medicine too. In order to truly have a profound experience one has to drink enough medicine so that it forces its way out of them in the form of vomit. Without the purging experience, there is hardly any effect. Inti convinces us that we're lucky to have found him, suggests that the plant probably drew our spirits towards it. "Many come here seeking the opportunity that I am offering you, but don't find it." How can we say no?

Inti instructs us to fast for the rest of the day. We make

plans to meet early tomorrow morning, then part ways. By the time we get back to our guesthouse, the day's already getting on, so resisting the urge to eat is easy... or maybe that's the cocaine that's still in our systems from the night before. Wanting to make the most of this opportunity, to have the most significant experience available, we go to bed early. I'm only just beginning to be able to sleep peacefully again.

We wake early and walk to the large open-air market to meet up with the shamans. Lynx is giddy; it's infectious. By the time we arrive, my nervousness has shifted to eagerness. "Buenos Dias," everyone says with smiles.

Inti introduces us to the other shaman, Fuego. We skip to keep up with Inti and Fuego as they navigate through the bustle. The stench of the meat section hangs thick in the air between all the plant stalls. The shamans barter and buy flowers, various curious herbs, bags of symbolic offerings, pure wild tobacco cigars. They finish gathering what is needed and the four of us hop into a taxi. We are whisked out of the city, up a winding mountain road. After a few minutes of driving past the last of the man-made structures, Inti asks the driver to let us out. From what seems to be a completely arbitrary location, we hike into the trail-free mountain side for about fifteen minutes. We arrive at a clearing, embraced by shrubs and boulders. Fuego stops in his tracks, turns to us and asks, "You like this space?" We nod. "This is where we shall do the ceremony."

Inti and Fuego start to clear the area of branches. Lynx and I exchange an excited glance and join in. The shamans chant and wave smoking palo santo wood around us and the land. A fire is struck with twigs and branches. Unfamiliar herbs are sprinkled on the flames with prayers. The aroma tingles and opens my lungs, causing a similar sensation of a eucalyptus cough rub. We sit by the fire as Inti and Fuego circle us, singing songs to bless our journey. Fuego takes a deep inhalation from a huge cigar and blows the smoke onto the crown of my head, and I feel shimmers flow through my cranium. We are told it's now our turn to say a prayer.

"Dear God?" I start, not even sure I believe in God. "Umm... if you can hear us, and happen to notice this prayer, well, um... please keep us safe. And, um... give us healing revelations. Thanks. Amen? Yeah, thank you."

Fuego takes a bundle of beautiful purple fabric and unwinds it to reveal a glass bottle filled with orangey-brown liquid. Inti gives us each a glass cup. The Ayahuasca oozes out, thick and sludgy. I take my first sip. It tastes like stomach bile mixed with chunky dirt. It's difficult to swallow, but we manage to gulp it down, motivated by the lure of its legendary magic.

I sit cross legged at the fire, excited and nervous. I anticipate the supernatural, but feel nothing, yet. I space out into the flames for a little while. Suddenly, gusts of wind from within bring me to my feet. I dance-walk, the breezes inside meander and control my motions. In an unexpected instant, my gut becomes cold and dense. I am overwhelmed by the need to vomit and reach the edge of our clearing without a second to spare. Projectile spew leaps from my throat. I fall to my knees and continue to hurl. It's excruciating. My throat burns, my belly quivers, my tongue is numb. My whole body trembles and aches. Fuego comes to me and rubs my back. "Muy bueno, muy bueno... solo un poco mas." My sensations are all magnified and his touch is incredibly soothing. The pain and the pleasant simultaneously overwhelm me. Then, the divide between negative and positive vanishes. The ground I'm barfing on comes alive. The grass and weeds start to spiral together, grow out of the mess in a beautiful whirl. My stomach is finally empty. I raise my head and look across the valley. The adobe huts in the distance transform into blue, cartoon-like blocks, then leap out of the mountainside. I feel them nudge me backwards.

The shamans each take a side of my body and practically carry my jellyfish-legs to the centre of our clearing. Walking is extremely confusing. Legs are as familiar as wings. I lay down and am overwhelmed by fear. What the fuck did I just ingest? Where the hell am I? Who are these men? I can't stand, or even sit. My body and brain melt into particles. Am I dying? Holy shit, I am dying! I curl up into a ball and my terror grows. Inti and Fuego gently roll me out of the foetal position and onto my back. They open my clench fists and open my palms toward the sky. Having my posture adjusted instantly shifts my experience. An epiphany flows into me; if I am dead then, clearly, I still exist. There is no point in resisting what is happening, I cannot change it. From the depth of my soul, wisdom whispers, "Take this transition with peace. Enjoy the ride." Fear disappears. Acceptance, curiosity, then excitement take its place. I surrender to, and welcome, Ayahuasca's spirit. My back is no more supported by the Earth and gravity as much as my front is resting on the sky, supported and held by air and galaxies. There is no up or down. Yet, somehow, there are so many directions. I'm being held in the centre of the cosmos and the centre of infinity. I fly through galaxies, watch time implode and explode into stardust.

Next, I spiral through the history of my life. Not only am I revisiting the past through my experience, I'm an incorporeal being that is entering and exiting the points of view and secret histories of the people in my past. People that were kind. People that were cruel. Perspectives begin to echo around my mind from countless angles, intersecting, extrapolating upon each other. Moments within worlds shape the worlds within moments, and I? I am Eye, the Seer of Seas. Nowhere to be found, but in between.

The sound of a train distracts me. It's zooming through the sky, directly towards me, approaching with increasing velocity. My thoughts can't reach my legs to move out of its path. I open my mouth and it becomes a portal. I swallow the train and am jolted into a reviving breath. The blast turns everything into familiar particles. The particles become more solid and dense. Next, my body returns to concrete existence, on a tangible planet. I open my eyes, and am back in our clearing, laying on the grass beside Lynx, who must have gotten carried over to me once his Ayahuasca took effect.

Lynx looks incredibly distraught. He moans, in distress. I take his hand in mind. "Maya?" he murmurs, voice cottony and frail.

"I'm here," I reply.

Speaking feels complicated and goofy. Lynx's face softens and smiles. We stay holding hands and move closer together to drift back into familiar consciousness. After what could have been minutes or hours, the shamans walk over to us and gently ask if we're ready to return to town. *Slowly*, we make our way down the mountainside. There are so many unique pieces of grass to look at! Back at the road, we stroll towards town. I don't want to return to the city quite yet, but the day is getting on. I'm as fragile and as indestructible as air. Refreshed and exhausted, I analyse the absence of thoughts, until a taxi eventually passes and Fuego flags it down to return us to Cuzco.

Inti invites us to spend the night at his place, and I notice for the first time that evening has arrived. Is it really night when the Moon is full? We float through the city, trust Inti to shepherd us. His home consists of a little bedroom and a small living room. There is a courtyard with a bathroom and a kitchen that is shared with neighbours. Our bodies take up the entire floor of the living room. I see Inti sip a cup of water, and am hit with extreme thirst. I guess that makes sense — I hurled up everything but my organs, then laid in the sun all day. I ask Inti if the water is safe to drink and he nods. I go to the tap and ravenously down litres.

A few hours later I ache with a chill all over my body. Next comes the diarrhoea. Hours of miserable and painful diarrhoea. Inti keeps filling the house with thick palo santo smoke, insists it will help me return to health. The air is so thick that breathing feels difficult. I need fresh air but am too weak to go outside. Everything is hazy and painful. I'm in and out of consciousness. When I do wake, it's brief, and I am too weak to get out of bed. I pray again. Pray for the pain to end.

Three days later, I'm well enough to get out of bed, and join Lynx and Inti in the courtyard. With my lungs finally getting the fresh air that they were desperate for, more energy comes to me. I sit in the courtyard all day, thawing my chills in the sun, and replenishing my cells with crisp clean mountain air.

The next morning, I'm much more alert, though my back muscles still ache severely. Inti says he has a cream that will help with the soreness. He turns to Lynx and asks if it's okay to rub it on my back — as if I were Lynx's property. But this man safely guided us to other realms. His moment of misogyny must be an accident, it doesn't suit. I shrug it off and continue to hold him in trust and reverence. I lay on the floor/bed, and Inti reaches under my shirt to massage the cream into my back. Lynx goes into the courtyard. Seconds later, Inti lifts up my pants and starts rubbing my ass!

    What the hell? Being a shaman, he should be able to feel the energy shift. He must know I'm not comfortable with this. My butt has no need for cream, and Inti certainly has no right, or permission, to reach under my pants. I leap to my feet, hold the wall to steady my dizzying body that wants to pass out, and scream at him in English, "Fuck you! You're a fraud! Fuck you!"

    Lynx comes back inside to see what the yelling is about. "We're leaving. Let's go!" Eyes on the ground, Inti dashes outside and skirts out of the courtyard, head hung low, not daring to lock eyes with the onlooking neighbour.

    My energy levels are still really low. Doing some of our leftover blow is our solution to get enough energy to trek our backpacks through Cuzco. We each snort a line in the courtyard, apathetic to what the bamboozled neighbour might think, not willing to go back into Intis' place.

    "I wonder if the Full Moon helps with that, too." Lynx says. I laugh feebly.

    "Whatever, let's just get out of here."

    We hop off a bus somewhere a few hours from Cuzco. While we walk out of the bus depot, everyone *stares*. No one smiles. My anxiety returns in full force. We do a one-eighty, go back to the bus station, and leave for Lima, Peru's capital city.

    Whilst in Lima, Lynx's dad decides to visit us. The three

of us make our way north on a cushy bus, to a sheltered hotel on a postcard perfect beach. Lynx and I try to portray how we're doing, but fail miserably. How I'm feeling is ineffable. I don't even understand it myself. The excitement, the terror, the aliveness. We have the beach almost entirely to ourselves. It's all very anaesthetic. Am I going through adrenalin withdrawal?

I rarely remember my dreams, but I have a vivid one that doesn't escape me upon waking. In the dream, I was holding my friend, Cody, as he sobbed uncontrollably. While I tell Lynx about the dream, his dad comes into the room, ashen-faced, and says, "Sorry, guys, I've got some bad news. Aubrey, Cody's brother, is dead. He killed himself a few days ago. Aubrey was being tortured by schizophrenia." Tears start to slide from my eyes. I don't understand what schizophrenia would be like. I don't understand how it would feel to lose a brother, a best friend, a son. I don't understand, but it hurts too much to fathom.

Morning goes by, slowly. It feels like I've woken up in black and white. Everything seems unfitting and hollow. Around mid-afternoon, Lynx finds me sobbing in bed. He puts on a CD that we bought in Lima, and turns the volume up loud. He dances around the room in forced exuberance. "Aubrey would want you to dance," he insists. I try to transform the pain into positivity. It isn't possible. So many different feelings come, I am unable to articulate any of them. My understanding of what people are has been shattered, and I'm left to grab the piercing shards and mosaic them into a different image with bleeding fingers. The world is as beautiful and magical then it is terrifying and cruel. Lynx and I dance insincerely for a long time and, through tears, slowly find

weak smiles. Excruciating, sad, unworthy smiles.
   A week of being on a quiet beach, passes. My grief ebbs and flows with the shoreline. Lynx and I are restless. Wanderlust takes the three of us on a three-wheel buggy up the highway, to Tumbes, the Ecuadorian border town. We walk around; there isn't much to see. A lot of bananas being exported, that's about it. When we smile at people we encounter, our smiles are not returned. I'm starting to clue in to the fact that third world border towns don't tend to be very cheery places. Or maybe it's just South American border towns. Or maybe I shouldn't have an opinion yet. Never mind, I don't know. I don't know shit-all.
   It's time to leave the beach. The three of us head back to Lima. In Lima, Lynx and I buy flight tickets to Iquitos. Even though it's on the mainland, one must either fly or take a boat if they want to go to Iquitos. There are no roads that go this deep into the Amazon jungle. In the 1920s there was a big rubber boom, and a bunch of Europeans came to Iquitos to work extracting rubber from the jungle. When artificial rubber was invented, the town was abandoned by the European workers. From the ghost of rubber boom prosperity, the downtown of Iquitos is filled with Seussical colonial buildings. Iquitos is truly unique.
   In town there is a giant bazaar. Folk spend days trekking things through the forest to sell at this market. There are countless unrecognizable plants, and even a few jungle animals for sale, dead or alive. There's an abundance of old, giant turtles for sale. They are becoming extinct but their meat is sold for a good price so people continue to hunt them. We pass a tobacco stall where a woman is cutting and rolling giant fresh tobacco leaves harvested from the wild. She invites us to

sample some of her hand made cigars. She shows us a wide variety of tobacco strains. Tobacco harvested and smoked in this manner isn't harmful to the environment, nor is it very addictive. Factory made cigarettes are a tragic and toxic devolution of this should-be esteemed plant.

 Lynx and I arrange a four-day canoe trip into the jungle. Our guides grew up in the jungle, thus are fluent in its ways. I think back to when I was a kid who had recurring dreams about comfortably running barefoot through thick jungle. A part of me wonders if those dreams were past life memories, cosmic reruns from another space and time. I also reflect back to young fantasies about exploring the Amazon. It's surreal to actually be somewhere I had visited in the imagination realm so many times.

 Early in the morning we load the canoe with food, water, tents, and ourselves. Most of the day is spent in the boat. There's a couple of sunburned British friends on the tour with us. So, here we are, six of us in a fairly large, hand-made canoe going upstream into the wilderness. The jungle becomes lusher and more enchanted with each stroke of the paddles.

 Day two. We pull into the river side for a picnic lunch. Our canoe knocks into a tree at the shore. A snake falls from a branch and lands right at Lynx's and my feet. The two of us shriek in panic. By some divine fluke, we manage to jump in perfect synchronicity. Our feet land on each side of our shared bench at exactly the same time and the canoe bobs in perfect balance. The guides burst into laughter. When they catch their breath, they wipe tears of comedy from their eyes and explain that it's a harmless water snake. Obviously. One of our guides nonchalantly grabs hold of the slithering serpent and tosses it back into the river. Embarrassed, we shake off our fright and laugh with everyone else.

On day three we visit a tribal village. They are mostly self-sustaining. Due to tourism in the area, they are beginning to participate in the monetary system. Most smile with friendliness, eager to meet us. Or maybe they're just eager to sell things, I can't tell. We almost have Spanish in common, but all speak it in an awkward, second-hand tongue. With hand gestures, more communication is found. I buy handmade jewellery, and bags, all the while questioning if I'm a positive or negative impact on these people. Change is inevitable, but the capitalist influence seems so disconnected and competitive opposed to communal living. I'm not sure if my actions are right or wrong. Maybe some things are not wholly "right," or wholly "wrong," just inevitable. Or maybe that's just my mind trying to justify my western guilt.

In the evening we canoe to a marsh. With bare hands the guides effortlessly scoop up a three-foot crocodile-like creature from the shoreline. They cradle the prehistoric animal like a babe in their arms. Holding it upside down they invite us to pet its belly. When I stroke it downwards from its head its flesh is smooth, the other direction is rough and scaly. Once we're done connecting with the reptile, it is gently tossed back into the water.

The fourth day comes all too quickly. We glide downstream, back towards Iquitos. Between lush canopies, deep shadows, and intersecting currents, I recognize nothing on the return trip. Only years of experience could acquaint one's eye and instinct with such a diverse, luscious, spread. Surely, I'm being a romantic, but am sad our time in the jungle was so short.

Back in Iquitos the clock is ticking. We have to be in Sao

Paulo for our flight home in a couple of weeks. We arrange a speed boat to take us to Tabatinga, a village in the Brazilian Amazon with a domestic airport. The traverse to Tabatinga is an uncomfortable twelve-hour ride. The tiny hull jolts against every… single… wave. Early in the evening we arrive, sore and spirited.

Tabatinga and Leticia are two villages that share the Brazilian and Columbian border, still mid-jungle. There are no roads into or out of here. A small street going through town provides the most inconspicuous border crossing imaginable. There is no need for passports or inspection at the imaginary line dividing the two countries. People come and go from the two places as if they are one. The atmosphere is relaxed and bright, chilled out people surrounded by lush beauty. The customs office in Tabatinga is closed for the day. A man notices us and says that it's no big deal, they'll probably be open tomorrow. We embrace the pace of village life and go for a beer with the man who told us not to worry.

The next day, at the customs office, we clue in for the first time that we made a mistake. All those months ago, we didn't get stamped out of Brazil when we entered Paraguay. Now, we are being told that this is a problem. The Brasilero customs workers say that they are unable to give us a re-entry stamp due to our blunder. It dawns on us that might be why there was so much hesitation from the Paraguayan officers. Surely that's what the hushed discussion and abrupt bribe was about. It was our first border crossing by foot and we didn't know that one's supposed to get stamped out of a country before entering another one. Our Spanish is decent now, but a few months ago, in that stuffy little gatehouse back at Iguacu, we had no idea what was being said to us. We are sternly told that it will take time for the customs officials to get in contact with authorities in non-jungle Brazil to figure out what to do about our situation.

We do our best to enjoy our precious time here. The end of our trip is near, and we want to savour every moment. The time has come where all the sweet stuff is also bitter. The sunshine is less soothing. The beer doesn't quite quench our thirst. And our next destination feels more melancholic than exciting. We check back with the customs office every day. After four days, we are presented with Portuguese documents and asked to sign them. We give our signatures blindly, not really having another choice. Next, we are each presented with a big, chumpy, five hundred US dollar fine. We call Lynx's family and ask to borrow the money. They transfer the money into Lynx's bank account. When we go to withdraw the money, we discover that the one and only ATM in Tabatinga is broken. We stroll into Leticia and retrieve the complete remnants of our bank accounts in Colombian pesos. We exchange what we need to pay for our fines and flights, then decide to wait until we get into Brasilia to change the rest, assuming that the exchange rate will be better in the city. After our fines are paid, our passports are finally bestowed with re-entry.

We catch a plane bound for Brasilia. We fly over the jungle, then over a vast stretch of cleared land. I've heard of deforestation, but it's terribly sobering to actually see it. Confused about whether or not I'm still an atheist, I pray again. A prayer that the jungle will become honoured and allowed to flourish. It is the world's largest, thus most needed forest. Not only is its well being essential for its people, plants and animals to continue to exist, it's also needed for the planet, as a whole, to thrive.

The Amazon Basin is roughly six million square kilometres and is spread throughout eight countries. An estimated one hundred and forty thousand square kilometres is destroyed per year. The rapid denuding of this ancient forest boosts local economies and generates money to pay off international debts by selling lumber and exporting minerals. Often, after areas of forest have been stripped, large scale farms are established in the empty space. Cattle ranches and soy farms for cattle feed are mostly what is being erected. Mines are also being set up, creating jobs, something that is much needed in this part of the world in its current economic battle. Due to this, many people here feel that deforestation is acceptable, even positive.

Tropical rainforests are extremely wet places. The layer of topsoil in rainforests tends to be very thin and is where most of the soil's nutrients —essential for regrowth — are held. When land is cleared, there are few roots deep enough, or canopy of trees, left to hold and protect the topsoil. Therefore, it quickly gets washed away by the rain, clearing the ground of nutrients and making adequate reforestation impossible.

The Amazon's ecosystem hosts an extremely exquisite variety of trees, plants and creatures. Often, areas are burnt after logging meaning that, in addition to Earth's loss of trees to create oxygen, the fires also create $Co2$, which also hurts the environment.

Please do your part to help this situation. Even if it's just the little things. The forest needs you. You need the forest.

Twelve

Brasilia, Brazil's governmental city, is an anomaly. The city was born in 1960, its development carefully planned, built in the shape of a giant bird. There is way less poverty than the other cities in Brazil. It feels unnatural, almost too presentable. It's grey and serious, opposed to a colourful melting pot.

None of the banks here will exchange Colombian pesos. They all say that Colombia's economy isn't stable enough. So we have no money and are obliged to take the role of freeloaders until we leave. Luckily, we have someone to stay with: Patricio — a middle aged man that's a friend of a friend from back home. It's all quite awkward, unsure if Patricio empathizes with our situation. Despite the uncomfortable moochiness of our stay, we are relieved to have shelter and to not be getting farther into debt.

After a week of beer and billiards with Patricio's friend's son, we thank our host that's certainly relieved to see us go, and catch our last epically long bus ride, back to Sao Paulo. At the airport, a flight attendant takes our boarding passes. I wish it were yesterday, that I had one more day to cherish this continent. I haven't had an adequate goodbye. It's all happening too quickly.

At our midnight connection in the Lima airport, we are told we don't have the necessary boarding pass and are denied permission to get on the plane. Right after the flight has departed, a flight attendant here realizes that one of the flight attendants had blundered in Sao Paulo. She took our Lima boarding passes prematurely. As compensation, Lynx and I get put up in a large, high-end hotel downtown. We're back in Lima again. It's as if the stars whisked my one-more-day woes into my wish.

As I tread through the streets in a jetlagged trance, I feel as if I'm meandering through a memory, instead of the present moment. The Spanish conversations in the background seem more distant today. The colourful buildings and squares are less crisp. It's painful to know that I may never return. We're penniless, but are living in luxury, until tomorrow's Lima — LA flight departs. The bed in our room is outrageously comfortable, and there's a deluxe buffet for us to graze at. But we spend the vast majority of our time walking around the familiar streets, devoted to our nostalgia. We are phantoms, floating through an intangible world. Lynx says it's got the same bizarre quality as how it felt to walk through the halls on the last day of high school, except this time it's sad instead of celebratory.

A complimentary taxi takes us back to the airport and we fly home. Washing my face in the airplane's bathroom mirror, I notice how different I look than from when we started this journey. I've lost a lot of weight and have the most dark and beautiful tan that I've ever had. I suppose there's that to smile about, in the midst of mourning our adventure. I guess I'm still, at least partly, a product of my society and it's programming.

Thirteen

As we drive through Vancouver, it's as if my vision is cracking and failing me. Where are all the hand-made shacks? Where are the crowds of people? The littered trash? The part of my brain that controls the periphery of my sight is superimposing them in brief flashes. The narrator in my mind insists on more South America. My eyes don't understand why, all of a sudden, these ubiquitous things have vanished.

Being back in Canada is confusing. The last four months blew my mind and heart into tiny pieces. I'm not who I was when I left. I'm not sure who or what I am any more.

I move in with my friend, Kai. I have insomnia most nights and mood-swingy depression most days. My heart feels discombobulated. One day, I just simply end things with Lynx, tell him that I'm not feeling it any more. His reaction is that he thinks I'm closed off because I'm going through Post Traumatic Stress Disorder and Culture Shock. His reaction barely strikes a chord through my numbness. He says he loves me and wants to remain close. He thinks I'm ending things because he's what reminds me of the shitty things that happened on our trip. I agree to stay friends.

This society is plastic. The people living in it are unworthy. When people ask me about travelling, I don't know how to articulate what I went through, and am going through, so I mostly don't talk about it. I feel all alone and miserable, unable to relate to anyone. My emotions aren't making a lot of sense. Maybe it is PTSD and Culture Shock? But I thought culture shock was supposed to happen when you're somewhere unfamiliar, not the other way around. It's hard to wrap my brain around the fact that the continents and societies that I am privileged enough to be able to hop in and out of on airplanes are simultaneously happening. I've returned to a bubble where practically everyone is living in abundance. There're so many different realities and realms on this planet. It isn't fair.

In the spring, Kai, Lynx, and I move back to Hornby Island together. Even though Lynx and I are not dating any more, we've remained good friends. We set up camp on Wanda and Herman's property. We share the outdoor kitchen and shower in my caravan's courtyard. Summer comes slowly, it doesn't have its usual effect of lifting me out of sadness. Kennedy comes and joins our camp for the summer. Her presence annoys me. She's just an entitled, sheltered, little girl.

Constant work keeps the worst of my depression at bay. Aside from paying off travelling debts, I'm also trying to put money aside to go away again. Travelling would make me feel alive again. Hopefully. I'm still not sleeping much, and when I do, nightmares jolt me awake in a cold sweat. Each day, I'm more and more worn out. My friends seem to be happy, silly, free. I can't find it in me to lift my heavy heart and enjoy the blessing that is summer time. My mood is too stormy to navigate.

There's a festival in the middle of August that, for years, so many people have praised. Shambhala Festival is an extensive electronic music festival in the interior of BC, about a twelve-hour journey from Hornby. Supposedly, it's an epic event that one must experience at least once in their lifetime.

Kennedy and I each buy a ticket. They're pretty pricey. It had better be worth it. Kennedy's mom, who her daughter has convinced that Shambhala is not a giant rave, meets us on the Big Island and drives us to Nanaimo to catch the ferry to the mainland. On the highway, we pass a girl hitch-hiking, and Kennedy's mom pulls over and we make room for her in the backseat. She calls herself Lakshmi. Lakshmi tells us she was mentally visualizing a nice ride. "Then your car, filled with women, with a bumper sticker that reads 'I believe in angels', pulls over for me." I want to be more like her. Brave, trusting, tuned into magic. The lot of us get dropped off at the ferry.

We take a bus to the small town nearest the party. The town is bloated with festival goers. We are invited to squish into an already full van of people on their way to Shambhala. The party is massive. There are six large, colourful, creative and contrasting stages in the forest, fields, and beach.

Most of the partiers have transformed their bodies into works of art as well. All my senses are tickled alive. All the sunshine and dancing uplift me significantly for the first time since getting back from South America. Or maybe it's all the Molly I've been taking? I don't know, but it's just so nice to feel light-hearted again.

I dance for most of my waking time, which happens to be most of the festival. My sadness shrivels into a harmless thing. By the end of the weekend, I feel like I've gone through genuine cleansing and have danced the sorrow from my bones. The festival ends and we sleep our way back to Hornby on a Greyhound bus.

Summer's coming to an end and I'm still not sleeping. One afternoon, Kai visits me at my van. She tells me about hooking up with a boy that I also have a tiny crush on, or at least did at some point, I think. Honestly, I barely care about him, and yet, when I hear this, I explode. I freak out at Kai. Scream at her for being selfish, tell her she's despicable. An awful friend, a liar, a phony. A horrible person! I ream her out for a while, each insult making less and less sense, but feeling justified, livid to the core of my being. I lose Kai and Kennedy, two of my best friends, two of my small circle of delusional kin. They want nothing more to do with me and I completely understand why. Lynx forgives me though. He seems to have stuck to the PTSD theory. He also seems to be calmly coping with life. Realm hopping hasn't toppled him over. He's travelled before and already had a broader understanding of the world. Or maybe he's being stoic. I don't know.

Goodbye summer. Hello autumn, the season that mirrors my sadness and internal deterioration.

Lynx's family are going to the South Pacific for six months to do medical relief work. They offer us their home to live in while they're away. Lynx and I leave Hornby Island and move into his family's house with a couple of friends from high school.

Everything is bothering me. I freak out again. This time at Vince, one of our roommates. I'm insanely mean about petty shit that doesn't even make sense. I project my own misery onto him, then blame him for it. "Turned the hallway light on in the middle of the night! His schizophrenic friend stopped by when I was home alone! Took up most of the room in the freezer! Doesn't use biodegradable soap!" I kinda just hover over myself and watch as I yell at my innocent friend, tell him he's heartless and evil. I used to think I was a nice person. Maybe I was. But now I've become miserable and mean. A cruel monster.

I find work at a little cafe down the road. The pay is low, but I live frugally and have no rent, so I'm able to put money aside. Most days, I live off of the meal that is given to me at work. The thought of future travels is the only thing that gets me out of bed in the mornings.

On the weekends, I usually go dancing with a group of raver acquaintances. I'm really shy until I'm drunk or high enough to tame my timidity. We don't have much common ground anyway. I mostly just dance. I tell myself that regularly taking M to dance all night is positive and therapeutic for me. It's a healing antidepressant.

I have a clay piggy bank that I bought at a little market somewhere in Bolivia. Every time I get a toonie, I put it in the clay slot. Mid-winter is approaching, and Lynx's family is going to return soon. I can't bear the thought of staying for the rest of this monotonous, grey, season. Surely the weather is at least partly why I'm so sour nowadays. Smash goes the piggy bank. Four hundred and eighty-two dollars. I gather my change from the shattered pieces of clay and bring it to a travel agent. I ask them where I can afford to fly to with this amount of money.

"Costa Rica?"

"Sure! Anywhere!"

I purchase a guidebook: "Central America on a Shoestring Budget." It turns out Costa Rica is one of the most expensive countries in Central America. One of my friends tells me that Costa Rica's ahead of most countries when it comes to taking care of the environment, that that's where he'd go if he were able to travel. I start to emotionally reconnect with the understanding that I'm more fortunate than most. The anticipation is helping my depression lose the power it had over me.

I read about a Spanish school in Nicaragua. Casa Xalteva uses its profits from teaching Spanish to feed, shelter, and school orphans that they find in the garbage dump outside of Managua, Nicaragua's capital. The garbage dump is seven square kilometres. There are an estimated one thousand people permanently living in squalid wasteland, half of whom are children. They scavenge through the sea of trash for scrap metal and glass to sell, as well as food to eat. It's a life I can hardly imagine. I make arrangements to spend a week at the school, alongside a homestay with a family. I have a few days after my plane lands in Costa Rica to make my way to Granada, Nicaragua. After the week of school, I'm not sure what I'll do. But having a start plan brings comfort.

Fourteen

The plane is nearly empty. Ten minutes after take-off, an American guy asks if he can sit next to me. "I'm bored and need someone to talk to, he insists" He buys us each a beer and shallow smalltalk ensues. Him and his buddy are going down for a week. Their sole aspiration: Partying. Internally, I criticize them for going to the developing world, isolating themselves in their culture, and likely leaving nothing but a mess in their wake. Honestly, though, a small part of me is envious at how comfortable they are with their hedonism.

We land in San Jose, Costa Rica, mid-afternoon. The guys from the flight offer me a ride all the way to the coast in their taxi. Glued to the window, I notice that there's garbage everywhere.

Where there are trash cans and recycling bins, they are all overflowing with and surrounded by unorganized piles of waste. In my imagination Costa Rica was spotlessly clean and green. It's sad to see that a country touted for "being green," doesn't actually have environmental care under control. If this is what the cleanest country in the Caribbean looks like, how bad must the other ones be? Our taxi arrives at the beach house the guys have rented. They invite me to stay. I use the excuse that I have to get to my school in Nicaragua, too uptight to give myself permission to retreat into a few frivolous days.

Fifteen

I have two options: Tica Bus or Chicken Bus. The Tica Busses cost more, but you're guaranteed a seat, a comfortable one at that. Also, they are much faster than the Chicken Busses, which stop in all the little towns along the way. The Chicken Busses are old American school busses that were sold to the people down here once they were considered outdated in the U.S. They are crammed with as many passengers as can fit, and sometimes animals, too, hence the name "Chicken Bus." I usually prefer the colourful liveliness of the slow, old, crowded bus rides. But, because I have limited time, I splurge and buy a Tica ticket. If I were being honest with myself, it's mostly because I'm afraid. Afraid of being dropped off by a Chicken Bus at a border town, all by myself, with no guarantee of arriving in daylight. Terrified of being lost in the dark, vulnerable, and alone.

Downtown Granada is all clean and first world shiny — refurbished colourful colonial splendour drenched in wet jungle heat. I feel like I'm in what I imagine Spain would be like. Supposedly, Granada stands out from the other cities in Nicaragua. There is more affluence here, mostly from tourism. People come here for its "European Charm." I ditch my bag on the top bunk of a dorm room bed and go out to its hostel's courtyard. I look up at the Moon and the stars in the pleasant warmth that lingers from the day and smile as I stare at the different constellations that are seen in Central America's sky.

In an instant, everything feels good again. For the first time since being in the Amazon, I am soulfully grateful to be in my unique set of circumstances.

A group of travellers at a table wave me over. They insist that I try a mojito. Rum, lime, and lots of fresh mint on ice soothes its way down my delighted throat then hops back into my dream spaced head. They fill me in. The Nicaraguan Flor de Cana rum is excellent, and Tona is the best local beer. We circle the table, announcing our names and where we're from. I mostly just listen to the others continue on with where they've been and where they're going. These people are way cooler than the party boys from the plane. They're here with a deeper purpose, openness, and respect. They're definitely also partying, but it's only a small part of what they're doing with their trips. My heart feels lighter and lighter with each round of rum. Around midnight, we decide to head to a bar.

There's a live salsa band. The dance floor pulses with talent. A Swedish surfer dude from the hostel asks me for a dance. We join in an attempt to imitate the people around us. They make salsa look effortless, hips roll like ocean waves, feet move in perfect rhythm. But the two of us... we just make a mess, sloppily trample into the other dancers. Out of consideration for the rest of the dance floor, we decide to return to just being spectators. A girl from Norway orders another round of Flor de Cana for our group.

In the morning, I set out to locate the Spanish School. I can't help but stop and watch a soccer game that's in play. The field is cinnamon-coloured. Dust leaps up from running feet, some shoed, some bare. Tin cans mark the goals. Their skills are next level. Isn't that a stereotype? Latin Americans being excellent soccer players? Well, it holds true for this field. The battered ball darts from player to player, as feet scramble for it. It looks like so much fun. I want to join in. But, I'd be the only girl... the dumb white girl that stumbles skillessly, ruining any chance of winning that my team would have. A mighty kick breaks the impasse and the ball pops high into the air. I look to the receiving goalie at the far end of the field only to find he's staring back at me. His eyes catch mine and with a smile he calls, "¿Que tal Bonita?" I blush as a few other heads turn and whistle. Seconds later, their focus is back on the game.

Early in the morning, I hoist my backpack onto my back and make my way to Casa Xalteva. A cheery eclectic bunch warmly welcome me inside the casa. I settle into the friendly Spanglish mingle. There are a dozen kids living in the old schoolhouse. About five teachers work here, some of whom were housed and schooled by Casa Xalteva as children. There are ten other travellers here, as students. After I meet everyone, one of the teachers walks me the few blocks to where I'll be staying.

My host family exudes the loving energy that all families should have, but so rarely do. After the mama, her son and daughter, and their female cousin welcome me with hugs, I am shown to a humble, spotless bedroom. The kids are all in their twenties, a little older than me. The house is large and clean, but barren with chipping stucco walls. My Spanish is better than I remembered it to be. Communicating the basic stuff happens easily.

At school I end up being given private lessons. Because I learnt the language half in high school and half by socializing while in South America, stringing together a broadening vocabulary without any comprehension of correct grammar, my learning needs don't match up with any of the other pupils. After a week of lessons my Spanish feels strong. I need to come up with some other excuse to keep my travels tame. My mixed emotions can't think of one. Time to dive in!

I venture to Isla de Ometepe, an island formed by two still-active volcanoes rising from Lake Nicaragua. An old ferry delivers us across the enormous lake, which casts shimmers back at the blazing sun like a myriad of gems. With the first step on Ometepe, I already get the sense of a slower pace and a bond with nature. The bumpy dirt roads are lined with mango trees, and they are in season. The ground is coated with golden mangos, they blanket the yards of small homes. It makes me smile to see a form of wealth showering down over here.

My first night is spent at a large guesthouse in the boonies. I try to read a Spanish novela on the large wooden platform that keeps the guests from being directly on the jungle floor. I hear some people shriek, then scamper towards the wall. A tarantula scurries out of the floorboards, one thick, hairy leg at a time. My heart pounds. I manage to calm myself by slowing my breath and reassuring myself that the odds of the tarantula torpedoing over to me and crawling on me to take a bite is highly unlikely. I do my best to silence thoughts like "what happens if one crawls up through the floorboards and onto me as I sleep?"

The second night on Ometepe, the guy that shared my salsa fiasco back in Granada shows up at the boondock guesthouse. He notices me across the deck and shocks me with an uncontainable smile. He walks over, takes the seat next to mine, pulls a half-drunk bottle of rum from his pack, and pours us each a glass. We catch up about the past week. He's pretty enthusiastic about everything that comes out of my mouth.

He's probably just trying to get laid. Distrust, or perhaps fear of happiness, inspire me to be progressively cold towards him. Conversation peters out and we go to bed alone.

In the morning I wake early, and leave without saying goodbye. Barefoot, I make my way along a warm, rock-laden, dirt road. As the day is starting to be too hot, I come across a sign that reads: "Finca(farm)/Hostel." Up the dirt driveway, I find myself surrounded by humble huts dispersed between trees. A few of the many budget travellers staying here are Woofers (people who travel by volunteering on organic farms in exchange for room and board). I almost become seduced into settling here, into the splendour of slow-paced island life and its bubble of safety. But I want to experience more of Central America, to do more than just take refuge in comfort. I want to immerse myself in other cultures, to do more than laze around with backpackers all day. I want to truly experience Central America.

I venture to Nicaragua's "best beach getaway," San Juan del Sur, already quite sure that it's absolutely the wrong destination for me. Everyone I meet is deeply disappointing. No one seems to have aspirations beyond partying and getting a tan. Out of boredom and loneliness I wind up playing drinking games with other backpackers that I met on the beach. In the morning, I set out with a massive hangover, destined for Guatemala. Last night someone said it's amazing there. Her eyes lit up like shooting stars when she talked about small villages on a lake. My new found plan is to start at the top of Central America and slowly travel back down to Costa Rica for my flight back to Canada.

Sixteen

Still too chicken to take the Chicken Busses across international borders, I catch another Tica Bus. My bus pulls into a quiet Guatemala City around six a.m. We're informed that there are no busses driving through or out of the city today. None of the drivers are willing to work. Yesterday, twelve bus drivers were shot. Gangs had been charging them for going through their neighbourhoods. The drivers decided to protest and refused to pay. Twelve men paid with their lives.

I get a taxi to take me to the airport, hoping that I'll be able to find others to share a cab out of the city with. Sure enough, I do, and follow them to their destination.

Lago Atitlan is sacred to the Mayan people. In some folklore, it is considered to be the umbilicus of the universe. The lake has several traditional Mayan villages dispersed around it. Though the villages are close to one another, for a long time the only way one could reach another village was by foot or canoe. For hundreds of years, visiting one of the other villages required a grand voyage, and the people were busy enough self-sustaining themselves. Because of this, each village has a varying culture, belief system, and sometimes even different dialects. The situation is *rapidly* changing. Now that there are roads and motorboats, the villages are no longer far from one another. Lago Atitlan is not immune to the steady shrinking of the world.

I quest through a not so long-ago village. There are stalls

vending tourist clothes, knick-knacks, and food all over the place. I walk around town to find the hostel with the cheapest fare. My room has about ten small mattresses on the ground, and that's it. No bedding, no pillows, no windows. But, at two bucks a night, it marks perfection. I ditch my backpack, then wander around town some more, past countless vendors and giddy children that vie for my attention. Outside the bustle, I chose an arbitrary foot path. At a quiet, grassy knoll I stop and sit cross legged to gaze into the Umbilicus of the Universe. I'm alone with the shimmering lake, until a traditionally dressed Mayan woman walks by on the trail in front of me. Her beauty is mystical and timeless, it teleports me into another time and place. I hear a cell phone ring. She takes a phone out of the folds of her dress and is now chatting with someone about something… So much for that enchanted moment. Modern life marches on.

Even though this is an international hotspot, it feels different. The backpackers I meet here generally seem to be wanting to learn from the local culture and to mesh with it, as opposed to solely coming here to get drunk and high because it's cheap and sunny. I guess it's kinda like they're travellers instead of tourists. There's just way too many of them. Well, too many of *us*, I suppose.

Because of all the backpacking hippies there's all sorts of random courses hosted around town. A dreadlocked white guy strikes up a conversation with me at a tostada stall. For ten minutes he goes on about how much the art of Tai Chi has helped him in so many ways. I start to show sincere intrigue and he says "I'm teaching a course tomorrow. It's only twenty dollars." I roll my eyes.

Seconds later, I shrug and say, "Sure."

The course is held on a flat rooftop near the edge of town. There's three of us, including the guy teaching it. Somewhere unseen, a dog barks in manic spurts. Our guide insists that the dog constantly interrupting our practice is just making us stronger practitioners. "The dog is our true guru." "Sure," I say again. A few moments of genuinely trying to feel the energy flow in the dancelike motions we're being led through pass before the dog erupts into another barking frenzy. "Outer noise to inner peace. The art of alchemy." Our teacher softly whispers. I can't contain myself, I burst into laughter. Soon the three of us are keeling over in fits of giggles. When we catch our breath, we decide our guru dog has implied we've done enough Tai Chi. It was kind of a ridiculous day, but admittedly, a good one that has left me feeling peculiarly serene.

A girl from my dorm asks if I want to go hang out on the shore. We get to the lakeside and she strips down to a bikini. Conversation starts with the boys she's attracted to from the hostel. From there she goes on to talk about how she needs to lose weight. She bats her mascara-laden eyelashes, asking for me to insist she's thin. Next, she points out how so many of the Mayan people are chubby and goes on pondering why, in a judgmental tone. I curl up in a ball up while she pines on, jolted out of my fairy-tale, la-la land delusion, again. The culture I'm trying to shed and escape finds me here. All that I loathe about my societal conditioning — all the superficial snobbery and self-importance — oozes from this girl. It isn't fair that rude, selfish people get to travel. Am I projecting my own lack of merit? Probably! Night comes and a bunch of us at the hostel get drunk together. In the morning, I wake to the smell of puke. There's a pile of it on the floor next to the shallow girl that needed company on the lakeshore so that she could tan. I don't know whether to laugh or to cry. I'm moved to carry on.

The sidewalks and roads in Antigua are packed with processions, Christians chant and wave frankincense in slow file. It's Semana Santa, the Holy Week of Easter. Enormous, heavy floats, adorned to represent Jesus's journey, are arduously being carried through the roads. People surround the floats, chant and sway-walk with the throng. I've never seen a religious ceremony of such grandeur. The only sentiment that this grand ceremony evokes in me is anger. Anger towards the European settlers and clergy that dismembered the spiritual traditions and culture that was alive here before they came and conquered.

Among bitter revelations, I'm hit hard with something else. I become feverish and weak. I should have stayed at the lake where it was calm and fresh. I spend days drinking as much boiled water as possible to try to flush sickness out of me. When I get out of bed, I become dizzy and usually collapse back down.

The better part of a week passes until I have enough stamina to walk to the market. I sit and people watch as I drink hand pressed orange juice from one of the many vendors. Another day passes and I decide I'm strong enough to carry on. Onward on my quest for something I don't quite know how to articulate. One thing I do know though, is that I want to get out of the city and off the beaten track. I suppose I'll head south, to Honduras.

Seventeen

I wind up in what seems to be cowboy country. There are no other foreigners in sight. Yet none of the horse-riding, boot-wearing, sombrero-sporting folk take a break in their dusty tracks to talk to me. Lonely and bored, I spend a few days drifting through a few small towns that blur together. I decide to drift on, and head for Honduras' capital city.

I meet one, and only one other person at my hotel. He's American, in Tegucigalpa on a Peace Corps mission. He expresses great surprise to meet me here. I'm the first backpacker he's encountered in the few months since he arrived. Despite him having been here for a while, he draws a blank when I ask for suggestions of fun or interesting things to do. "All I really do is work." He asks me where I'm headed next and I blurt the first idea that springs to mind.

"El Salvador, I suppose!" He gives me a hard stare and a serious lecture. El Salvador hosts some of the most ruthless gangs in the world.

"Coming to Tegucigalpa, alone, was bold and risky enough, but nothing compared to El Salvador." His words strike a chord in me. I heed his advice, and let it deter me from going to El Salvador blindly. The next morning, my cowardice and self-loathing are on a Tica Bus, trundling back towards Nicaragua.

On route the bus breaks in San Salvador, El Salvador's capital. From my window seat I watch a Coca Cola truck deliver soda to a small store. The truck has three men, each holding a large rifle, guarding the beverages. I ponder how desperate the situation here actually is here. Is life that cheap? Physically, I'm here, but I'm not really here. Looking out the window feels like watching television.

Eighteen

On the bus, I flip through my guidebook and decide on a destination: Little Corn Island. Squished between two locals on the bench of a speedboat, I zoom down a river lined with thick tropical forest. I look up at the sapphire blue sky, and at the vivid lush lime vegetation that whizzes by, and can't help but smile ear to ear. I think about all the people that I know. None of them know where I am or what I'm doing. It isn't scary; it's blissfully liberating. For the first time in my life, I feel fully free. Light. Unburdened. Gloriously insignificant. Overcome with gratitude, I'm tempted to burst into song. I am soulfully satisfied with life. The purpose of everything bad in my life was to make me able to feel as blissful as I do at this moment.

As dusk starts to dim the crisp tropical colours, we all pile off of the speedboat at the Caribbean city of Bluefield. The guidebook insists that it's seedy here. There were no other backpackers on the boat, no one to accompany me on the hunt for safe shelter. Anxious to get off the streets before they're fully enveloped in the dark of night, I scamper over to the first hotel that I see. I pay a small sum of cordobas and they point me towards a room with a metal door. It's filthy. There's an empty condom wrapper on the floor beside an overflowing trash can. It's gross, but I'm not brave enough to go back outside and find a different hotel. I bolt my door shut and remain fully clothed as I spread my sarong over the stained bedsheet. Sleep comes instantly, probably from being in the blazing sun all day.

As soon as I wake I head straight for the dock. The one and only passenger boat that leaves for Little Corn has one seat left, and leaves promptly after I take it. Mid-afternoon, the boat slows and motors to the shore of the tiny island. The last packsack is tossed onto the sand and the captain promptly does a one eighty for the mainland, not to return for a week. My feet dig into pristine white sand as I hike the shoreline. I seek out a guesthouse, and after inquiring at what feels like most of the places to stay, I finally find one with a vacant room. The floor is sand, the low ceiling has gaping wooden boards, about a foot under a patchwork tin roof. There's a mosquito net with several large holes hung over the bed that takes up most of the room. It's perfect. Outside the door lies paradise.

Little Corn is special. White sand beaches and warm, clean water, far from society and its stresses. The locals are remarkably chilled out, and I'm accustomed to island folk. Many of them have golden jewellery with diamonds that sparkle alongside their eyes and easy smiles. It's a tad curious for such an isolated place. I can't help but wonder if they're retired pirates.

At night, I hear and see the outline of giant rats scurrying around the ceiling boards. I calm my breath enough to sleep, tell myself that they won't fall... crap... or piss... on me... hopefully.

Several relaxing days on the beach go by where I notice the same man walk past, a few times, every day. His head is always lowered and he's always on the tideline. I point him out to the traveller I'm having afternoon beers with. He laughs and explains that the man is looking for the "white lobster."

Supposedly, bricks of cocaine occasionally float ashore. Boats smuggling from the south are sometimes too laden and have to drop some of their wares off of their ships to lighten the load. We giggle a little, while we watch the man walk past, head down, staring at the tide, seeking his ivory fortune.

Reluctantly, I make the decision to leave after a week, while the opportunity is there. I'm forced to decide as the speedboat captain's fingers drum on the side of the boat impatiently. He won't be back for another seven days. I would regret not visiting more places if I stay here for too long. To Panama City! Boats, boats, busses, and busses.

Nineteen

Panama City is wealthy and gentrified. The only striking differences from cities back home are the language and the climate. Barely after arriving I am yearning to be back in nature and arrange a trip to the Archipelago de San Blas. The Archipelago is a string of three hundred and sixty-five small islands off the Caribbean coast.

A half dozen other travellers and I are taken on a jeep ride across bumpy mud roads lined with lush forest to the Caribbean Sea on the brink of the Darien Gap. The Darien Gap is a stretch of jungle, "no man's land," shared by Panama and Colombia. It's inhabited by guerrilla soldiers, drug smugglers, poachers, and jaguars. It is said that those who enter seldom exit. The jeep stops at the end of the road. There's a small makeshift dock with a small ramshackle dinghy waiting for us. We hop out of the jeep and into the boat, and slowly motor out to sea.

We are brought to a small island inhabited by the Kuna Yala people. They are adorned with an abundance of piercings and tattoos. Their hand-sewn, colourful, psychedelic clothing enchants me. About fifty inhabitants live on this island. It is an honour to be here. These people are mystical, sacred and supernatural.

We visit some of the archipelago's other islands. One is inhabited solely by a married couple. They've chosen to live alone. How romantic. I couldn't imagine being hedged in by an ocean, solely with Lynx, or... anyone, for that matter. We spend our days going to and from islands, breaking to swim and snack on coconut. I am truly in awe of the beauty of this magical place.

On our last evening, the children perform a traditional dance for us. The old American man who is part of us six visitors, starts making appalling comments. Out loud he wonders how much it would cost him for the locals to let one of the young girls go to bed with him. Shocked, infuriated, and devastated I'm filled with fiery hatred for this man. Why does this monster have the ability to travel? This isn't okay. Rich assholes come for a week or two, whining about their pampered lives, and, in the blink of an eye, peaceful innocent people and their beautiful cultures are raped. I scowl at him viciously and tell him he's disgusting and pathetic. He drops it and shuts the fuck up. The night ends and the group of us see to it that he goes to bed alone.

Back in Panama City, I spend a couple of days roaming tame streets at random. At the hostel I meet backpackers who've just come through Colombia. They tell me it's safe and incredibly friendly. I trust them way more than the media, which always portrays Colombia as being treacherous. Little do I yet know the extent of the media's deception. Unfortunately, I don't have the time or funds to go to Colombia on this trip. Bummed out, I catapult myself north to catch my flight back to Canada.

Twenty

At home on Hornby, the mirror makes me smile. I'm thin again! Losing weight was intentional, for purposes of vanity and finances. A smaller belly is cheaper to fill, after all. Looking good seems to have helped me shed my shyness. With new-found comfort in my own skin, I become closer to the people here that I admire and used to find intimidating. I'm happy, my heart is light, life is good. It's the polar opposite of how I felt returning from South America last year. Time to restart my lifestyle of working like a maniac. I cook, garden, and serve coffee, whilst living minimalistically, back in the hollowed out van that Wanda offered me when I was struggling in highschool. My rusty bicycle takes me everywhere I go. I am beyond content with the pattern of working then travelling that I've established. The extra vitamin D that I got from skipping winter must be what's making me so happy and alive. Why else would I have so much energy even though I barely sleep?

Skylar and I start a romance. He's this gorgeous boy who's also travelled through South and Central America. He's ten years older than me but the gap's invisible. Neither of us consider age to be a viable way to sort people into categories. Our evenings are spent drinking beer and snorting blow while talking about travels. It's nice for a little while. He always struck me as mysterious and intimidating. But the more time we spend together the less and less smitten I am. He's a drug addict that's fixated on the past, disinterested in creating a positive present or future for himself. He repeats the same stories over and over again. I'm left wondering if he's too drunk and high to realize he's already told me his choice travelling tales, or if he really has nothing else interesting to talk about. Has he just been a hermit in his cabin, drinking beer and snorting coke, since the "good ol' days"? Disenchanted, I stop going by his place. I want a healthy, dream-actualizing life, not a life of poverty, drug addiction, and nostalgia.

One day at work I go to take the plastic wrapper off a cucumber with a knife. Cucumber in my left hand, knife in my right, I aim down. The cucumber slips, and I end up stabbing my left pinky finger. I tape the wound and return to my tasks. Strangely, I'm unable to bend my finger, but it doesn't hurt. At the end of my shift, I take off the bandage, and my finger starts gushing deep, dark red blood. My boss drives me to the doctor. Turns out I severed a tendon and need to go to the Big Island for surgery. The innards of my hand are sewn back together, and I'm given a brace to wear for the next six weeks.

With my injury, I'm given worker's compensation for the next three months, two months more pay than I would have made at the bakery that's only open until the end of the summer season. I relax and watch the dollars pour in. My first autumn on Hornby is lovely. The atmosphere changes drastically once the tourists are gone. I slow down and become one with the ocean and forest.

At least once a week, my friends and I get together to play some serious hacky sack. It's really fun and we're getting really good at it. There's a boy. He's got the sparkliest of sparkly eyes. His name is Nile. When he's around I can't not smile. Whenever I'm near him I butterflies. Rarely have I encountered people who've had an effect such as this on me. I love his energy. The more we get to know each other, the more massive my crush becomes. I can tell by the way he blushes and smiles that our sentiments are mutual.

It's Halloween and there's a party. I make myself a jellyfish costume out of a white cloth bag with lengths of purple, white, and blue fabric hanging down as tentacles. Late into the festivities Nile shows up dressed like some sort of cosmic shaman. Hand carved wizard staff, a mix of exotic clothes, jewellery he fashioned from crystals, topped with a halo-crown made from plants, he catches my eyes and blushes his way over to me. We end up talking for hours. There's something fiercely special about him.

On one of Hornby's many mellow days, I look through old diaries of mine. I come across a Bucket List that I had written in Montreal. Snow-covered memories of my first breakaway spring to life within my mind. At the time, I hadn't thought I'd accomplish, or even attempt, most of what's on my list. Some are more ambitious than others. Free Tibet. Go to the Amazon. Sing in front of an audience. Speak five languages fluently. Make an elaborate cake. Hang glide. Do volunteer work in Ethiopia. Overcome fear of snakes. Put on an art exposition. Experience psychedelia. Learn what requited love feels like. A long travel through India... Huh! India! I hop on my bike and glide to the ferry. On the Big Island I find a travel agent and purchase a flight to Mumbai. I stare at the plane ticket in my hands with exhilaration. I can hardly believe that I'm going for six months.

My friend Lila throws a farewell dinner for me. Nile and I spend hours glued to each other at the campfire. For the most part, deep and interesting conversation flows easily. There are only a few moments of small talk to fill silence with mundane things like, "Where are your flight layovers?" Once everyone else has gone home, Nile and I leave on our bicycles together. He lives at the opposite side of the island but makes the huge detour to see me back to my caravan.

We glide slowly on the moonlit empty roads, still talking and laughing, until we reach my place. We share a long hug, not wanting to say goodbye. I find the courage to kiss him on the cheek, then my courage vanishes, and I flee inside.

In Vancouver, I stay with friends from high school. When we were young it felt like we had so much common ground. Now they're burying themselves in student loans for courses they've already lost passion for.

Once through customs, I spend the wait walking around the airport. I want to burn enough energy so that the hours of sitting on planes will be as pleasant as possible. A flight attendant makes the announcement that my flight is starting to board. I sit at my gate and wait for my section to be called. A woman walks up to me. She smiles and says, "Are you Maya?"

"Yes," I say, a little taken aback, as the name on my passport reads "Sarah." It turns out to be Nile's sister. She's on her way to Europe and at the last-minute thought to phone her brother to tell him that she's going to be away for a few weeks. She hands me her cellphone. Nile is on the other end. The synchronicity feels like a magical confirmation that we are meant to be in each other's lives. Nile wishes me bliss and safety, then it's time to board the airplane. I guess the kiss I planted on his cheek was appreciated.

Twenty-One

Jet lagged and sore from twenty-seven hours of sitting through flights and transfers between them, I finally alight in Mumbai. It's midnight here. I take a look around the terminal and see that I'm the only foreigner, the only person with no one to receive them and no known place to go. I sense eyes on me. This doesn't feel how landing in Costa Rica did. There isn't anyone looking to share a taxi into a warm and tranquil afternoon. My guidebook suggests Colaba. Supposedly it's one of the nicer parts of the city and has plenty of cheap guesthouses. I take a deep breath and step out of the placid airport.

Even at night, Mumbai's warm air is thick enough to swim through. I find myself in a loose cluster of people. Taxis and rickshaws abound, competing for our business. It feels like most eyes are on me. Everyone can see I'd be easily fooled into overpaying my fare. Overwhelmed and intimidated, I try to look confident as I take in the surroundings.

A man walks over to me and shows me a hotel business card: "In Expensive and Good!" He asks if I'd like him to take me there. "OK," I say, needing to pick someone. I can't loiter around here till the security of the sun comes, can I... should I...? The man returns with a van, leans over to open the passenger door, and motions for me to get in. I climb into the front seat and hug my backpack that I've hoisted onto my lap. We start to drive before I notice there's no hotel logo stickered to the windows, nor anything else implying a business vehicle, associated with said hotel. This feels fishy. A year ago, I might've swallowed my suspicion. But now, wise enough to choose the assurance of safety over the fear of being rude, I tell him that I've changed my mind.

He says, "No, no, we go to hotel." I tell him to stop the van.

"No, I bring you to hotel."

"Stop the van!"

I become saturated with fear. Who is this man and why won't he let me out of his van? Where the is he taking me? I command him to stop once more and am given the same reply. I lean over and start honking on his horn like a maniac. He looks at me bewildered, then after about ten honks he complies and pulls over to the shoulder of the driving strip. He shouts indecipherable insults at me as I hop out and run back to the small huddle of people outside the Arrivals gate.

There are still too many rickshaw and taxi drivers to count, but hardly any potential passengers left. Now I'm even more conspicuous. All I have to do is vibe out a taxi driver, no big deal… right? I walk over to one of the quiet ones and ask for a ride to Colaba. He nods silently and helps me with my bag. I settle into the seat beside him as we set out into the gargantuan sleeping city. Why did that seem so complicated and scary a minute ago?

My driver stops at several small hotels until we find one that I can afford. He double checks I'm okay then drives away, into the night. The guesthouse has six basic rooms and one shared bathroom. My room cost one hundred and fifty rupees, less than four Canadian dollars. Around nine a.m. I wake and instantly leap out of bed. I should be tired — I've barely slept the past forty-eight hours — but the excitement of being here is all powerful. Still dressed from yesterday, I grab my shoulder bag, and become one with the hot, busy streets.

Holy cow. The rocket ship ride is over, and I'm in India.... I feel like I'm swirling through a kaleidoscope. Everything and everyone is morphing its way through each other like magical dancing puzzle pieces on the congested streets and sidewalks. There're so many vivid colours. Cars, rickshaws, poor people, rich people, business suits, skinny jeans with glitzy tank tops, turbans of every hue, bright saris, dark burqas, billowing salwar kameez. Everyone's weaving in, out, and all around the city streets, seething in a dense crowd between stores, kiosks, hotels, guesthouses, restaurants. Every inhalation brings with it new surprises: incense, spices, gasoline. There are slummy shacks and humble restaurants, interspersed with fancy hotels, clothing shops, and high-end jewellery stores. The crowd thins slightly towards the shoreline that gives way to the populous harbour. On the streets of Colaba, I feel like I'm seeing all the contrasts I imagined India to have, except the cows. I thought there were supposed to be cows. Where are all the sacred cows?

About ten minutes into giddily strolling through the compact crowd, a man wearing orange robes crosses my path. He stops, smiles, and nods for me to do the same. I do. He tells me he's a Brahman Priest and asks me if I'd like him to give me a blessing.

"Yes, please."

He says what I think is a prayer, and gently waves his arms around me. A palpable breeze of calmness flows into my seemingly solid body. I am deeply impressed, intrigued, and a little bamboozled by the energy this man effortlessly invoked.

He ties a red piece of yarn around my wrist, asks for one hundred rupees, then is gone as quickly as he came. Yearning to understand the energy that the priest made me feel, I become even more excited for the mystery of this journey that has barely begun to unfold.

I come across a sign that reads "The Taj Mahal." Confused, I say to the guard, "I didn't know the Taj Mahal was in Mumbai! Where is it?"

"Yes, yes, here, come," he says. He steps aside and waves me through a metal detector that's arched just inside the doorway of a large building. There's a knife in my bag that should have set it off. I shrug, find it comical, and continue through, finding myself in a fancy restaurant leading to an extravagant hotel. It's just a tribute, not the actual Taj Mahal. I do a one eighty, back into the streets for some more whimsical wandering.

Hunger hits as I pass a large and crowded open-air restaurant. I sit at the only available table, order a curry, then take out my journal and start to draw. I begin to feel exhausted from the heat and jet lag. Eating a hot meal makes me even more tired. The bustle around me dulls to a muted blur as I nearly nod off. As I leave the restaurant, I glance back to read its sign: Leopold's. The name seems familiar, my guidebook may have recommended it. I shuffle back to my guesthouse, climb up to my room, and fall asleep within seconds of laying down.

I wake to the distant sound of fireworks somewhere in the streets. I stir in bed and try to sleep through the ruckus. But the fireworks continue to pop and whistle. All of a sudden, I hear voices echoing in the hallway. The TV is turned on and the volume raised obscenely high. I look outside — it's pitch black. How rude! It's the middle of the night! After about five minutes of trying to stifle the noises under my pillow, I roll out of bed, and storm into the hall determined to get those inconsiderate jerks to turn down the volume. All six rooms are awake, everyone is huddled in the lobby.

"What's going on?" I ask. A long second ticks by.

"The city is under attack."

Those weren't fireworks. Bombs are going off. Dazed, we watch the local news. Shootings and bombings took place at a dozen locations throughout the city this evening. Scattered in their response to this initial wave of raids, the police have been slow to respond to the armed attacks against the Oberoi and Taj Mahal hotels, where men with machine guns stormed in and struck without warning. These hotels are just a couple blocks down the road from our guesthouse. They've started a fire in one of them. The news is saying that the assailants are the Indian Mafia and that they are targeting foreigners for ransom and worse. Inside the hotels people are being shot and held hostage. One of the other backpackers turns to me and says that the attackers are pulling people with American passports off the street and shooting them.

"I'm Canadian," I reply, feebly, wondering if that matters.

We are right in the area where most of the incursions happened. If there are more to come, they will probably be in Colaba too. Luckily, everyone in this guesthouse is present and accounted for. At the guesthouse on the floor below us, someone is already missing.

My ears ring as I gaze at the others. Their lips form words I cannot hear while they pace in frantic circles. I'm buzzing, wide awake, in shock. I stepped into the Taj Mahal Hotel just this afternoon. The restaurant I ate at suffered a grenade attack, mere hours after I left. A British boy in the guesthouse trips out with me. He had planned to go to the cinema that had a bombing. At the last minute, he did something very out of character, and decided to stay in and catch an early sleep. We both narrowly avoided catastrophe tonight.

He calls his family, reporting to the rest of us that the BBC is blaming Al Qaeda. Really? Here? The Mumbai News station was blaming the Indian Mafia. My distrust of the media solidifies. The networks are jumping the gun. When the Irish couple phones home, their media hasn't chosen where to place blame yet. The broadcast media machines of the world are scrambling to convince their populations of a story that suits their political agendas. I find this strangely soothing. Analysing the press brings me into my head and distracts me from being terrified.

Morning comes slowly. Through a window I look down at the dawning street. It's miles apart from the rainbow whirlwind of yesterday. The roads are completely empty. No fabric to be measured, not a bangle to be sold, no incense to inhale, no rickshaw to be rode. It's eerie, ghostly... haunted.

The guesthouse owner insists that we need to get out of the city. As foreigners, we are prime targets. If the Indian Mafia sets out for another attack, we fall directly in their path. Our host phones everyone he can think of, determined to help us to safety.

In the corner of the lobby, I crumble to the floor, close my eyes, and, for the first time in my life, pray with everything I have. With all my might and all my grace, I visualize the seven of us leaving the city safely. After doing this for at least a half hour, I come to let myself relax and trust that that is what will manifest. Just to make sure, I spend much of the day pre-

thanking the Universe for giving a safe exodus to the people of my guesthouse. Extending my intent on the people beyond these walls feels too ambitious, too difficult. This room is all I can handle.

The hotel clerk makes dozens of phone calls. Late in the afternoon he finally finds us a bus with room. But there's one problem: it's on the other side of Mumbai and is scheduled to leave in less than two hours. The six of us agree that getting to that bus is our best option. The Irish guy and the older man volunteer to find us a taxi. Their plan: get to the edge of Colaba as quickly as possible until they come across a taxi. I try to keep conversation flowing with the Irish girl, to distract her from worrying about her lover as he hunts down a ride for us all. The wait is maddening. The threat of death has never been so real.

After what feels like forever, there's a knock on the door, and a thick Irish accent announces that there's a cab below. We sprint down the stairs, to not leave the driver waiting in the warzone. Within seconds we are all piled into the car, zooming towards the outskirts of the city. Slowly the streets thicken with life. As the immediate danger trundles further and further behind us, I wonder how desperate for money our courageous taxi driver must be. He drops us off at the bus station and we leave him with a handful of cash. I can't help but question how desperate for money our driver must be, to be willing to give us that ride. How many weren't so lucky? How many people are here but don't have the means to get out of the city?

This experience, along with common sense, has taught me to be wary of the media and its "news," so take this with a grain of salt: This catastrophe came to be referred to as the Mumbai Massacre. A convicted attacker, Ajmal Kasab, confessed to be from Lashkar-e-Taiba, a Pakistani terrorist group. Not the Indian Mafia, nor Al-Qaeda, like the media initially proclaimed. CIA double agent David Headley was revealed to be the mastermind behind the events. The hotel occupation lasted three days. At least one hundred and sixty-six people were killed. Nearly three hundred others were wounded.

Twenty-Two

Our escape bus is bound for Goa, a small state on the west coast. The movement of the bus lulls me to sleep as adrenaline subsides. Before long, I'm floating through tall, deep red mountain walls that jut into a crisp blue sky. A speed bump knocks me awake. How peculiar, I think, I seldom remember my dreams.

Early morning light graces the calm white sands as we pile out of the bus. Normally, Goa is India's party zone. But warnings of more potential attacks have spread here, so the area is unusually tame. There are as many cows as people on the beach. So, here's where all the cows go! Five of us that escaped Mumbai together settle into a row of basic beach bungalows. The live-in workers are very friendly. Short, smiley Shankar and I forge a bond over beach walks and bidis.

In need of more appropriate attire for this culture and climate, I buy a couple of loose, light, colourful outfits from one of the many street vendors. The women here generally dress quite modestly. Oddly, though, the ubiquitous sari leaves the belly area uncovered. I think back to Jr. High in Canada, where exposing the belly was considered inappropriate and unpermitted. It's interesting what different cultures adopt as acceptable. Looking at my smooth flowing saffron pants and baggy golden shirt with pretty hand sewn embroidery in the mirror, I start to feel like I belong. I like this version of me.

At the end of the market lane, a poster advertising

"Tibetan Astrology Readings" catches my eye. Sitting at a humble wooden table just below it, a bald monk in robes smiles at me with a subtle head bow. Intrigued, I approach. After collecting my birthplace and location, he tells me he needs time to calculate my astrological chart. It'll be ready tomorrow.

When I return to his kiosk the next morning, he welcomes me with another smile as warm as the sun. According to his calculations, I was an elephant in my most recent life. In my next life, if I stay mostly virtuous, I will probably be a wealthy Western man. He goes on to inform me that in this life I am going to be a teacher, and a celebrity. I become filled with doubt. What do I have to teach? And what could possibly make me famous? I can't sing, or act worth a damn. Fame feels intangible, and also a little undesirable. Definitely not an ambition of mine. I thank him, sceptical, but with fragments of wondering if and how his prophecy might unfold. Does he tell the same thing to everyone? Probably not. Being a monk and all, he probably has a higher moral compass than most.

The more the group of us hang out, the more it becomes evident that we don't have much common ground, other than escaping the Mumbai Massacre together. The Irish girl says she hates India, that her whole time here has been hell. The first day she got to Delhi a cow pissed on her and, from that moment on, she knew she was going to hate it here. I tell her that I know that I am going to love being here.

"Why?" she scoffs.

I shrug. "Just a feeling."

She rolls her eyes.

One evening the five of us go to a large market a few beach-towns over. At last, an opportunity to have my palm read finally presents itself. Interested and excited, I have to remind myself to not take it as absolute certainty. I'm sure you can find everyone from true prophets, to bullshit artists, to the genuinely delusional, making their way in the business of fortune telling. The first thing the woman reading my palm tells me is that I might be a descendant master.

"A descendant what?" I ask.

"A famous guru, or healer," she says.

She strokes the sacred and rare symbol marked in the centre of my right palm, the triangle within the triangle. I listen, camly bewildered. It's hard to believe, but that's the second time I've been told that I have an exceptional and divine fate scribed in my flesh. On the return rickshaw ride, I stare at the "Eye of the Universe" in my palm, while the Mumbai crew tease me for spending money on a palm reading. When we get dropped off, I hurry to my little hut and scramble to write everything that was said at the market. But it slips away, like the dream on the bus. I try to grasp the oracle's words as they trickle away. One of the things that stuck with me was, "You are going to go through some *very* tough times. When things are difficult, remember you chose a life where you wanted to learn a lot."

After a few more days at the beach, Jessica, the british girl, invites me to join her on a migration to Hampi. A mere four hours past scheduled departure time, we hop on a crowded train with cramped wooden benches. I'm giddy with excitement, not really sure of where Jessica's leading me.

Twenty-Three

Hampi feels like what one would imagine Earth to have looked like when the dinosaurs roamed. The town is surrounded by clusters of gargantuan boulders, shaped like gently closed fists of the gods. There are temples in and outside of the town, hewn right into the rock itself. The walls surrounding are etched with beautiful, meticulously detailed carvings of creatures, geometric patterns, esoteric symbols, and other designs. The carvings are so intricate and abundant it's hard to fathom how much time and labour it must have taken to chisel this otherworldly place. Hampi is an ancient town holy to Hindus and draws many pilgrims.

On our first walkabout, Jessica and I are waved into a jewellery shop. The stones and crystals within cast shimmers that dazzle. Among the geodes of royal quartz, nuggets of lapis lazuli, and sultry carved rubies, I find the most magnificent and magnetic to be the Star Sapphire. It is a small, round, sky-blue stone with a flawless white six-stemmed star that glimmers from its centre. The jeweller tells us that the Star Sapphire is September's stone. Jessica and I both simultaneously voice that we're September babies, and are each charmed into buying one. I feel like I now have a piece of the cosmos on my thumb. After our purchases, we end up chatting with the shopkeeper for some time, and he invites us to his home for dinner.

There is no furniture in the living room of his two-room

house. On the ground in the centre of the room there is a lavish feast that his brother's wife prepared for us. The three of us sit on the ground in a triangle and eat with our right hand, as is the custom here. The right hand is always used for eating. The left hand is never to touch food, nor to be offered when shaking hands. This is because the left hand is used to clean oneself with water after going to the bathroom. One has to be mindful when meeting new people to never offer their left hand to be shaken, as it is a very degrading gesture. It would really suck to be left-handed in India. We spend the evening trying to keep conversation flowing about our different lives, filling the awkward gaps by clumsily stuffing more morsels into our mouths.

The next morning, Jessica leaves to catch her flight back to England. I want to find a guesthouse that's more communal, a place where it's easy to meet other travellers. This turns out to be as easily said as done. I find just such a place, with an inviting courtyard filled with young backpackers from all over the world.

As I wander around town some more, a young man on a motorcycle stops abruptly next to me and invites me to a lunch celebration. One of the men in the village has just finished building his new home. He's invited everyone in the village to celebrate and bless his new house by serving them all lunch on his flat rooftop.

"Everyone's invited!" he insists.

I trust him. His energy feels pure. I hop on the back of his motorbike: to be appropriate, I grip onto the back of the seat instead of hugging his waist. He takes me to the edge of the village, where there's already quite a crowd of people waiting. I'm the only non-local here and I feel honoured. Once the kids take notice of the oddity that is me, I'm stampeded. They jump all over me and ask me to take pictures of them, then to show them the pictures on my digital camera. We do this for quite some time as none of them seem to even tire slightly from all the picture taking and viewing. They're deliriously hyper and happy. Eventually, my motorcycle buddy comes to get me. The men have finished and it's now my turn to eat.

There's only enough room on the roof for roughly thirty people, so the crowd's eating in turns. I peel the giggling children off of me and climb the stairs to find myself with only women. We smile at each other. A banana leaf is put in front of each of us. Next, people come around doling out dollops of colourful and unfamiliar food onto our banana leaves. I sigh relieved, as I notice that everything's vegetarian. I'm not very good at eating with my hand. It's trickier than it sounds and half the stuff escapes between leaf and lip. The women sitting around me laugh at and with me as I spill rice, veggies, and sauces down my front. They mime proper technique to show me how to one-handedly ball and scoop the food, yet still, much of the feast spills onto the vibrant hues of my baggy clothes.

After my group finishes eating, we are whisked down the stairs to clear the space for the next round of people. The man who invited me has been waiting. We zoom back into town to roughly where he found me, and I hop off the back of his bike. He says, "Nice to meet you," without the desire for anything further: no tip, nor kiss. Impressed, I smile and wave goodbye as he rides away.

Back at the guesthouse I meet a Colombian guy named Jorge and an Israeli girl named Chave. The three of us rent bicycles and pedal around Hampi. A group of three young children wave and ask for a ride. We each take one of them on the handlebars of our bikes and swerve them through the maze of people, laughing as we narrowly avoid collisions with pushcarts and potholes. At the edge of town, we stop at a humble restaurant, and treat the kids to little glass bottles of ambiguous, fluorescent-coloured juice (their choice, not ours). After they finish their drinks, we pedal them to their home. The three of them share a one-room clay hut with their impoverished mother. There's a mattress-less broken metal bed frame and a few cooking pots, and that pretty much sums it up. Her husband, their father, has abandoned them. It's sad. Yet they seem to smile sincerely, and all have sparkles in their eyes.

Scratch the thought that being left-handed in India would suck. True hardship would be life among the many poor people, the ones considered to be untouchable, the lowest class of the often abided-by caste system. The highest caste are the Brahmins, the priestly scholars among Hindus. The second class are called the Kshatriyas, or Rajanyas. They are the rulers, administrators, and warriors. Next in the hierarchy are the Vaishyas, which include artisans, merchants, tradesmen and farmers. Lastly, at the bottom, are the Shudras, the menial labourers, with the most undesirable jobs — if they can even find work. The castes are considered inherited callings in life. They are not chosen, and they seldom change.

Jorge and I end up hooking up. We spend the evening in bed together. I haven't had casual sex very many times. At the start, I am uncomfortable in my body, despite Jorge treating me like I'm outrageously beautiful. Still, though, I feel fat and gross. His affection can't be genuine. Using the sobering magic that culture hopping brings, I tell myself to let go of the beauty standards that I have been brainwashed into feeling. This actually works, and I transform my mind to relax and to be at peace in my skin. I know that I have been conditioned into perceiving various things in certain ways. The more I travel the more I notice the ways my society has wired me — and the more I realize this, the more I'm able to let go. But I still have much work to do to unravel the power that cultural conditioning has over me.

The next afternoon Jorge and I hang out downtown, in front of the main temple. I take my attention away from the pyramid, and all of the art and story imprinted into it, and notice a raggedy man with his three small children in tattered clothes. I ask if I can photograph them. The father smiles and nods a sideways yes. That's how people nod "yes" here, with a vertical jiggle from side to side, instead of a straight up and down. I take several photos. We pass the camera back and forth to look at the pictures. I tell them they're beautiful. They blush, eyes lowered. Their ragged clothes and unruly hair imply that they're from the Shudra caste. I do my best to show them the decency and respect that all humans deserve. I look up and I notice a family with brilliant, crisp, clean clothing, adorned in golden jewellery, with perfectly pampered hair. They glare at us disapprovingly. Because we're treating poor people as equals? I ignore the unfriendly looks. When we part ways, we hold our hands in prayer in front of our heart-centre, bow slightly and say "Namaste," the ubiquitous greeting, that translates as "the divine in me recognizes and honours the divine in you." I'm left wondering if, and when, a revolution of equality will come. And if, perhaps, we played a miniscule part in the revolution.

Jorge gets clingy. It's annoying. I need room to breathe. I

end what we have and cross the river to another guesthouse with Chave. We go for a short hike out of town to a Hanuman Temple. Hanuman is a Hindu God that is part monkey. Naturally, people bring bananas as offerings. The monkeys come in droves. I'm pretty sure it's the piles of bananas that draw them here. But who knows? Maybe Hanuman's partly responsible for alluring the monkeys. Here at the temple, there are more monkeys than I've ever seen in one spot. They peacefully chomp away at the piles of bananas.

It's time to carry on, there's just so much to see. There's an ashram in the far south that's been recommended to me by Angela, a friend back home. Still not totally clear on what an ashram is, I decide to find out, and arrange a train going to Trivandrum, a city in the southeast. I sit in the boiling hot open-air platform and chat with other backpackers as we await our train that finally arrives six hours late. As was also recommended, I buy Second Class Sleeper tickets. Most trains have a variety of class options, ranging from overcrowded and sweaty to incredibly luxurious and elite. Second Class falls somewhere in the middle.

The inside of the train is a long corridor with tiny bench-like beds stacked on top of one another in little compartments. I follow the number on my ticket to my empty, faded blue bunk. The compartments are shared between men and women, children and elderly. There doesn't appear to be any obvious gender or caste barriers. We're all in this ride together. I climb up onto my bunk and lay down, using my backpack as a pillow. The heat and motion of the train loll me into a lovely reverie that soon turns to sleep.

Twenty-Four

Luckily, I wake up five minutes before the train arrives at Trivandrum. I flag down a rickshaw to take me to the Sivananda Ashram. My driver's face softens when I tell him where I'm going, and he asks an unusually modest price for the ride. Perhaps this is because I'm going to do spiritual practices, something which is generally regarded with reverence here. Or perhaps because many people here believe in karma and it repercussions.

As I step through the gate onto the ashram's property, I feel a current of serene energy flow into my being. It's not unlike the sensation that I felt when the Brahman Priest blessed me in Mumbai. India seems to have a prevalence of access to a strong and magical energy that the eye doesn't do justice to. Maybe energy wavelengths are easier to feel here because people believe in, and acknowledge, them, thus giving them more power. My culture has trained me to not feel invisible frequencies, that they don't exist. But they do exist. I am starting to regularly experience their subtle presence. The sun is setting. It's a vivid red, more intoxicating than wine. It looks larger and closer than it ever has. Watching the sunset, I feel a deep sense of awe and gratitude. I whisper a "Thank you," not quite able to define whom or what I'm thanking.

My backpack and I saunter past a big, beautiful, open-air yoga pavilion, then a tidy courtyard with well-tended flowers and plants. I locate my dormitory building. My super smiley bunkmate is from Japan. She tells me that travelling to Canada is a dream of hers. It occurs to me that Canada is also an exotic and interesting place, providing you don't come from there. I make a little vow to treat Canada with more appreciation and enthusiasm when I return.

As I continue to try to figure out what an ashram is, I read the daily schedule. We are required to participate in its entirety each and every day:

Five thirty a.m. Wake up.

Six a.m. Meditation and Bhakti Yoga-Satsang (Devotional Chanting).

Eight a.m. Hatha Yoga (Practice of Asanas(postures)).

Ten a.m. Brunch.

Ten forty-five a.m. Karma Yoga (Selfless service to purify the heart. E.g., cleaning, gardening…).

Twelve p.m. Varying spiritual activity

Two p.m. Lecture (Yoga, Ayurveda, Meditation…)

Four p.m. Hatha Yoga.

Six p.m. Dinner.

Seven thirty p.m. Meditation, Bhakti Yoga, Satsang.

Ten p.m. Silence and lights off.

During our meditations, we are instructed to let all of the sounds flow through ourselves without labelling or reacting to them. I have moments where I feel like I'm doing it successfully. The birds and breezes become as much a part of me as my breath. We are told not to think about time. When thoughts do arise, we are to stop them without judgement and to return to the free flow of unlabeled sounds arising and passing. I don't know it yet, but in a few years this meditation will prove to be incredibly helpful in coping with psychosis, and the voices, spirits and demons that psychosis brings.

Satsang is call and response chanting, mostly Sanskrit names of various Hindu gods. We aren't so much praying to external gods as praying to awaken the various qualities of those gods within ourselves. One of the lines towards the end of the long chant is translated into English.

Being able to understand the words makes this part my favourite. I feel it far more powerfully than the rest of what we chant.

"I am bliss. I am bliss. Bliss absolute. Bliss I am."

There is something disarming about singing you are bliss. For the first time in my life, I sing without judging the sound of my voice. I can feel the vibration change the chemistry in my body. I am mending.

So, from what I gather, an ashram is a place where a spiritual community lives and constantly practices different forms of divine unity. This ashram's form is Jain. In a lecture, I learn the three principles of Jainism: Non-violence, Ahimsa; Non-possession, Aparigraha; and Non-Absolutism, Anekanta. One way in which Jainism contrasts to Hinduism is that Jains do not support the Caste System. In this, I am drawn to it.

Until now, I thought that yoga was simply just stretching exercises, that the more flexible one is, the more "good at yoga" one is. It turns out the word "yoga" translates as "union." The goal of yoga is to harmonize one's body, mind, and spirit, in peace and wholeness. There are various methods of yoga, various ways to attain such balance. At the ashram, I've counted four kinds of yogic paths that we are practicing daily: Hatha Yoga, the practice of various breathing exercises and physical postures; Karma Yoga, the discipline of selfless action as a way to purify one's heart; Bhakti Yoga, the cultivation of love and devotion toward God, often through chanting; and Raja Yoga, the yoga of knowledge and mental control.

Every two-hour Hatha class is a mountain. We start with dizzying, difficult breathing exercises that my lungs just aren't accustomed to. Next, we do sun salutations, arching ourselves between a plethora of postures to warm up the body. They on their own are an extremely exerting exercise. Then we bend, stretch, balance, in pretty much every way I can imagine. Despite it being quite difficult for me, each time a class finishes, I feel accomplished, and a little closer to being who I'd ideally like to be. As the days go by my body aches a little more, a little less, then a little more again. I've woken up muscles that have gone ignored for quite some time. It's a good hurt.

We break our regimen for New Year's Eve, and everyone stays up 'till midnight. Cups of pepper tea are poured to help us stay awake. At about eleven thirty we start chanting "Om Namo Narayanaya," a prayer for World Peace. We chant it into the New Year. As we sing, I try as hard as I can to feel and to visualise what World Peace would be like. Warzones become amicable communities. Food and water is brought to areas of famine and drought. People everywhere smile. Vegetation thrives in cities. People from different countries hug and hold hands. As the last note concludes, the room rings with a beautiful resonance. I go to bed filled with hope for our planet and its people.

After about a week of being here, the community quadruples. The ashram is hosting a Yoga Teacher Training. The atmosphere of the ashram shifts from calm to cluttered. Quite a few of the students are carrying the fast-paced, stressed-out wavelengths of the cultures they've just jetted in from. An English girl named Amy and I decide to leave together. Best to remember the ashram as serene.

Twenty-Five

Downtown Pondicherry, Amy and I sit at the sunny shoreline sipping chai. A man with eyes locked on Amy strolls over from the sleepy restaurant he was tending. He peels his trance-like gaze off her, turns to me and says, "Wow — your friend is really fat. Wow, she's so fat!" He resumes staring at Amy, all googly eyed. Awkwardly, I say, "Yeah, she's beautiful."

Often in India, big women are considered to be more desirable than thin women. My theory is that whatever is most difficult to achieve in a society becomes idealized, so that the capitalist rulers can sell more personal dissatisfaction in the form of makeup, clothes, etcetera.

Being content and fulfilled with oneself is not good for business. In the west, where thin figures are what we're taught to see as most beautiful, people generally have money and vehicles, are surrounded by an abundance of food, and work immobile jobs, making it difficult to achieve a slim figure. In India, where poverty is abundant, a fuller figure implies wealth and comforts. The man's words were intended to complement her. He even exaggerated her "fatness." Really, she's just a strong healthy. Unfortunately, his attempt at flattery no doubt made her feel hideous and insecure. She comes from a different societal conditioning.

That evening, I sense Amy is now in duality about whether or not she wants to eat. I invite her to a nice dinner. At the mostly empty restaurant, there's one other foreign girl, sitting by herself at a table, sipping a glass of white wine. A little while later I get up from our pillowy table in the corner and walk across the restaurant to ask for more water. I notice that the girl who was sitting alone is now surrounded by half a dozen men competing for her attention. Assuming she's overwhelmed by her crowd of pursuers, I walk over and invite her to join us for dinner. She excuses herself and makes her way to our table. Her name's Daisy. She's vegan, except for chai. She's just arrived from Sri Lanka, where she lived at a Buddhist monastery for a couple of months. The three of us laugh into the evening. Amy and I walk Daisy to her guesthouse, then the two of us walk the quiet streets to ours.

    A little way out of Pondicherry, there's an international eco community built in the shape of a galaxy named Auroville. Aurovillians are attempting to manifest human unity and equality, through cooperative, self-sufficient communes. Intrigued, Amy and I decide to go there for a day trip. We catch a bus that leaves us on the highway at the turnoff of the small, dusty road that leads to Auroville. There are a few basic stores and huts at the junction the bus left us, nothing more. There are no taxis or rickshaws in sight on this sparse stretch of highway. As we sit at the side of the road pondering what to do, a group of four young guys in swish clothes, on two motorcycles, zoom out of the distance. They notice us, ease off the acceleration, and roll to a stop beside us to chat. They're on vacation from Delhi. We explain our conundrum, and they offer us a ride to Auroville.

    The six of us share two motorcycles, and one helmet. Amy and I ride on the back of one of the bikes, while three of the guys squish onto the other one. In a flurry of giggles and exhaust, we rip down the narrow, winding road. Through the sporadic, eclectic congestion, the other bike whizzes ahead, out of sight. We wind around a sharp corner and see the three other guys, and their bike, sprawled across the road. They wiped out from taking the turn too quickly. Our driver cranks the handle bars and swerves to avoid them. Too late. Our motorcycle spins out in slow motion. The guy driving leaps forward, out of the way of the bike. I boost my butt up off the seat, and the bike careens forward out from beneath me as I fall backwards. Amy, stuck in the middle, has nowhere to jump to. The bike falls on her, and she starts screaming in pain. The other guys jump up from their daze and rush over to lift the heavy machine off of her.

About twenty people appear from the bushes lining the road. Some are carrying buckets of water, which they generously use to clean our scratches and minor wounds. Some of them start to chant and pray as they wash our cuts. Amid the commotion, I barely make out the back of a girl bicycling past. She must have clued in that there was a crash, because she turns around to join the cluster. It's Daisy! On her cellphone, she calls a cab to come get us. While we wait for the taxi, we exchange numbers, and make plans to meet up back in Pondicherry. Back at our guesthouse, Amy and I tend to our injuries. We're in a bit of pain, but have no serious wounds, and are feeling more lucky than sore.

The next day, Amy has a flight to catch. Daisy tells me that, while in Auroville yesterday, she heard whispers that the Dalai Lama is going to come for a visit.

"What! When?"

"Tomorrow."

I notice a deck of Tarot Cards peeking out of Daisy's bag, and suggest asking the cards if the Dalai Lama is in fact going to be here. We pull the High Priestess, then do our best to interpret it together. A holy person in robes, sitting on a chair against a red and yellow backdrop (the Dalai Lama's colours!), as if in front of an audience, ready to teach, looks back at us from the card with a loving gaze.

"She's sitting beneath the number two," I say. "Do you think that could be mean 'TWOmorrow?'" For us, it's confirmed. We set an alarm clock for sunrise.

We walk and hitch-hike our way to Auroville on the same road I crashed on a couple of days prior. In steadily rising heat, we finally arrive. We ask the first person we come across if the Dalai Lama is actually here. To our glee, it's confirmed! He has been invited to inaugurate the Tibetan Pavilion that the Aurovillians have just finished building. His Holiness is also here to thank the galactic community for taking in four Tibetan orphans and raising them. We ask directions to where his speech shall take place, and are led to a blocked off clearing with a lineup of Aurovillians, and a handful of other fated travellers. Each person that enters the cleared area has their bag thoroughly searched. Cameras and cell phones are banned. After a short wait, we get to the front of the line, hand over our cameras, then go and find a spot on the ground to sit.

The area fills with about four hundred of us, hushed in anticipation. A giddy woman, almost in tears, walks to the microphone at the front of the clearing. She welcomes His Holiness in a voice quavering with elation. Everyone stands as he approaches the microphone. I pinch myself. This is actually happening.

The Dalai Lama graciously thanks Auroville for inviting him. The crowd cheers and slowly returns to sit on the ground. With eyes, ears, and heart wide-open, I listen to his speech on

World Peace and Human Unity, his advice to the Aurovillians on how to contribute to this goal. As always, his words are beautiful and inspiring. I've read some of his prose before and was deeply moved. But today I was graced by his auric field.

After, Daisy and I buzz with childlike giddiness. We skip and laugh our way back to Pondicherry. What are the odds? How many other people would have been astounded and soulfully grateful to stumble upon a free afternoon with the Dalai Lama? We try to articulate our wonder. Why us? Divine synchronicity perhaps? Utter fluke? We fail to understand why we were so blessed. My cells are still humming with bliss.

At our hotel in Pondicherry, we meet a guy who's in the midst of a mild panic attack. His skin is pallid, his nerves frayed. He's just been told that he is going to be in a fatal car crash at the age of twenty-seven.

"Who told you this?" we ask. He goes on to tell us about the Library of Leaves.

Two thousand years ago, a prophet wrote down the fortunes of all the people who will visit the Library in the future. The foretellings are scribed on palm leaves that have been preserved with much care over the centuries, while they await their destined visitor. The library's in a village, a few hours from here. Although the fortunes are potentially grim, the thought of ancient divination is too alluring to pass up. Daisy and I look at each other... "Let's go!"

Twenty-Six

Our destination requires a journey on a slow, battered, old bus. The rollicking, see-saw groan of the axles over untamed road is familiar and soothing. The street sort of smooths out as we emerge from dry trees and bushes and enter the village of Vaitheeswaran. The first person we ask points us to the Library of Leaves.

I poke my head into the unassuming building. The librarian at the front desk seems like your ordinary, bored, sleepy, librarian. Clearly immune to the mystical enigma of such a place, she quietly tells us to come back later in the day. At the moment they're with a newly married couple. A reading costs two thousand five hundred rupees (about forty-five Canadian dollars); "no bartering." Usually, I'm unable to resist esoteric divination, but today, for some reason, I'm not feeling it. I change my mind, and decide not to have my future read to me. There's something that I'm not ready to hear.

Daisy remains enthusiastic. I sit in while they hunt for her prophecy. They ask her a series of yes or no questions. As soon as a "no" rolls off her lips, they put aside the faded brown bundle of meticulously preserved leaves, hand scribed with ink, and grab a fresh one from the neatly packed, abounding shelves. Eventually she answers "yes" to a string of questions: Were you born in December? Is your father currently ill? When you were young were you an atheist? Are you from England? Do you paint? Did you break your right leg when you were seven years old? At last, the oracle pauses, bows his head and announces that they've found Daisy's bundle of prophesized prose. I leave the room for Daisy to hear her fate in privacy.

Outside, I smoke a couple beedies to pass time. Beedies are tobacco wrapped in tendu leaves. They are considered to be the poor man's smoke, but I actually prefer them to regular cigarettes. They're way less expensive. But mostly I like them because they just feel much more natural and closer to being sacred. Sacred, the way tobacco was considered to be for centuries, before the big companies morphed it into a highly addictive and highly toxic substance to profit off and enslave people into chemical addictions.

Later, we saunter around the village and order dinner from a stall on the street. There are many items we've never seen. We point and ask their names, mostly unable to make out the pronunciation, or recall the name of the dish that came before. We decide to just ask for one of everything that's vegan. The vendor's eyes light up as he grabs several banana leaves, and piles mountains of food onto them. It turns out the whole menu was vegan. We eat our fill, far past the point of satiating our curiosity, not wanting to offend the vendor. Unable to contain any more food in our bursting bellies, we ask to have the leftovers packed. Within seconds of walking towards our hotel, we come across a mother asleep on the street, wrapped around her three small children. I put my hand on her shoulder and gently stir her awake. We give her the food, and say our namastes. As we walk away, she wakes her children. They bolt upright and voraciously inhale the food, smile and laugh as they gorge. We head in for the night, reminded of how fortunate we are. We always have shelter, privacy, food.

Twenty-Seven

In the morning, we leave for Chennai, a city on the east coast of Southern India. We aren't sure what part of the city we are in but, from our long, arbitrary stroll, we conclude that Chennai is a dirty, dusty, grey sprawl. The streets are lifeless for Indian standards. Eventually, we happen upon a travel agent's office. It seems out of place, as there are no other businesses in sight. We enter and inquire about what there is to do. The lone woman operating the slumberous business recommends going to the Andaman and Nicobar Islands. They form an archipelago, one thousand three hundred and fifty-four kilometres off the coast of Chennai. The Andamans are much closer to Myanmar than the continent of India, yet most of the islands belong to the latter. One must have a government-issued permit to go there and, even then, one can't stay longer than four weeks. Most of the isolated islands are off limits to visitors, to protect the tribal people that still inhabit the region. The thought of islands in the middle of the sea, far removed from modern culture, is too seductive to resist. It seems exotic in a different kind of way than the continent of India is. In my imagination, it is a unique, multi microcosmic area, in virtue of its remoteness. I buy a plane ticket on the spot. It's only two hundred dollars for a flight to the Andamans, then one from there to Calcutta. My plane departs tomorrow morning.

Back at our hotel, Daisy mourns her dwindled travel fund,

wishing she could come along. I take a shower, and when I get out, she hands me a handwritten letter, saying that I'm easygoing, kind, and humble, and that she hopes we cross paths again. I'm really flattered as she's someone that I found to be admirable, even a little intimidating. Saying goodbye to a kindred spirit would normally be sad, but I'm too excited for the mystery that awaits me.

Twenty-Eight

The plane surprises me in its modernism and size. I'm the only foreigner on the flight, which also comes as a pleasant surprise. Am I off of the typical tourist trail? We land in Port Blair, a small city on one of the larger islands, from which I arrange a ferry to Havelock Island. The ferry is an old rusty boat that loads on as many passengers as possible, and then a few more. The boat will take half a day to get to our destination. The water is very rocky and the humidity downright nauseating. A passenger a few spaces down the bench has brought a large cardboard parcel of meat with her. A few hours into the tumultuous ride, blood starts melting out from the cardboard, trickling down the tightly packed bench of commuters. I watch as beads of blood wobble back and forth, closer and closer, in almost hypnotic rhythm with the heaving of the deck. One final lurch forces me out of my seat to let the red ooze pass. I finish the remainder of the ride standing. This passage would have seemed very long and unpleasant, but the other option was a four-day boat from Chennai. As my legs flounder onto shore, I realize how glad I am to have splurged for a flight.

Havelock Island instantly impresses itself upon me as a tropical paradise. My backpack and I walk down warm, calm, palm-lined roads for about a kilometre, until coming across a row of beach huts for rent. There's one left that's vacant. My hut is the size of the double mattress in it with a roll-up bamboo screen as a door — there is no way to lock it. It's less than four dollars a night. My deeper knowing is completely at peace with my hut being lockless. One needn't have a lock on Havelock.

I quickly find companionship among three other young women that are staying on the same property. Talya from Finland, Bee from England, and Nicky from Toronto. Nicky and Bee had also been at the Ashram in Trivandrum and took the yoga teacher training course which caused such a buzz as to, scare me off. We set the intention to start every day with a yoga practice together. The four of us soon feel like dear old friends. We spend most of our days together, wander, talk about our lives and dreams, as we bask in the island's serene energy and spectacular beauty. One evening I bring out my colouring pencils, and the four of us fill pages from my notebook with colour. As Tayla doodles, she freezes.

"Wait..." she says. "What's the date?"

We share a fit of laughter. Combined, it takes us a couple of minutes to remember what month it is. We've all been travelling for a while now. The feeling of liberation from clocks and calendars is intoxicating.

There's a three-day festival going on. The island comes together to cook, eat and celebrate. We are waved off of the road to join the celebration. We sit on the floor with hundreds of people and enjoy the vegetarian feast served on banana leaves. My fingers snap shut like Venus Flytraps around neat and tidy little packets of rice. My hand eating skills have become way less sloppy.

We keep hearing talk of "the Lagoon." Between yoga sessions, swimming, and frolicking in the sun, we find the time to rent bicycles to and seek out the lagoon. The four of us pedal the quiet, stunning, tree lined roads under singing birds. We breeze past bright vegetation, until we reach a gargantuan hill that requires us to arduously pump our legs. Fuelled by joy, we actually make it up on our gearless bikes. Then comes the glorious finish of flying downhill from the summit, to arrive at the most gorgeous, huge, and empty beach any of us have ever seen.

From the sublime beach, we walk a trail that weaves between tide and trees. It turns out not to be a true lagoon, but a beautiful, soft sand beach with a deep incline into the sea that blossoms out to a rainbow coral reef with cosmic fish fluttering freely in the flow. Here the ocean is as warm as bath water. While in the sea, I feel like I'm flying more than pumping myself through water. Everything is perfect. I pray that all people get to feel like this at least once in their life. Bee and I stand waist-deep in the tide, and both agree that this is the happiest we've ever felt. My bar for jubilance has been raised. I wonder if the law of karma is in fact what determines one's circumstances and, if so, what I did to deserve this.

The next day at a little open-air shop, I purchase hand carved wooden spiral ear stretchers. The shop owner takes me over to a lemon tree and breaks off a spine. He instructs me to stick it through my ear, that it'll stretch my earring hole while disinfecting it at the same time. It slides in, slowly, painlessly enlarging the gap. Nature has much magic to teach me.

Thanks to Nicky, my body is getting good at yoga. We actually stuck to our goal of doing the two-hour Sivananda practice every day. But, all too soon, the time has come for Nicky to catch her flight back to the main continent. Talya, Bee, and I have half a week left before our permits expire. We peel ourselves off of Havelock to go check out another island.

Our next island is newer to tourism. We find a place to stay at an aspiring guesthouse. The men here build us a tent out of clean, plastic sheets and beach logs. The materials are modest, but the result is impressive. We've got a spacious enough shelter. We paint a sign with sunshine, sea, and spirals, advertising their new "hotel," in exchange for staying in the plastic palace. After a few dreamy days of dazzling dips and wonderland walks, we leave in a dreary trance. The problem with happiness is the inevitable parting of ways with the things that made you happy. I'm trying to focus on gratitude for these life-peak weeks, instead of sadness that they're over.

On the ferry back to Port Blair, dolphins come out of the sea and dance in the sky alongside the ship. The three of us laugh, and agree that it feels like the dolphins are jumping just for us, as a beautiful omen that more amazingness shall follow.

Twenty-Nine

Bee and I fly to Calcutta together. Calcutta is India's second most populated city, and our portal to the north. From the airport, we find a rickety old city bus to take us to Sudder Street, the "backpacker ghetto." Instantly, I get over my longing for the Andamans and relish my return to the kaleidoscope of colourful, bustling India. This time I realize that Indian cities are not only a visual kaleidoscope, but a motley of the other senses as well... the plethora of aromas and sounds... perfumes, spices, cow shit, trash, sacred music, cheesy jingles, honking horns... I take a deep breath as I gaze upon the psychedelic chaos.

Bee and I rent an inexpensive double room in one of the hotels. The walls in our room are covered in art from travellers who have come before. We take out my art supplies and add to the decoration on the walls. I write "Follow Your Bliss" arching above the doorway, and smile sublimely as it occurs to me that I am doing just that.

While exploring the dusty, crowded streets, I come across a bookstore. There are a couple decks of divination cards. Intrigued, I saunter over and hold one of the decks in my hands. "You want buy?" the shop owner asks. Already enchanted, but not quite feeling like they're befitting, I ask if he has others. He goes to the private closet behind his desk and comes back with another set of cards. He places them in my hands, and right away I feel a deep and mystifying resonance.

These cards were waiting for me. I ask the price, trying to seem only half-interested. We barter and he insists I pay one thousand rupees, which is only about twenty dollars, but twenty dollars feels like a lot when you're accustomed to Indian prices. He tells me if I'd like to pay less, then I can buy one of the other decks. My heart is set on the deck from the back. I agree, knowing he's getting a really good deal, but I'm okay with that. I want the cards more than I want the money, even though one thousand rupees goes a very long way here. All the better for the shopkeeper.

Back at the hotel, the first person that I strike up a conversation with tells me he's funding his travels by doing tarot card and palmistry readings along the way. Synchronicity just feeling normal now, I tell him that I just bought my first deck of Tarot Cards. He rolls his eyes in a snobby fashion then asks me to show him. As soon as I produce the box of Rider-Waite cards from my shoulder bag, his eyes light up and his attitude changes. "This is the most powerful deck." I smile, intuitive confirmation also coming to feel expected now. "You want a palm reading, don't you?" He says.

Ultra-eager to hear what his take on my odd palm will be, he takes me to his small room, clears the bed and lights a stick of incense. We take our seats on the mattress. I hold out my peculiar palm. He doesn't comment on the triangles. But, upon seeing that I don't have a separate heart or head line, he explains that that is because I don't have a duality between the two, that they are more of a team than most people's. Though, as the reading progresses, he concludes that my heart is my governing energy. The hill under the thumb is the Mount of Venus, and mine is huge. Venus is the planet of love, and the planet of Libra, my star-sign. He tells me my aura is pink and green, another confirmation that my heart is my boss, as those are the heart chakra's colours. For a moment, I am flattered, but quickly conclude that that definitely doesn't portray me.

I'd like to think of myself as being like that, but it'd be delusional. I am as selfish as anyone. I mean, here I am, hedonistically backpacking in a third world country. Not to mention, my moments of being really mean, for instance berating friends that summer after South America, or all the times I've walked past beggars... he notices my attention wander and tells me to come back to the present. "You have dragonfly and hummingbird energy; those are your spirit animals."

"That is why you were just spacing out, and also why you travel in spontaneous, random patterns. You need to read the book *Animal Speak* to better understand yourself."

After we're done with the reading, he invites me to his weeklong course on Tarot Card reading that he's hosting in the Himalayas a few weeks from now. Because what he said didn't feel one hundred percent accurate to me, I decline but ask if he could give me a few pointers on tarot.

"Well, seeing as you intuitively picked the best deck, it would be wrong not to." He grabs the instruction booklet from my deck and pockets it. I open my mouth to say "Hey!" but, before I have the chance to, he insists that he's doing me a service. "Let the cards speak to you. Trust yourself. They will communicate something different every time. It's a medium to the divine, not something black, white, and academic. You've either got it, or you don't."

We say our namastes and I go back to the hotel's rooftop courtyard to join the suddenly not-so-arbitrary-feeling bunch of people. I can't help but wonder if we were destined to intersect paths and help each other along our trails, towards our destinies.

On a street corner near the guest house there's a Chaiwala. He's there every day, all morning, all afternoon, and stays well into every evening. No one ever comes to relieve him. He remains still within the bustle: The view aperture of the kaleidoscope. He serves chai in rough pottery cups for pennies. He doesn't wash and reuse the cups after serving tea in them. I suppose clay must be plentiful around here. While drinking a warm, creamy, sweet and spicy mug, I notice some of the people throw their cups onto the pavement, smash them once they're empty. The Chaiwala sweeps the broken pieces of pottery into a pile, then someone comes and takes them out of sight. This seems silly, but seeing as he never reuses the cups, breaking the cups has a fun, childlike novelty to it. I join in the tradition. Smash!

Bee and I roam the streets. Big streets, small streets, all of them congested and loud. Days into our stay in Calcutta, we finally locate one of our destinations, the Botanical Gardens. The huge park in the middle of the mammoth metropolis claims to host the world's largest tree. It's a Banyan tree. Their branches produce aerial roots that become mini trunks, which look as if they're dripping down the tree like candle wax, so it's larger in width than height. But, still, I'm feeling privileged to be walking under and alongside the gigantic tree. We carry on and come to a magnificent pond, bejewelled with enormous lotus flowers with wide, heart-shaped leaves. And, sure enough, there are tons of dragonflies, my little spirit messengers letting me know that I am where I'm supposed to be. Bee and I sit and share an open-eyed meditation at the pond's edge, then eventually pull our sweaty, tired bodies from the oasis and return to the smoggy, loud, cluttered sprawl.

Calcutta's downtown market is made up of tons of little booths crammed chock-a-block together. Here one can find many things. Luxurious jewellery, tacky knick knacks, incense, saris, brand name jeans, Bollywood movies, Britney Spears CDs.... The menagerie is endless. As I try on a pair of sunglasses, I look back at Bee and see her talking to one of the other travellers from our hotel.

Breathlessly, he sputters out, "You'll never guess who I just saw!" All gaga, he tells us about how he spent all morning following Michael Pollan around the city.

"Oh wow!" says Bee, as if stalking someone is a sane and reasonable thing to do.

"Who the heck's Michael Pollan?" They turn to me, bewildered.

"He's a writer, and an activist! Ooh, I bet he's probably here for a documentary or something amazing like that!" We have a laughing fit, not so much with each other, but at each other. To them, I appear to have come to India from living in a cave. "I mean, how could you not know who Michael Pollan is?" While I laugh at him for spending his day secretly following around a celebrity.

The elusive clock is ticking, and faintly talking; I'm over halfway through my trip. Bee and I have both come down with the customary "Kolkata Cough." Each day, by mid-afternoon, we're coated in grime from the humid smog, from our skin to our oesophagi. We need to leave the city in order to return to health. We've been getting along really well and decide to make the pilgrimage to Bodhgaya together. Bodhgaya is the village where Siddhartha Gautama, the first Buddha, attained enlightenment, fifteen hundred years prior. It hosts the Bodhi tree that was planted from the sapling of the very tree beneath which the founder of Buddhism was meditating when he reached enlightenment. Bodhgaya is a far-reaching pilgrimage for Buddhist monks, nuns, and laypeople alike.

We have one last chai before heading out. As pottery clatters into shards at my feet, a man turns to me and, in a surprised tone, asks if I support the caste system. "Of course not!" I reply. He explains that the cups are meant for single use to ensure people from higher castes don't touch their lips to the same cup as a lowly Shudra, even if they are washed. Extremely ashamed, I look at the pieces of smashed clay and the aristocratic disdain it represents. I awkwardly try to make eye contact and whisper "sorry" to all who return my gaze. From a place of self-hatred, I'm yet again shown the lesson that I should travel more informed and less blindly. Even though I know that my intent behind smashing my chai cups wasn't inline with its symbolism, I feel horrible.

Thirty

On the train, Bee and I dip into her guidebook. We learn that Bodhgaya is in Bihar, India's poorest state. From the train station in the city of Ghaya, where we debark, there is a thirty-minute drive to get to Bodhgaya. The book warns of occasional highway robberies. We concur that intuitively, we both feel that we don't need to splurge for the extravagance of a taxi. We hop off the train and hire one of the many eagerly waving rickshaw drivers at random. Crammed into the back of the buggy with our bloated backpacks we glide and bump through the evening's lovely warm breeze. No trouble comes our way.

We locate a monastery that rents basic rooms and ring the doorbell at its tall metal gate. After a long moment, a smiling monk in red robes approaches from the other side. We bow our heads and ask if they have any beds available. He nods, and unlatches a giant padlock, turns a key in another lock, and swings open the heavy gate, all in complete silence. He gently motions for us to follow him. As we step through the humble, immaculately maintained courtyard, I become regretfully aware of how grimy I am. We're shown to a spotlessly clean room where the atmosphere is beyond tranquil. The thought of armed robbery seems ridiculous and improbable anywhere within miles of a vibration so peaceful as this. The sun has barely set, but we are unsure if it would be appropriate to go into town and ring the gatebell later in the evening. We wash our hands and faces, stretch quietly, then lay down on our firm beds. From reverie, I drift into a deeply refreshing sleep.

We wake, wash, put on fresh clothing, and start the short walk to the Mahabodhi Temple that encompasses the legendary Bodhi Tree. Near the temple gates we pass a blind beggar with stubs for hands and legs. His skin is etched with intensely painful-looking cracks from the dry heat. He is in the roughest shape of anyone I've ever seen. Shaken from his condition, I drop a handful of coins in his bowl. His sight is too deficient to even take notice of the alms. I can't help but feel an immense sense of gratitude, wonder, and guilt, for being in my current karma.

On a garden path, we walk towards the narrow, tall pyramid that is the Mahabodhi Temple, and slow our already relaxed pace, calmly in awe. The air feels fresher with every step. Beautiful wavelengths pulse into my cells as we walk through the temple and arrive at the Bodhi tree. It slowly sheds its heart shaped leaves onto the ground. We join the still meditators under the boughs of the tree. I sit in sparkles for some time. When we rise, we make our way to a towering statue of a meditating Buddha. There's quite a crowd meandering, yet everyone is serene. I'm in a lovely dream state, feeling a calm this heightened and mighty is a first for me. Proof in invisible but tangible energy presents itself again.

Later, on the outskirts of town, we come upon the Root Institute for Wisdom Culture. Due to the poverty in the area, the centre is guarded by men with rifles. They smile at us and wave us in. We step through the divide, back into a peace zone. In three days, they're hosting this season's last Ten-Day Introduction to Mahayana Buddhism Philosophy Course. I apologize to Bee for bailing on our plan to carry on together.

My dragonfly spirit is drawn to this course. Bee's wanting to buzz toward another sweet hive.

My next few days are spent under the Bodhi Tree. Grime leftover from Calcutta's foul air makes its way out of my body in the form of a coughing fit. I feel a tap on my shoulder, and look up to see a glowing, moon-faced monk smiling at me. He motions for me to open my palm. I do. He pours about a tablespoon of brownish-orange powder into my hand, then gestures for me to swallow it. With the water I have beside me, I swirl the slightly bitter powder around my mouth and gulp it down. My lungs are suddenly strong and clear. I bow my head, place my hands in prayer in front of my heart and say, "Namaste." With a radiant smile, he slowly strolls away.

The first day of my course arrives. The program is going to consist of philosophy teachings, various kinds of guided meditations, and a little bit of hatha yoga. There are approximately twenty of us here for the ten-day course. Half of the students are teenagers from affluent families in the US, on an exchange trip organized by their school. The other half of us are long-term, solo backpackers. We're an odd bunch. Getting to know each other is slow since most of our time is spent either meditating or listening to teachings. We are asked to not talk in the dining hall, so we familiarize with one another more through the overlaps in our energy fields than how-do-you-do's. Our teachers are lovely. There's a nun who exudes gentleness and a forthright monk with a clever sense of humour.

One of the philosophies that is introduced to us is that of Precious Human Life. Precious Human Life basically means not taking for granted being in the circumstance where one is free to consciously better oneself, and also to be able to help others. Only certain human incarnations provide that opportunity. One should take heed and act when in such a rare and blessed condition. Samsara (the cycles of death and rebirth in various forms and realms) can often be torturous. One can go through lifetimes of helplessness. So we, in our current karma, are encouraged to devote ourselves to peaceful and positive evolution, as much for ourselves as others.

Our nun guru reads us a text written by Robert K Hall, a psychiatrist and lay-Buddhist priest. The philosophical prose is about how facing fear is facing life and about how transformation only happens in the present moment. The writings are brilliant to me. After class, I ask for the book and copy the text into my journal.

I learn that there are many different branches of Buddhism. In the Mahayana tradition, some choose the path of the Bodhisattva. A Bodhisattva is a person who is able to leave samsara, and reach a state of enlightenment and bliss, but delays this transcendence, and instead, returns to the pain of cyclical existence to help others who are still in realms of suffering. This really moves me. It seems so beautiful, well, angelic, really. Naively, hardly even grasping the basics of Buddhism, if at all, I pray that I, too, become a Bodhisattva.

Near the end of our ten days, we are guided through an evening meditation that begins by filling ourselves with the sentiment of absolute and unconditional loving kindness for ourselves. Patiently, we are instructed to take that feeling and extend it to the people sitting beside us. Breathing in, we brim ourselves with love, then, as we exhale, we send the sensation and intention to those beside us. We continue for quite some time, inhaling pure love, then sharing it with our surroundings. As we progress into the practice, we extend our love further.

We deliver loving kindness to the room of meditators, then to Bodhgaya, to Bihar, to India, to Earth. By now we've cultivated a powerful sensation in the room, almost overwhelming. We continue. We are guided to send our love to the Moon, then the planets and stars. The intention becomes a tangible force, projecting out from us. I am seeing a crisp vivid image of the cosmos in my mind's eye, and start to wonder if I'm astral travelling. I drop that question and return to concentrating. This sensation of love is stronger than anything I've ever felt. It's flowing freely, being shared with infinity so naturally, so completely. A millisecond after we are guided to stop, a very loud sound of thunder erupts and heavy rain begins to pour, restoring life to the desert around us. In the glimmering resonance one of the teenagers shifts our silence back to sound...

"Did we generate the rain?" he asks, with a voice of awe. The room starts to giggle. We can't help but speculate that possibility, the connection between all.

The course ends. Most of us backpackers linger at the centre, wanting a gentle transition back to the extraverted and action-packed reality of travelling. You can't help but smile when backpacking through India is your return to normality. We spend a couple of days just hanging out, finally able to get to know each other through verbal conversation. I notice a Nepalese guide book on the shelf, and soon, a few others are flipping through the book with me. Three of us decide to set out for a hike together. But, first, I want to visit Varanasi, the "spiritual capital" of India, while I'm relatively close and the option is there. Semu, the boy from Malaysia, and Elisa, the girl from Norway, have already been to Varanasi. We make plans to meet next week in Pokhara, a town in Nepal where many treks begin. The two of them head to Kathmandu together, while I leave for Varanasi.

Back at the Ghaya train station, I realise that I am alone for the first time since landing in Mumbai. It's a little intimidating. I visualize meeting someone to travel with. At the huge train station, I wander around for a minute or two, then, sure enough, I spot one other backpacker in the sea of people. She looks as lost as I feel. I walk up to her and introduce myself. Her name's Teesta and she has the same destination. I ask her if she wants to get train tickets together, and she's delighted by the idea.

"Thank you," I whisper to my best friend, the Universe.

Thirty-One

Despite the trains almost never being on time, one is advised to buy tickets in advance, as they are almost always filled to the brim. But, to our fate, there are a few Second-Class-Sleeper tickets still available on the next train to Varanasi. The train is scheduled to depart momentarily, and happens to actually be on time. On the ride, Teesta and I get to talking. She was raised in the UK by a Buddhist family. She resonated with Buddhism and kept it as her way of life. I express envy of her upbringing.

Varanasi is believed to be at least three thousand years old. We make our way through the city towards the Ganges riverbank. We start to feel like we're being taken through a giant labyrinth. The roads are narrow, with old, tall rock walls, making the non-gridded side streets invisible. Varanasi is one of the most highly-sought cities in India for locals and foreigners. Finding a guesthouse is effortless; there is an abundance to meet the demand.

It's an aspiration of many Hindus to be cremated here. It is believed that the Ganges river is a source of spiritual purification. Every year, countless Hindu pilgrims come to Varanasi seeking just that. It is believed that if one dies or is cremated here, they attain Moksha: Liberation from the normally endless cycles of death and rebirth. Every day, approximately two hundred and fifty bodies are cremated in Varanasi. Cremation Ghats line the river. The wood for cremation is outrageously costly, making it so that sometimes the process isn't one hundred percent complete before the ashes are given to the river.

The Ganges is exceptionally polluted here. The coliform bacteria count, which includes E. coli, is three thousand times higher than what is considered safe. Despite this, hundreds of people bathe in the river here daily. There are many accounts of people with various illnesses going in and emerging miraculously healed. To me, this feels like logical evidence for magic, the divine, or however else you want to go about trying to articulate the supernatural with mere words.

Teesta and I arrange for a rowboat ride at dawn. By cover of darkness, our guide takes us down to the river through the city, confidently weaving us through the winding maze of streets and alleyways. The buildings and carts of Varanasi lay still as if abandoned. At the river's edge, we step down into a small wooden boat. The first faint hints of blue and orange blush their way into the morning sky, catching folds of water where they whorl around the oars. We drift down the river and watch the sleeping city stir from its slumber. Out from a shadowed alley comes a man on a bicycle, the first sign of life. Next, a woman laying out a bright rainbow of freshly washed saris on the steps of the riverbank to dry. Slowly, others start to trickle into view. People, monkeys, cows. Now that the sun has risen out of the horizon, we can see how filthy and debris-filled the water is. Although it's not the first extremely polluted river I've seen on this trip, the sludge is still horribly mesmerizing. The trance is broken when we drift by what I'm quite sure is a half charred human thumb. I dart my eyes up from the river and try to not gag.

Later, I go for a long walk across the city, glued to the river's edge to ensure I'll be able to find my way back. At a creek off to the side, I stop dead in my tracks, horrified. There's a swamp that's inundated in trash, it's a foot deep and covers at least fifteen metres squared. A mother with her two young daughters, rifle through the garbage, competing with a few scrawny piglets that are feasting on the choice edibles in the trash. A steep slope that leads down to the river is also laden with layers of litter, guiding the slurry of refuse into the Ganges. There is no garbage disposal service in the holiest city, on the holiest river.

Back in the bustling tourist district, I notice a sign for "Chakra-Balancing Reiki." I don't understand what all that means, but I'm compelled to find out. I knock on the door and a tiny woman with dark sparkling orbs as eyes answers. I ask her what reiki is.

"A healing technique where one channels energy into the patient's body to restore balance in the chakras and activate the body's natural healing processes."

"Chakras?" I ask.

"Energy wheels within the body that harness power. Many traditions believe that there are seven main chakras. Beginning with the root chakra at the base of the spine, that grounds one with earth, and ending with the crown chakra at the top of the head, which harmonizes cosmic connection."

She instructs me to lay on my back, close my eyes, and to breathe deep and slow. Her hands scan my body, an inch or two above it. A pleasant breeze flows from her palms. When her hands arrive at my lower abdomen, the sensation shifts and I feel a dense clog. She hovers here longer. After a minute or two, the stiffness suddenly leaps from my abdomen and floats away. My whole body feels open and free. She tells me to remain laying on the table until I'm ready to be back in the city. I stay for what could have been three, or thirty, minutes. In a dream state, I thank her. She instructs me to do yoga and meditation regularly, to give my chakras a better chance of remaining in balance.

Afterwards, I ponder cultural differences. Where I come from, there's so much most people don't understand or acknowledge. We've been conditioned to not feel the invisible connection between one another, our planet, and the galaxies beyond. We are victims of programmed desensitization. Why? Probably for the sake of keeping the economy fuelled, to keep the capitalist competition alive. We've been taught to believe our school teachers, doctors, and media dogmatically. We're told we are solid and separate, that energy that isn't instantly seen with the naked eye doesn't exist. In the west, mystical phenomena is considered ridiculous, even stupid. Maybe people are afraid to acknowledge that they don't understand everything? Western society has conditioned us to feel that confusion is weak and stupid. It's nearly ineffable. I have much hardwire to unravel, and unlearn.

Varanasi is extraordinary and unique. I could easily spend months here. But I don't have months if I want to explore other places. Teesta decides to join me towards Nepal. There's a city in the north called Gorakhpur that has trains to the Nepalese border.

Gorakhpur is the most obnoxious place yet. A rusty, creaking, cog in the clockwork of my journey. The traffic here is somehow even more helter-skelter than the other cities of India, feverish and furious. Cars, trucks, bicycles, rickshaws, pedestrians. They all fight through the chaos, only show grace and give space for the cows. It's filthy. There's trash scattered all over the ground. The dust in the air is one with the thick smog. My opinion could very well be unfair, as I'm only seeing the area where the train station is. Hopefully, there's an oasis, somewhere, in this city. Teesta and I are glad to leave as quickly as we arrived.

Thirty-Two

A long slow bus ride on narrow winding roads lined with sheer drop-offs drum up memories of Death Road in Bolivia. I breathe deeply and try to transform anxiety into excitement; supposedly they are physiologically the same experience, just with positive and negative labels given to them. Near Pokhara, the foothills become coated in pine trees; for a moment I feel like I'm back in British Columbia, Canada.

The bus crests the final incline without plummeting off the steep roadside. I welcome the clean, brisk air into my lungs, relieving them from all the dry dust they've inhaled since the Andaman Islands. This small city is a tourist hub. There are more trekkers than townsfolk. An abundance of restaurants, bars, hotels, internet cafes and hiking gear stores fill the town. Any luxury a privileged person would want while they wander the wild sierra can be found here, in Pokhara.

Teesta and I had arranged to meet Elisa and Semu for dinner. But Pokhara's tourist district is small enough, and we bump into them before we even drop our bags in a hotel. Under a crisp, blue sky, amidst a gorgeous green mountain backdrop, I introduce them to each other. Elisa and Semu are friendly to us, but have stone cold faces towards each other. I suggest going to get chai. They bicker pettily about where to go, daggers in their eyes. It's obvious, they hooked up whilst in Kathmandu. I really hope Teesta decides to join us on the hike, so that I don't wind up spinning the third wheel in this already uncomfortable dynamic.

Over chai, three of us agree that we don't need a guide or a Sherpa. Six eyes turn to Teesta for her agreement. She falters, and anxiously declines her invitation to trek with us. As soon as Teesta leaves, Elisa starts saying that Teesta needs to pluck her unibrow. Her shallow cruelty shocks me. I ignore the obvious omen that we might not be compatible trail buddies. The lure of the mountains is just too magnetic. This opportunity is far too exquisite to pass up. I'm not brave enough to go alone, nor do I want to splurge for a guide.

The three of us buy jackets and hiking boots. There're loads of cheap North Fake and Pataphonia for sale in the shops, no doubt carted in from nearby sweatshops. The hike we've decided to do is called the Annapurna. The three-week walk presents little risk of getting lost, starving or freezing to death. Supposedly there are basic guesthouses and restaurants along the well-marked trail. All of the food, and the fuel needed to cook it, is hiked in by porters.

We set out the next morning. Town trickles away. All that's in sight is the elephantine entry into the mammoth mountain range. It suddenly occurs to me: We're going deep into the secluded, tempestuous summit of the earth with nothing but our flimsy boots and each other. Even if it is on the comparatively gentle Annapurna, it suddenly feels bold and intimidating. I close my eyes and say a prayer to be protected during this hike. I open my eyes and a dragonfly is right in front of them. Everything will be okay.

We walk all day. It's beautiful, as nature always is, but the surroundings are still familiar enough. Supposedly the sublime spectacle really starts a few days in. As sunlight weans from the sky, we pass a house with little sleeping huts to the side of the trail. There's no village here, just one woman and her two young children. We spend the evening indoors trying to converse. Our host seems to relish the reprieve from isolated mountain life. As we help her stack the dishes, lightning splits the sky, and a thunderstorm erupts. The innkeeper explains that it's angry dragons in the sky. I love that that is what thunder and lightning is for her. Call me ridiculous, but western scholars can't know everything. There's a slight possibility that there were dragons here, some day long past, legend keeping them alive.

The three of us retire to our small hut for the night. The thunder and lightning bears down with winds so strong that our flimsy sheet metal roof starts to flop in the wind. Semu stands on his bed and literally holds the roof down. If the dragonflies blessed our passage, surely the dragons will too? Eventually the storm passes, and our tired bodies return to slumber.

A few, mostly pleasant, days go by. I'm a slower walker than Semu and Elisa. I feel bad, but I can't maintain their stamina. Elisa makes it clear that waiting for me is annoying. Every half hour or so they have to stop and wait for me to catch up. Elisa whines about my pace. I tell her I'm trying. "Try harder," she says, irritated. Now that it's begun, I stop denying the obvious: This is going to be a bittersweet three weeks.

Even though we don't cover much distance per day, the landscape changes significantly. The road ended a couple days into our hike. From here on in, it's only footpaths. The distant mountains become taller and steeper. The snow to vegetation ratio has met its tipping point. The townships now have longer distances between one another. We're encountering fewer and fewer other people as we ascend.

On day five, I round a corner and see Elisa and Semu waiting ahead, *again*. Semu's shouting, arms in the air. When I catch up, he turns to me and says, "I'm sorry, Maya, I can't stand being around Elisa any more!"

As soon as those words leave his mouth, he speeds ahead. I half expect him to apologize and turn around. He doesn't even look back as he disappears into the distance. For a moment, we stand silent in the breeze. Then Elisa starts freaking out. "We're gonna get raped! Two white girls alone in remote mountains with no guide! We're dead!" I try to calm her down.

"We've got each other. It's an extremely peaceful culture." She does simmer down, and agrees to continue forward. I'm not worried about our safety. I'm worried about having Elisa as my sole companion for the next two weeks.

Small temples and beautiful archways built from stone with prayers chiselled into them are plentiful on the practically deserted trail. More and more, we pass prayer wheels, meticulously hand-chiselled metal cylinders built into stone supports. Every single time we pass a set of prayer wheels I walk to its left and spin them with my right hand, as was instructed. I pray for whatever comes to mind. Usually, it's just the typical stuff... world peace, happiness, health, love... Elisa ignores every single prayer wheel. Sometimes, I get the impression that she's choking back laughter.

Short, lean, bulging-thighed men, pulling loads easily three times the weight of our own, speed past us with incredible momentum. They're porters, carrying goods to the guesthouses and villages further ahead. Some of them have crowded cages of live chickens on their backs. Most have cheap flip flops as footwear, if that. Their feet have ravine-like cracks that look very painful. Nepal's economy is struggling. This backbreaking work is their only option to make a little bit of money. They humble me. The soreness that's accumulating in my back, legs and feet would normally bring me to whine, but the porters are a constant reminder that my situation is actually quite cushy. I am increasingly in awe of this landscape and its tough and beautiful people. But Elisa doesn't seem to be moved at all. The porters walk too briskly past her. The sun is too bright in her eyes. Her zipper keeps getting stuck. She always has something to complain about.

As the scenery becomes more and more stunning, Elisa and I become more and more sick of each other's company. We don't have anything left to talk about. We're both begrudgingly aware of the fact that we still have days and days together. All day, every day. Usually, this situation would be difficult to stay positive through. But I've become a tiny creature frolicking on the top of the world. I am practically in disbelief to be here, to be doing this.

A few days from the Thorong-La Pass, which is at five thousand, four hundred and sixteen metres above sea level and is our highest peak, we meet an American girl and a hired Sherpa. Jasmine, Vishal, good ol' Elisa, and I, group together. It's an extremely welcome reprieve to have more people to share energy with.

At midafternoon, we arrive at "High Camp," the last place to stay before the Thorong-La Pass. No village here, just a lodge and trekkers. With a mouthful of rice and lentils I burst into uncontainable laughter. My group looks at me, perplexed, as I keel over, in guffaw about things that really aren't that funny, or even funny at all. Though, I suppose being stuck up here with Elisa is, at its essence, quite funny, but I don't vocalize that one. I look out of the window of the lodge and have a vertigo-like floating sensation, which just makes me laugh more. In severe cases, altitude sickness can be crippling. Despite having a whole lot of fun, I become lucid again by the time we finish eating dinner. If the altitude sickness had persisted, I would have had to turn around and hike back the way we came to recover. I wonder if Elisa would have stayed by my side if that had been the case. Probably not. She'd probably say that it's my own fault, leave me to head down by myself, and scurry on up the hill with Jasmine and Vishal.

Tomorrow, we're going to have to wake up before sunrise. Often, by early afternoon, the winds become so strong near the top of the pass that they render the hike treacherous. We crawl into our beds wearing literally all of our clothes: jackets, mittens, toques, everything layered on top of one another. We tuck in under several thick, dusty blankets, then pull the blankets over our heads to avoid freezing. In the night I wake, needing to pee. I go outside to find the toilet.

The sky is crystal clear. I have hiked up into the heavens, where the stars are extraordinarily bigger and brighter. I'm among them, below, and beside them. I lift up my arms to touch the stars, and they twinkle in reply, just beyond my grasp. The crisp snow I'm standing on becomes thousands of stars condensed together, reflecting the ones above and around my head. I'm not sure if the snow's making the stars shine or the stars are making the snow shine. I stand in the middle, dazzled by their light. I prolong my break from the dreams that come with slumber, reality far more spectacular. I stand in awe. This is what perfection is. Never have I experienced such splendour. This is why one would choose to incarnate on Earth, to go through all the pain and struggles, just for an occasion as beautiful and magnificent as this. I'm more at peace than I've ever been. My standards are bumped up another time. When the unforgiving chill becomes too intense, I retreat indoors, back to bed.

At three thirty a.m. Elisa's alarm goes off. We peek our heads out from under the covers, tighten our toques, and stroll out of bed. Half-convinced I'm still asleep and dreaming, I hoist my pack onto my back. Seconds later, we are outside, marching the ascent up the steep, snow-laden mountain, under the now dark and cloud-filled sky. Sun comes slowly from below us, and soon we are taking off our layers, sweating from the climb. Now it's Jasmine that's having a hard time breathing. The altitude must be getting to her too. We round a corner, and, amazingly enough, there is someone prepared for just this situation: A man and his yak. Elisa and I watch her and Vishal disappear ahead in the distance as she gets carried towards the pass on the back of the yak.

A couple of hours later, my body starts to fail me. Walking has become arduous. Each step takes tremendous effort. My legs are as stiff and heavy as the rock that makes up the mountains below.

And, what's more, we're alone. The others that left from high camp this morning were all accustomed to mountaineering, thus much quicker than us. They're long gone. I'm starting to worry, wondering if I'll be able to make it. But, between laboured breaths, I can hear words of encouragement. Elisa's cheering me on. This is the kindest she's ever been to me. I'm surprised she hasn't rolled her eyes and motored on ahead. She offers me the last of her water, says it'll give me more energy. But it doesn't. We can't ignore the reality any more. Conversation turns dark. Are we even going in the right direction? Shouldn't we have come across the pass by now?

A bone shaking thought creeps into my mind. Did I have the peak experience of my life just hours ago because I was on the brink of death? Was this trek up the mountain a send-off?

Just as I'm trying to accept what's happening, someone appears out of the distance ahead. Oddly, they are walking towards us, down from the pass. Maybe someone else got altitude sickness and had to turn around. If that's the case, we've still got a very long way to go. They're moving quickly, almost running. In a couple of minutes, we can make them out in the distance. Tears fall from my eyes. It's Vishal.

He had waited for us at the pass. He asks if we're alright. I tell him that my legs are lead, and my lungs are deflated balloons. He takes my backpack, hefts it easily onto his shoulders, tucks his arm under mine, and lifts me slightly to help lighten my steps. "We're *very* close," he insists. With Vishal's help, walking becomes radically different. It's still laborious, but I am able to keep going. He insists that we need to hurry. Elisa playfully pushes me in the back. I give it my all. Five minutes later we make out colours ahead, prayer flags fluttering in the wind.

Vishal points. "That's the pass."

As if by magic, the tension and strain float out of my body while we near the countless Tibetan prayer flags. Bright new ones, and old wind-battered ones, dance in the wind. Hundreds of people have hiked up here and hung them. Hundreds of people care. Now I'm sobbing. I don't know why. Tears for Tibet? Tears for making it? Tears for being alive? We take a couple pictures, then are urged to hurry down. We are lucky. "The winds are exceptionally calm today." But the wind can pick up without notice. One last look at the surrounding mountains from our platform of snow, and, within seconds, we are off.

Vishal double checks that Elisa and I are all right. From my tear-stained face I express another, inadequate, "Thank you so much." He giggles a little. I wonder how ridiculous I must seem to him. The thought actually makes me burst into laughter, again. Vishal walks ahead to catch up to Jasmine. She was carried up, over, and down the pass as quickly as the yak could take her. As I watch Vishal disappear into the distance again, I can't help but wonder if he literally just saved my life.

Elisa and I forget the rift between us. We skip down the mountain like little girls deliriously high on sweet, sweet, sugar. Elisa starts singing, I join in and we sing several songs together as we skip our way down the mountainside. The descent is far easier on our muscles and lungs.

Days breeze by. The sensation of aching muscles has come to be a constant, but it doesn't bother me anymore. Despite having less and less to talk about, and becoming more aware of how drastically different our personalities are, Elisa and I have grown to appreciate and respect each other, bonded by this adventure. We even get lost once, but in under an hour realize that where we're stepping definitely isn't a trail any more. We trace our steps back to the path and laugh it off. A few more days of hiking through dwindling hills then, all at once, the journey is over.

I feel odd. Confused. Directionless. I'm exhausted. But I would do it again in a heartbeat. Even with Elisa.

Back in Pokhara I bump into Teesta. She's radiantly happy. She's been in Pokhara the whole time, and has fallen in love with a man from Australia. I smile and feel a bit like the matchmaker, as I was the one who suggested she come to Nepal.

Elisa wants to party. She offers to buy me drinks and keeps whining for me to go out with her. Reluctantly, I agree, mostly to get her to stop whining. The thought of drinking alcohol feels immoral. We're in an impoverished place and in a culture that doesn't condone futile intoxication. The bar is filled with travellers from all over the globe, realm hopping to party in cultures similar to their own. Something in me has shifted. I'm not interested in talking to others and hearing their stories that will all be forgotten with tomorrow's hangover. I'm bored. Bored of yet another evening of, "What's your name? Where are you from? How long are you travelling for? Where have you been? How hardcore are you?" I might be being kind of standoffish, but I'm just no longer interested in, or impressed by backpackers getting drunk together. It's the same everywhere I've been. Isn't the whole point of travelling to experience different realities?

The night moves me to re-immerse myself in India's spirituality. I register for a ten-day Vipassana meditation course. It starts five days from now, making it time to venture to the city of Dehradun, back in Northern India.

Thirty-Three

I stop in Rishikesh, en-route to Dehradun, mostly because other travellers have insisted on Rishikesh, another sacred city on the holy Ganges River. It's sort of a Mecca for yogis. The glacier-fed, fast-flowing river, still in the Himalayan altitudes, makes the water crystal-clear, unlike the brown, waste-choked waters of Varanasi downstream. I find an ashram to stay at. It turns out to be an ordinary guesthouse with phony ashram airs. Other than a couple of yoga classes held here each day, nothing about the guesthouse and its environment reflects spiritual focus.

After being disappointed by the boring yoga classes at the guesthouse, I try a class in town. I'm the only student. Under the pretence of checking my alignment, the man teaching keeps patting my body enthusiastically during the asanas, repeatedly saying, "Wow! Very good! You are very strong!" I walk out shortly after the class commences, wondering how many money hungry pseudo-gurus could be in this town.

Wandering the streets, I see a poster that reads "Palm Readings." On the quest to confirm if my palm actually indicates an exquisite destiny, I can't resist. A studious man at a wooden desk in an otherwise empty and small room gestures for me to take the seat across from him. He holds my hands in his and traces some of the lines with a red pen, while circling other markings scattered in my flesh before speaking. "You are going to have a very good life. But that will come later.

I'm sorry to say, but you have very difficult times ahead." He looks deeply and compassionately into my eyes, before continuing.

Whatever it is he's seeing makes me shiver. His face tells me that it's something no one would envy. "When times are hard, you must remember that you are going to have a very blessed life." He pauses again. "Always remember that." In a lighter tone, he goes on to say that I have a "crazy nature," and should do my best to tame my "crazy tendencies." I will have many careers, and will not have children until I'm significantly older. And there it is again: "Your name will be known." Hearing that I'm bound for fame, yet again, curiously, makes it feel more likely.

It's time to leave, my Vipassana course begins tomorrow afternoon.

Thirty-Four

From Dehradun's train station, I find a taxi that takes me out of the city. We bump down a winding dirt road. There're a few other sign-less roads branching off from it, like twigs confused about what direction to grow. I'm dropped off at a large, white, circular complex with a golden temple reaching towards the sky in the centre of its dome. Through the entrance, I find myself in a simple room with a man at a desk, signing in the mismatched group of meditators. Most of the people waiting in line are middle-aged Indian folk. There're a few younger people, and a few foreign travellers. Everyone seems to have come alone.

When my turn comes to sign in, I am asked to leave my camera, all of my books, journals, and my pens. The man at the desk locks them in a cupboard, assuring me that the key will be given to me at the end of the ten days. I am assigned a bed and room. "Silence begins now."

For the duration of the course, all of us meditators are forbidden from speaking or writing. Nor are we to do any other spiritual practices, such as yoga or other meditation techniques. And, to top it off, making eye contact with each other is also a no. Basically, all forms of interpersonal contact are not welcome here. The rules are so we can experience solely the effects of Vipassana meditation. Once the ten days are over, we are then free to be extraverts and to decide for ourselves what to do for spiritual practices.

The men and women are separated to avoid further distraction. In silence, I slowly ball my dinner of rice, dhal, and chapatis into my mouth, trying to eat meditatively, among the twenty or so other women. The sounds of chewing, swallowing, breathing, and especially the clinking of dishes, seem so loud with the absence of conversation. After that, we are left with nothing but ourselves until we fall asleep. Sleep takes hours to arrive. I'm very bored, already. The course hasn't even begun.

Our daily schedule:

Four a.m.: Morning wake-up bell

Four thirty — six thirty a.m.: Meditation in Dharma Hall

Six thirty — eight a.m.: Breakfast

Eight — nine a.m.: Meditation in Dharma Hall

Nine — eleven a.m.: Meditation in Dharma Hall—

Eleven — noon: Lunch

Noon — one p.m.: Rest, or private Q and A session with the teacher

One — two thirty p.m.: Meditation in Dharma Hall

Two thirty — three thirty p.m.: Meditation in Dharma Hall Three thirty —five p.m.: Meditation in private cells

Five — six p.m.: Tea

Six — seven p.m.: Meditation in Dharma Hall

Seven — eight fifteen p.m.: Teacher's Discourse

Eight fifteen — nine p.m.: Meditation in Dharma Hall

Nine — nine thirty p.m.: Rest, optional private Q and A session with the teacher

Ten p.m.: Lights out

The first few days, I yo-yo between strain and calm. We are asked to spend all of our sits focusing on the sensation of the air coming in and out of our nostrils. When our minds wander, we are to stop our thoughts without attaching to their story and return to focus on the air flow in and out of our noses. This is supposed to strengthen our mind's ability to be quiet, concentrated, and unobstructed. It's impossible to do it for more than ten seconds at a time. I meander in and out of trying. Each day, there are three, hour-long, sessions where we are not to reposition ourselves, no matter how badly a leg falls asleep or a back aches, from staying upright with perfect posture. And the heat doesn't help. Other than the early morning and late evening session, it's so hot that sweat drips down my back all day long, despite being motionless.

My room is shared with a young Indian woman. While taking a pee in our private bathroom, I notice a large wolf spider scurry out of the shower drain. I cringe as it scuttles about. Soon, multiple wolf spiders are creeping up from the drains, and into our bedroom. My roommate is terrified of them. With petrified eyes, she breaks our no-interaction vow. With wild hand gestures, she summons me to help her de-spider the room. We fan them back towards the drains where they were dwelling. I don't break the silence vow to voice the obvious futility, as they just keep scuttling back up from where we exiled them. It's nice to have something to do.

Every three days, the meditation practice evolves. It's day four, and we now are instructed to slowly scan our bodies, from toe to crown, and stop at every little place along the way, then give that area our undivided attention for a little while. We are to not label its sensation as pleasant or unpleasant. If another part of our body aches, which is happening most of the time from the hours of sitting, straight-spined, cross legged, on a small cushion, we are to ignore it and exclusively experience the tiny area on our body whose turn it is for attention. How I feel varies drastically from day to day, even from hour to hour. This meditation is a psychic tightrope juggling act.

I try to focus on the subtle breeze on my right cheek, while ignoring the tingle in my deadened left leg, while also trying to ignore the thought that it could actually be causing severe, irreparable damage to ignore a sleeping limb for so long. I have a moment of being enraged at myself for signing up to do this. Staying for another week seems like a torturously loooong time.

But I will stay. I ride the emotional and physical rollercoaster. It's not all difficult. There are moments where I have pearls of thoughts and realizations. It's frustrating not being able to capture them on paper. All I can do is set them free and accept the possibility that I may not have that groundbreaking revelation again, that I will never be able to benefit from its wisdom. Moments of physical agony, of sadness, regret, hatred, self-hatred, love, self-love, forgiveness, anger, confusion, bliss, deep relaxation, come and go, like wind blowing through a forest. You name it, I've felt it in the span of these past five days.

One of, if not the, main goal of Vipassana meditation is to reach equanimity. We practice equanimity on the physical plane to reach it in the mental plane. When a muscle has fallen asleep, or aches from trying to hold proper posture, we breath into those places without labelling the sensations as negative. It works some of the time. I suppose I'm taking baby steps on the journey of mastering attitude, to liberate myself from drama. Things that would ordinarily be uncomfortable become accepted, even welcome.

Each day, we spend one meditation session in a private cell. I've started cheating, and do yoga quietly during our cell sessions. I'm convinced it's helping me enjoy sitting more — or is it hate sitting less? — while also enabling me to concentrate and have deeper meditations. I feel a tad guilty and blasphemous about the yoga. The Universe will surely forgive me.

On day seven, we progress from pinpointing places on our body to slowly scanning the body as a whole. Up and down, then back again, and again. Today, for the first time, I succeed in not budging during our afternoon hour-long sit. When the hour is over, I am left surprised. It felt like no more than twenty minutes and was actually quite pleasant. So much for the theory of "Doing the same thing and expecting different results," being a definition for insanity.

I am sitting outside during one of our ever so sweet breaks. I close my eyes and look inward. My cells are universes and galaxies. I feel space between them as they move the way the Earth and the other planets dance around the Sun. I feel the reality of not being solid. The Universe is inside of me as much as I'm inside of it. I'm discovering what I truly am. I'm remembering where I was and how it felt to be formless and unlimited. How existence feels before taking a respite in human form. This is one of the moments where the tedious agony of the past week feels worthwhile. My ego congratulates itself then laughs at itself for the pride. Even though there are only two days left, it still feels like an epically long road lies ahead. There are no shortcuts through Vipassana. I set the intention to try to stay focused for the rest of the course.

The tenth day is really beautiful. I'll let you take the course to experience it.

Our guru rings a soft bell and gently announces that the

last meditation is over. I open my eyes in dreamy disbelief, as if stepping out of a plane into a new and exotic place. A palpable wave of contented satisfaction ripples through the room. I linger in the silent, now empty, hall after everyone else has stood up and walked back to rejoin planet Earth. Despite many arduous moments of extreme restlessness, now all I want is to stay in the tranquillity that I've cultivated. When I think about speaking, it just seems absurd and goofy. As soon as I start talking it will probably be a boring waste of energy, a string of pointless, shallow shit and vague opinions. More minutes pass, and, mostly out of feeling obliged, I reluctantly stand up and walk out of the meditation hall.

    The soft murmur of small talk roars in my ears like a flock of migrating birds taking exodus. I introduce myself to my roommate. She's twenty-two and has recently been arranged to marry. Before she gets married, she wanted to have some time to herself, which is why she chose to do this Vipassana.

    It's my turn to respond, but I don't know how to. Though I do notice that I don't see her situation as good or bad. Before, I probably would have passionately pitied her, overcome with rage by my ignorant opinion against the oppressive tradition of arranged marriages. I surely would have felt entitled and right in my perspective. But now? I don't know what to think. I think?

    Another woman who did the course lives in an ashram. A real ashram, not a hub for privileged people to go through their spiritual crisis in a pampered atmosphere. She's lived there for over twenty years, since the time she became a widow. I find myself envious of her. It sounds so connected with peace. I'm probably being a romantic, though. I really have no idea what it would be like to live in an ashram year after year, no end in sight, except death. Here I am again, trying to fathom the mystery of how I arrived in my unique karma.

While talking to the others, I come to regret cheating in the form of yoga during our private cell meditations. It's just that now I have no idea what I would have experienced if I had done the course properly. A bickering duality inside of me says, "That's okay, you'll just have to do it again to find out," while another part of me says, "Heck no! It's done!" Already, conversation has swept me up again, within and without. But a voyeur behind the internal and external chatter has been resurrected, and she is unconditionally non-judgmental.

Before I'm ready, I'm hopping out of a taxi in the city centre. I sway through the chaotic streets of Dehradun and notice that my mind is slower than it was ten days ago. With my eyes, I'm barely noticing all the bikes, rickshaws, cows, and cars hurtling by. I just float through the mayhem by some kind of tuned-in grace. Or maybe it's just a spaced-out delusion. Same, but different? Maybe.

Thirty-Five.

I find a night bus to the small conjoint city of Dharamshala/McLeod Ganj. It hosts the Dalai Lama and the Tibetan Government in Exile. As dawn's light is blanketing the Himalayan foothills with warmth, I walk up the valley to the edge of town. Legs still strong from the Annapurna, I find a guest house overlooking the clutter of the city. Morning shifts to day and I watch the steep, narrow streets fill with quasi-pilgrim hippies from all around the world.

At least once a day, my feet carry me down the descent into McLeod Ganj. I'm ritualistically going to the Dalai Lama's temple and circulating it with the other monks, nuns, Tibetans and travellers. Whether in motion or while sitting, I practice clearing and purifying my mind at the spacious red and golden temple. Clarity comes easily, probably because I'm physically absorbing the wavelength of the serene atmosphere. I recite mantras and prayers, for Earth, for Tibet, for myself, for the people I love, and even the ones that I dislike.

One day, while sitting close-eyed in meditation at the temple, I feel a presence. I open my eyes to see a man waiting patiently before me. In a soft voice, he asks if I could teach English to some of the Tibetan refugees. I start to go off on a tangent about how English feels wrong to teach. That it just contributes to the whitewashing of the world and the disempowerment and destruction of other cultures. His face lights up at my thoughts, before he goes on to explain a different point of view. English is becoming the language of the world. Tibetans who learn to speak English will then be able to tell the world of the horrors happening inside their homeland. Raising awareness with a global language is a non-violent tool to help their country's salvation. Perhaps it is the only solution. My opinion of teaching English shifts completely. I agree to start tomorrow.

I walk down the valley to a plaza on the outskirts of the temple where the lessons take place and wonder how it'll be. The group size varies daily. It depends on how many teachers volunteer and how many students attend. I arrive a little early. There are far more students than teachers. We divide ourselves into similar sized groups. I have about a dozen people in mine.

Not really knowing what else to do, I sit in the circle that has organically formed on the ground. Everyone is smiling at me. I become nervous, and stutter out, "What do your other teachers normally do?"

Kind faces calm my feelings of inadequacy. One of the girls suggests I ask a question, then the group can take turns answering it. This way they will all get a chance to practice and I can help by correcting grammar and by introducing new words to help them elaborate. I ask them what they did this morning, disappointed with myself by my boring question. Some of them speak fairly well. Others struggle to string together sentences. Most people reply with pretty much the same answer: "Had a shower, made my bed, ate breakfast, walked to the lesson…" I am heartened, and saddened, by their patience with sharing me, their very-lacking teacher.

It occurs to me to ask about their journeys fleeing Tibet. One of the more fluent young men goes into great depth about his experience. He and a small group walked for a month through bitterly cold mountains. Amazingly, his guide had succeeded on three prior occasions of leading groups like his to freedom. The guide heroically returned to Tibet to attempt a fourth escape party, risking his life to help others out of the bleak situation inside of Tibet, instead of choosing to stay in India with the others. There was no trail. The route was arduous, cold, and frightening. They were blessed enough to avoid Chinese border patrols. But one of his good friends got frostbite one night, and was forced to walk the last week in terrible pain, battling to keep up with the group. His friend actually made it to India and, upon arrival, received surgery to remove his dead, frozen foot. He has no way of contacting his family back in Tibet to tell them he made it safely. He thinks of his family every day. He hopes and prays that he will be able to see them again. He hopes and prays that they are okay.

The girl who taught me how to teach at the beginning of our circle tells of similar horrors. The fear before, and throughout the exodus. When she gets toher arrival here and how she got to meet the Dalai Lama, her face turns from sadness to joy. The beloved spiritual and political leader takes time to meet with every single Tibetan refugee that makes it here. But, still, the heavy pain from all that she's endured, that was in her eyes moments before, lingers within me. She is so young and so kind. I can't wrap my head around what these innocent people have gone through. It all sounds like such a nightmare. Yet, here they are, traumatized yet unbroken, trying their hardest to save the others that are still in Chinese occupied Tibet.

I educate myself more about the situation.

***

Tenzin Gyatso, the fourteenth Dalai Lama, is considered to be the Enlightened One of Compassion. He is the adored spiritual and political leader of the Tibetan people. The culture he leads is one of dedication to aid all. All. Having realized that violence leads to more violence, the Tibetan philosophy and way of life is pacifism, and respect for all living beings. Before China's invasion, one of the main focuses of Tibet was developing inner strengths like wisdom, kindness and, of course, compassion. Therefore, Tibet had no army. Unlike China today, which has the largest army in the world.

In 1950, China began the invasion of its neighbouring country, Tibet. China's army totally overpowered the unarmed Tibetans, resulting in a nearly instantaneous and full occupation by forty thousand soldiers. By 1959 the situation had become so dangerous and oppressive that the Dalai Lama had to flee to ensure his life, and be somewhere where he could have a voice to help his nation. He disguised himself and hiked for three weeks through very dangerous mountain terrain with a group of other Tibetans. Once they made it to India, the Dalai Lama established the Tibetan Government in Exile, here in McLeod Ganj/Dharamshala.

The Chinese invasion led to much more than a robbing of territory. After the Dalai Lama's escape, the Chinese bombed Lhasa, Tibet's capital, and destroyed many sacred scriptures and art that were vital to Tibetan culture. It gets worse from there on in. The military actually forced monks to destroy their own monasteries and relics and denounce their beloved leader. When people refuse to rebuke their culture, or often even if they do, they are tortured horrendously.

The current persecution of Tibetans, and other ethnic

minorities in China, is part of a wide-scale purging mission known as the "Chinese Cultural Revolution." Thousands and thousands of lay people, nuns and monks, have been beaten, stripped, raped, and imprisoned. Beatings are often with electric batons or lead pipes. Limited video footage is available depicting these abuses because the Chinese government censors so much of its media. There are accounts of soldiers defecating and peeing on the faces of Tibetans. Forced sleep deprivation is also used as a common torture method. Many monks, nuns and even lay people have been imprisoned in appalling conditions for reasons that do not make sense; sometimes there is no reason given at all. Something as harmless as having a picture of the Dalai Lama warrants imprisonment and torture.

Most Tibetans inside Tibet have become too afraid to speak of their experiences, and are especially afraid to be filmed, because they've seen countless atrocities being done to those who've tried to rebel against the violent Chinese government. So far, all protests within Tibet and China have resulted in more people being tortured, imprisoned, or killed. An estimated one and a half million Tibetans have been killed since 1950. There are now approximately five million Tibetans left. The population is shrinking as you read this.

During the 2008 Olympics, mass protests broke out again. They were silenced. If at all, the world barely got a glimpse of the many protests, nor were they shown the extent of the gruesome ways the protesters were treated. The Chinese government clamped down with an iron fist in an attempt to terrify the masses even more. Since then, human rights have continued to become even more bleak.

In 2009, there was the first documented self-immolation

protest. A monk named Lobsang Tashi literally doused himself in gasoline and set himself on fire in public to protest at the fascist invasion, dictatorship, and genocide. Since then, there have been a reported one hundred and thirty other Tibetans who've self-immolated as an urgent and utterly desperate protest to be heard and seen.

Half of Lhasa's population is now Chinese, and is estimated to now have more brothels than any other city in Asia. As for other "livelihoods" for Tibetans, there are forced labour camps: people are literally being captured into slavery. As for the "free" Tibetans, often they are only able to find extremely difficult work, for abysmal wages, if that. Building roads, for example. Chinese nationals are paid significantly more for the same work, which not only traps Tibetans in unimaginable poverty, but also perpetuates class division in tandem with race division, in a country that claims to be communist. The Chinese government could achieve Tibetan genocide if we idly stand by.

China is destroying Tibet's natural environment. Tibet is huge, making up over a quarter of China, and is rich in mineral resources that China is profiting off, whilst torturing the people they stole it from. The Chinese government is using Tibet as a nuclear waste dumping ground, and invites other nations to do the same in exchange for massive tariffs. Vast deforestation is also happening.

The Chinese Communist Party calls the Dalai Lama a separatist, a terrorist, and a dictator, and regularly denounces Tibetan culture, calling it backwards and superstitious. The Tibetan language has been banished in schools and, nowadays, Tibetans are taught to feel ashamed of their heritage. All discussion and literature on the topic are subject to scrutiny and censorship by the Communist party.

This horror has led Tibetans inside Tibet to fear expressing their ideas and opinions. The Chinese Government is trying to break the spirit of the Tibetan people. Most Tibetan nationals live in constant fear, with very little hope available.

An estimated three thousand Tibetans attempt to flee China every year. The journey is a three to five-week hike through perilous mountains. Often, the refugees sleep during the day and walk during the night to avoid Chinese soldiers that patrol the escape routes. The soldiers have snipers, and often maim and kill Tibetans attempting to exit "China." Despite the very real dangers of fleeing, the situation inside Tibet is so dire that many still attempt to escape Chinese oppression. Often, the aspiring refugees get some form of frostbite on the journey because they do not have the appropriate clothing or gear for such a trek. During some expeditions, snow largely makes up what they have to eat and drink. Some literally freeze to death. It is unfathomably desperate.

There is now an estimate of over one hundred and fifty thousand Tibetans living in exile. India is the country that hosts the most.

China tells the international media that Tibetans are now enjoying freedom. This couldn't be further from the truth. What is happening is one of the most horrific massacres done to humanity in modern times.

The Chinese media does not give the Tibetan people a voice. The government is incredibly dishonest about what they are doing in Tibet. Because of their economic and army scare power, China has thus far been successful in intimidating other nations into having the Tibetan situation silenced and allowed.

Peaceful dialogue has been attempted many times from the Tibetan Government in Exile. China hasn't budged. When the UN asks to have discussions about the situation, the Chinese representatives do not attend.

It is astounding and terrifying that, in this modern-day, world leaders are letting this atrocious situation continue. We must act, and we must act now. Without the aid of other countries Tibet has no hope. Apartheid in South Africa, or the Nazis of World War Two, are examples of situations that would not have been stopped if it weren't for other nations stepping in. We don't even know the full extent of what is happening inside China, similar to how, before action was taken to free the Jews from the Nazis, most of the world was unaware of how inhumane the situation actually was.

I know nothing is black and white but, sometimes, it feels like there are two kinds people: Those who sacrifice themselves to benefit others. And, those who sacrifice others to benefit themselves. Which one do you want to be?

Tibetan culture is geared towards the achievement of inner peace and world peace. Humanity *needs* those kinds of teachings and wisdom to evolve in the direction of wellness, and to maybe even to survive as a whole. Please, I urge you to take action and help stop the attempted genocide that is happening right now, in China.

***

Back to my rich, white girl, la-la land experience...

One morning, I meet a girl who's been studying and seriously practicing yoga for over a decade. She has met her all-time top teacher here. I sign up for his five-day course. It's expensive, even though one of the yogic principles is non-greed. But, compared to recent disappointments, his instruction might be worth the cost. I learn new posture techniques. What's most valuable is the lessons on underlying psychological, physiological, and spiritual healing aspects of different asanas. He, and most of the other students, are incredibly inspiring. I vow to myself that I will continue to practice regularly.

Between yoga classes, teaching English, and just having fun with the other world wanderers here, the days are going by so quickly. Too quickly. I could stay forever. I've never felt that anywhere.

I meditate in the mid-afternoon sun. Tears trickle down my face as I become overwhelmed with gratitude for having got to live out my childhood dream of travelling through India. Every experience feels precious. From surviving Mumbai, to being whisked on the back of a motorbike to a rooftop feast, the motorcycle crash that led me to seeing the Dalai Lama, the bliss on the stunning Andaman beaches, the wisdom and calm of Bodhgaya, weaving through the ancient maze of Varanasi, the literally breathtaking mountain peaks of Nepal, and all of the friendships I made. The countless train and rickshaw rides through rainbow cities and countryside, all of the cups of spicy sweet chai, roadside samosas, the cow and monkey encounters, to the awe and overwhelm of this present moment. Abruptly, my emotions shift. I am devastated and torn to pieces about this trip being on the brink of its end. Joy suddenly jumps back into my cells, and I spontaneously break into song. "Mother Moon, I'm yearning for wisdom! Shall I become a Sadhu?"

...Lalalalala land...

Later, as I weave my way through the backpacker landia on the outskirts of town, I accept that my time in India was spent wearing swish, rose-coloured glasses. Life here is a battle for many. I have no idea how difficult poverty actually feels. Perhaps that's one of the reasons why the Universe takes me through a torturous reality a couple of years from now. Maybe I am in dire need of truer comprehension.

I travel to Delhi and savour every moment of being a part of the chaotic kaleidoscope. Too soon, it's time to make my way to Mumbai. I pray that, one day, I can return to live in this beautifully contrasting and contradicting country, maybe even call it home.

In the airport, I meet a woman from Sao Paulo. She gives me her contact info and invites me to visit her some day when I'm able. The world feels so beautiful and friendly right now, like it will always be wide open to me, and that all of my dreams will surely take shape.

The plane starts to rush forward. I look down and touch the worn faded piece of yarn that the Brahman priest tied around my wrist when he blessed me my first day in Mumbai. It comes undone and gently falls off. Amazed, I whisper a thank you to that man for helping to keep me safe on my six-month journey that felt like six years' worth of experiences and transformation.

Thirty-Six

As I step out of the Vancouver Airport into its carpark, I'm struck by how fresh the air is. In the past, when I'd visit Vancouver from the islands, I'd be appalled by how thick and polluted the city air felt. But now, coming from Delhi and Mumbai, the air feels remarkably clean. Yes, that's right, in the airport's carpark.

After a few brief encounters with flight attendants, bus drivers, and passers-by, it's a sharp shock to switch from prayer-hands-namaste-ing greetings for the past six months. A spiritless, "Hello," with a limp-wristed flailing of fingers feels so shallow and empty. "The divine in me recognizes and honours the divine in you," is no longer my normal greeting. I miss India so much already. The last six months were shared with people that were practically strangers, yet we shared such strong affinities. Brief but deep connections, earnest conversations, and shared such peak experiences. It hits me all at once that I'm a very different person from whom I was before.

Memories from my younger years feel like blurred reflections of someone I wouldn't even recognize walking down the street. I don't know what I am any more, what it means to be human. Is this culture shock again? Shouldn't I be over that by now?

On the ferry I bump into an acquaintance and catch a ride going north up Vancouver Island with him. A small part of me wonders if he somehow knew I would be on the ferry and he deliberately came to find me. I shake that thought off and tell myself it's just more synchronicity. We cruise down the highway and the radio plays a pop song that has the lyrics "Thank you India" in it. It's as if the radio DJ is playing an anthem for me. Another faint whisper in me wonders if the DJ knows I'm listening, and is, in fact, literally playing the song for me. The lyrics remind me to try to focus on gratitude that the trip happened, and not indulge in sadness and self-pity because it's over. Even so, as I look out the window to the impeccably orderly highway, I miss the cows, the rickshaws, even the trash.

    I push myself into work mode... cook, barista, farmer. I need the money. I'm flat broke. I persevere through, and remind myself that they'll end soon enough, when September comes. I hate myself for complaining, I'm luckier than most. But I'm tired of working low-paid, dead end jobs. It's getting old, as I also grow older.

    There's an upcoming music festival on another one of the Gulf Islands. Lila arranges a speedboat from Hornby to the shore of the festival for our group of friends. All of us nature hermits are due for a good dance. I hitch a ride to the dock to meet everyone, and notice Nile sitting and waiting with the others. My heart skips a beat. We somehow haven't crossed paths since I've been back. I think back to the insane synchronicity of our goodbye phone call while I boarded my flight. I send him a shy smile and wish I wasn't turning tomato-red. He returns the smile and my giddy eyes dart away in shyness.

    The lot of us pile into a small speedboat. The sound of the motor and bashing of the waves prevents any chance of catching up with Nile. The boat drops us off on the festival's beach. We find a shady clearing under some trees and pitch our tents. An ethereal, rhythmic warbling rises up and beckons us down the shoreline. We pass around a bag of magic mushrooms, chew them to an earthy mulch, while me make our way towards the music. The trees surrounding the dance floor start to shimmer, while the dancers swirl in pretty patterns. Lila and I lock eyes, then burst into laughter. Soon after, the other stage starts up, and the two of us go and dance to some reggae. The high-spirited vibration here is contagious. The medicinal weekend of dancing, swimming, and just chilling with friends is over as quickly as it began.

It's Monday morning, and our group has packed up our stuff, waiting at the shore for our water taxi. I go for a little walk, assuming there's ample time. When I get back to the shore, the boat to Hornby has already come and gone. The water-taxi captain must not have been willing to wait. I sigh as I accept that I'll have to take the long way back... alone. Three ferry rides, plus hitchhiking across the islands in between, carrying thirty pounds of disorganized stuff, with no backpack. I start to stress, I'm going to miss more work, the people who've already been covering my shifts are gonna be pissed. I tie my stuff in a blanket, hobo style, then embark on the regrettable detour. I set out up the beach past the now disassembled first stage, and then, at the edge of the second stage, nearly off the festival grounds... I bump into Nile.

"Looks like you missed the ride home too." He smiles. "I went looking for you, you know?"

"I guess we'll have to journey back together." I hold in a little scream of delight.

Our conversation goes on uninterrupted, except by

outbursts of laughter, through all the ferries, roads, and waits between them. I wish that the route was longer, so we'd have more time together. We make the last ferry to Hornby with less than a minute to spare, shouting thankyou over our shoulders to our hitch-hike driver as we sprint towards the ship. Once ashore, Nile invites me over. I start to skip, unable to hide my delight. We stay up, cuddling, until the sky starts to lighten, and it's time for me to head to work.

The next few weeks fly by in a wonderful whirlwind. I work more than full time, cycle across the island daily. But it's not exhausting or bothersome any more. I'm not sleeping very much, yet I have tons of energy. The sunshine must be fuelling me, in place of all the sleep I'm missing. Or maybe it's the prana from doing yoga regularly. Or maybe it's that I'm in the midst of falling in love. Practically all of my free time is spent hanging out with Nile.

Shambhala's time rolls around. Three of us plan to sneak into the festival this year. I ask the Tarot if we'll succeed. Most of the cards I pull are wands: various numbers of magical staffs on each of them. The only major arcanas are the "Lovers," and the "Wheel of Fortune." The "Lovers" is an obvious omen: Nile and I are going to deepen our connection. The "Wheel of Fortune" is a menagerie of winged beasts around some kind of clock thing, under the roman numeral ten, X. ...X?-tasy? The Wheel of Fortune part probably just symbolizes karma. It could either be negative or positive. I draw one last card from the deck: Wands, again. I leave it at that, unsure of what it all means.

With three ferries and eight hours of driving ahead of us, four of us cram into a car and head out Thursday afternoon. Windows down, we delight in the breeze as we cruise through the muggy August heatwave. I have everything I want except for beedies. I feel like they would help quell my nostalgia for India. In Vancouver, we stop at a tobacco shop and ask if they carry the small cigarettes hand-wrapped in dried leaves. No luck. The shop owner tells us that they're becoming impossible to import because beedi packages aren't labelled with a "Smoking Kills" warning, so they are now illegal to sell in Canada. A little disappointed, but still in high spirits, we carry on.

Just before dawn, we get to the outskirts of the festival. Nile, Jeff and I hop out of Zaben's car at the riverbank, and she drives our stuff into the festival for us. We have to cross the river in order to sneak in. Uncertain what direction to take, we pick a path across the river where it looks most calm. Lasers appear from the forest. Bright beams of colour crisscross through the canopy, illuminating the way ahead. Onwards! We forage wooden staffs to help balance in the fast, cold current. This must be what all the wands were about when I consulted the Tarot! The river comes up to my bellybutton at its middle. It's tricky, chilly, and slippery, but we make it across. We brandish our wands in victory. We see the beach stage and shiver our way to it, as casually as one can when tromping through the bushes, soaking wet. We slip into the crowd victoriously.

Jeff sits at the river's edge with a big grin on his face. He looks to his side and spots two twenty-dollar bills. Laughing, we all agree that the spirit of Shambhala smiles on our shenanigans. Nile and I go for a walk. I check out a vendor while he waits in line to get us coffees. I'm overwhelmed by a sudden headrush. I have to stop and stand still for a few seconds, dizzy. I look down to my feet and see a full pack of beedies, laying at my feet. I pick them up. My world may still be a magical wish-granting vending-machine, after all.

I go back to Nile to show him the beedies. He smiles and says, "But of Course!" We kiss. Life is perfect right now. A different version of the perfect that it was in India. Am I simply emanating and magnetizing to the vibration of love and bliss? I don't know. I just hope that life will feel like this forever.

Nile and I spend the whole weekend glued to each other. We keep it chill at the beginning. Wander the beautiful forests and beach, between dancing to music at the various fun-qi stages. Fun-qi. We've started redesigning language into metaphors and omens. It almost feels like tapping into magical spells. Sunday night we decide to take molly and LSD so we have the energy to keep celebrating. We freestyle silly poems to each other as we flutter barefoot from stage to stage.

Morning comes and we're still on the dance floor. Tired and inspired we clasp hands as we dance to psytrance. We ground score increasingly elaborate attire. It starts with tacky party stuff. Glowing bracelets, a "cat-in-the-hat" type toque, a turquoise feather boa, a paisley sarong. What we find next we both feel is sacred and that the Universe intentionally left for us to find, like the beedies. Two playing cards. A three of hearts and an eight of hearts. It's my third Shambhala, and Nile's eighth. These cards were waiting for us, to assure us that we are on the right path, that we are meant to be together. This journey began and is ending with the Universe speaking through cards.

We ride our jellyfish legs up onto a platform beside a path and perch ourselves above the passers-by. Everyone below gets called over. "Hey You!" Once they stop to listen we call out: "You're perfect! Keep changing!" We eventually tire of that, and go back to dancing until all the stages have finished their final set. What we share is more than love. It's magic.

Wide-eyed and pleasantly exhausted, the four of us pile into Zaben's car for the drive back to Hornby. On the ride I sleep for hours, something my body hasn't felt the need to do in weeks.

The last three weeks of August, Lila leaves Hornby to go for a summer vacation and escape our island that is bloated with tourists. I move into her room in the house she shares with our friend Nala. Clive's living in our driveway, in his van. Clive's presence annoys me. He isn't very evolved. He doesn't seem to think deeply about anything. All he does is skulk around, drunk and stoned. In theory, I know that separating and judging people to be on some imagined pecking order of consciousness isn't very evolved of myself. Still, though, as his housemate, I feel entitled to my opinion.

I've hardly slept this whole summer, yet I buzz with unlimited energy and inspiration. Labour Day arrives. My work season grinds to a halt. Most of the tourists leave. I skip home after my last shift at the cafe. Clive's inside. "I'm free! No more work!" I sing.

"Freedom's just another word for being broke," he smirks. I start to like him a little more, and realize I should give the guy another chance. Why am I so pretentious? I'm probably just projecting my own self-hatred, insecurities, and areas where I lack.

Thirty-Seven

I have ample free time now, more than enough to catch up on sleep. But I'm still active most hours of the day and night. Between spending time with Nile and other friends, I do yoga, draw pictures, ride my bike, and go for long beach walks and swims. There's so much to enjoy! Sleep is a waste of time! I must be tapping into yogic prana, accessing the wellspring of source energy that's available to us all. Maybe that's why the state of being enlightened is often referred to as being "awake."

Work enabled me to put a significant amount of money aside. Practicing yoga has become a regular, easy and joyous part of my daily life. I've cut out all animal products from my diet to honour the philosophy of nonviolence. Fat has completely vanished from my body. I am strong, and more bendy and energetic than I've ever been. I'm proud of myself. My confidence has soared. Every day I do at least an hour and a half of asana. It has imbued me with crisp vitality.

Lila gets back and I move in with Nile. The transition is as easy as breathing. Waking up next to him feels like the most natural thing in the world.

Time passes joyously. Suddenly, a month's gone by. It starts to feel bizarre and wasteful to stay on Hornby. There's just so many places to discover. So much time to live instead of time to kill. Life is really good right now, but I can't help but get restless. So I go to Salt Spring Island, spontaneously.

At Salt Spring's commercial hub, I wander into a used bookstore. The shopkeeper links eyes with mine. "I have a book for you." He hands me a gently used copy of Animal Speak. I recognize the title. It's about Native American Totem Animals. The guy who read my palm in Calcutta told me I should read it. Normally, I'd be delighted to stumble upon something I've been seeking, but it feels different this time. I'm tinged with suspicion. Are people talking about me? How does he know about the experience I had in Calcutta? Did Bee somehow get in contact with people here and tell them? Is there some sort of plot afoot?

I brush the bizarre inkling aside. How ridiculous! My moccasins, braids, and feather earrings obviously display reverence for First Nations culture. I smile, thank him, let him know that I've been wanting to read this book for a while now. It must have been my expanded attunement that guided me here, to the book, nothing more. I go back to Hornby, already missing Nile, even though it's only been a few days.

With all of the summer tourists gone, I become closer with the locals, bonding in shared isolation. Despite the island and its population being small, it's hyper social. Every time I go out, I bump into people I know. Everyone knows everyone. Most of the people in my tight knit group of now close friends are older than me; this boosts my confidence. My ego convinces my brain that I am special and mature. I haven't had this kind of fond affinity with a group since high school. Having inspiring friends is such a blessing and is surely contributing to the bliss that has become my constant emotional state.

Living in nature with tons of free time is medicinal. I'm returning to source, remembering and reconnecting to the fact that I am nature. The people, animals, plants, and planets all seem to be tuned into each other, and I, to all of them. I'm harmonizing with psychic connection to all. I breathe the world in, and the world breathes me out.

Lila and I make plans to go to a Halloween dance party in the forest on Vancouver Island. She invites Robyn to come along. At first, I just assume it's just because he's going to be on the Big Island tomorrow anyway, to pick up his partner, Freya, at the airport from her month in Hawaii. At the party, the three of us take some M. We're just barely coming up when Lila and Robyn slip away to have sex in the car, Freya's car. After Lila comes back to the dancefloor, in her disinhibited state she admits that she and Robyn have been hooking up pretty much the whole five weeks that Freya has been in Hawaii. She dances through this confession, clearly free of qualms.

In the morning, the three of us go to pick up Freya. I want to say something about the affair. I look at Freya's huge smile, and can't find my voice. I decide to keep my mouth shut for the car ride. The four of us head back to Hornby in a heartbreaking, false, but friendly celebration. Wanting to tell Freya consumes my thoughts; it's the right thing to do. But if I tell Freya, I'd hurt her, betray two friends, drill a fault line into our group, and create unpleasant drama on our tiny island. But, if I don't tell Freya, I betray her, the innocent one. In the backseat of the car, I theorize that monogamy is possessive and unevolved, a by-product of historical patriarchy. I try to ignore the fact that few people with our societal conditioning are emotionally strong enough to be at peace with their partners loving others, and that it only works when people are being honest about their actions. This meditation unlocks my telepathic powers. I hear the voices of my friends in my head as we cruise towards the ferry. Freya telepathically tells me she knows, while Robyn tells me I'm being a baby. Lila telepathically orders me to keep my mouth shut, and not to tell Nile.

I've admired Lila for some time. She's been sort of a role model to me. She inspired me to go vegan. She's kind to everyone. She is deep and philosophical with original thoughts. She's a good artist and is always up for an adventure. The past little while I've started to consider her as my closest friend. I don't want to lose her. I force tears back as I begin the silent mourning of a friend I adore and admire, someone who I could effortlessly relate to about anything. I begin to hate myself. I'm a bad friend. I still haven't said anything to Freya.

Autumn settles deeper and deeper around me. Finally, I open up to Nile about my struggles with the Lila and Robyn situation. He shuts me out and tells me he doesn't want to hear about it. He's completely apathetic to the wrong that is being done to our friend and the terrible effect that it's having on me. It's faint, but I can make out Nile's mind desperately trying to dodge the subject, because he knows that I'm telepathic.

Then it hits me. It's probably because he had sex with Lila, too. My mind taunts myself with what's likely the truth. Lila's more sexually desirable than me. She has more experience, she's exotic. I do not deserve honesty anyway, because I left Freya in the dark. My breath stops, my heart blackens. I shake my head and retreat into delusion. Maybe I'm imagining things? I swallow the sorrow. Nile loves me. He's a good person. He wouldn't hurt and deceive me. We're soulmates. I'm the one he loves.

Life is still pretty good.

This all changes in an instant.

Nile and I go to the store one night. We walk past our friend Rainbow sitting at a table with some people I don't recognize. Normally I'd say hi, but she seems absorbed in intense conversation. I notice static around her head, as if her face is coming in and out of blurred focus. Later that night, Nile and I are sitting on the couch, drawing. Out of nowhere, my skin starts to crawl. I jump up, uncomfortable, afraid. Forces battle inside my body, like strong winds fighting for control. I haven't felt panic like this since Lynx and I were taken by the narcotic officer in Bolivia. I shudder, this time completely oblivious to what is causing the turmoil. I pace around, uncomfortable.

"Something horrible is happening!" I proclaim to Nile, ashen faced.

The next day, we learn that Rainbow was murdered in the night. I wasn't very close to her, so the most difficult emotions for me aren't so much losing someone, but sympathetic agony for the community members who have just been brutally robbed of someone they loved dearly. I don't know what to say or do to ease the pain of Rainbow's family, lover, and closest friends. I'm a useless little girl.

The island is battered by storms and strong winds for two weeks after Rainbow's death. The sky embodies our grief as it howls and bawls. We sit inside for days at a time, stunned, shocked. Our world has been transformed. Everyone's traumatized. Hornby is no longer safe. It is no longer a haven from worldly trials. It's a black hole.

I feel helpless. I lose touch with joy. I start to project and blame. I conclude that Nile has a role influencing my misery. He wants me to stick around Hornby, guilt trips me when I voice the desire to travel. He cares more about keeping me in his domestic life than encouraging me to pursue my passions. He's being selfish, values his contentment above mine. Our different ambitions hang like a veil between us.

I start to go squirrelly as winter really sets in. I now regularly hear the voices of my friends and other islanders inside my head. It used to happen from time to time, but it's becoming more frequent. Surely it's a telepathic awakening from all the yoga and nature. Since I've had experiences throughout my life where my psychic abilities were confirmed, I trust that everything I've been hearing lately is real. Little do I know, I am descending into full-blown clinical insanity.

I go to visit Nala and Lila. Through stunned tears, barely coherent, they fill me in on the latest tragedy. Three days ago, Clive went for a walk along the island's bluffs. The ground crumbled away below him, and he fell, breaking a handful of ribs, and both his legs. He dragged himself as close to the public trail as he could, and was stuck outside for three days and nights in torrential downpour. A walking group finally found him, on the brink of death. He was airlifted to critical care in Vancouver.

Lila, Nala, Skylar, Heather (Clive's current lover), and I go to Vancouver to visit Clive in the hospital. En-route, we stop at a gas station. Skylar uses the washroom before me, then hands off the key. When I close the door behind me, I notice his forgotten bag of blow and his straw sitting on the counter. He's still addicted to coke, and not openly admitting it to us. This just makes my wall of numbness grow. He used to be someone who really lived. He actually walked his dreams of seeing the big, bold, beautiful world. Now he's thrown everything away for drugs. I pull Nala aside to tell her. She says she knows that Skylar, her partner as of late, has addictions that he tries to keep secret from the rest of the island. It seems everyone has something to hide these days. What's become of our island paradise?

As we get off the ferry in Vancouver, Lila, Skylar, and I have a moment to ourselves. Lila fervently whispers that we could ditch Heather and Nala and go party. Because I used to hold Lila on such a pedestal, I'm once again baffled to see her acting so selfishly. Did she actually just suggest to Nala's boyfriend that we should blow off Nala? And also, Heather, whose partner just had a traumatizing near death experience, and not to mention Clive! You're gonna blow off visiting him? This glimpse of Lila's shadow turns my heart colder. For reasons beyond me, I still love her. Maybe it's a deluded kind of love that wants to believe in her goodness so I don't lose a friend that I'm attached to. Or maybe it's because I half-realize that we're all traumatized right now, and handling it in our own ways. But this just makes everything feel more fucked up and miserable than it already was.

Seeing Clive bludgeoned and bandaged flabbergasts me. He winces as he tells us about how he wanted to give up, to close his eyes and sleep, to let the pain drift into death. But he pushed to stay awake for those three hellish days and three agonizing nights so that the ones that love him wouldn't have to endure his loss. That was the force that fuelled him to drag his broken limbs up and out of the storm battered cliffs. He even fell once, injuring himself further, and started again. I am blown away. I vow to stop judging people and lumping them into categories. Maybe Clive's more evolved than Lila, who I'd ranked highest. I halt that tangent as I realize my brain's dividing and judging people again. Shut up brain!

We attend no parties. Our drive back to the island is sombre. Looking up at the storm clouds, I remember Rainbow and burst into tears. Lila looks over at me from the driver's seat, and her face splits like glass as she notices me crying. In my head I hear her say, "Maya — you're anorexic," then she bursts into tears, too. I look down at my body and, for the first time, realize that I might be. Life feels so far from the healing love-realm I was basking in only a few weeks ago. That realm feels unreachable.

Nile started to retract emotionally when I tried to bring up my inner conflict about Lila and Robyn, but ever since Rainbow died, he's withdrawn into his cave of quietude even further. This is too much for me. I feel all alone most of the time I'm with Nile. I'm accustomed to frolicking in tropical sunshine, free as a bird at this time of year. Instead, this winter is all cruel realities, cold, grey, and emotionally repressive.

I continue to practice yoga seriously. It's become my escape. I've become more flexible than I thought possible. I take it up a notch, push myself harder and harder into poses, reach away from all the outer misery. It occurs to me that I'm advanced enough to teach now. I'm twenty-one years old. It's time for me to find a "real job," one that I'm passionate about, and make more than minimum wage at. Becoming a teacher would ensure keeping yoga as a regular part of my life. In need of a break from this especially dark winter, I google yoga teacher trainings and click on the first tropical one I find. It's a four-week course that begins late in December in Baja, on the north-west coast of Mexico. I register immediately.

Nala needs to get away, too, and impulsively arranges a trip at the same time as me. She's going to study dance in West Africa. The suffocating cloud of gloom that has settled over

Hornby has affected her as strongly as it has me.

When I tell Lila about my plans, I add that I'm going to stay for a couple of weeks after the end of the course. I'll be all the way over there, it'd be ridiculous to not explore a little. She lights up and says she wants to meet me there and travel together. With silence, I blow her off. Cold vengeance sparks in her eyes behind a wincing smile. Whatever, I don't want her as my best friend any more.

Nile tries to guilt trip me for leaving, the hypocrite. He's already distanced himself emotionally.

I need a break. I fear a heavier depression coming on if I stay for the rest of this season of decay. I explain that I need to figure out how to make a livelihood for myself that I am actually passionate about. I don't want to cook the same boring things, serve the same lattes, and weed the same veggie patches for pennies any more. I'm not a teenager.

Once on Vancouver Island I stick out my thumb. Within a minute a car pulls over. The older couple giving me a ride are also yogis, visiting from Vancouver. This trips me out a little. Is it a coincidence? Synchronicity? Or, did they know I'd be on the ferry and come to meet me to inspire me to stay on the yogic path? I no longer am convinced that these happenings are all divine synchronicities. Is there some sort of conspiracy afoot? If there is, though, it must be a benevolent one, what with all the yogis involved. I am really confused. It's becoming very unsettling.

In Vancouver, I meander a long route on foot to meet the friends that I'm staying with for the night. On my walk through the city, I stop at a coffee shop, seeking caffeine for the long walk. They have vegan cookies and bars on the counter. I buy one of each, thinking that it's okay to treat myself today. I haven't eaten anything yet, and I'm about to embark on a month of multiple hours of daily yoga. I step outside and put the cookie into my mouth. It's so delicious my head arches back in disbelief. My brain buzzes alive, and my saliva gushes in delight. I savour the bar next. Still hungry, I beeline to a nearby falafel stand and order one. As soon as the last bite is swallowed, I need something else to eat. The long walk goes on, and I find myself snacking the whole way. As soon as I finish one thing, I buy another. It's as if I can't stop and can't be satiated. I feel like I'm watching my body go through the motions, voraciously chewing, swallowing, eating, eating, eating. Veganism gets thrown out the window by my untameable hunger. Ice cream, pizza slices, brownies... is it the city's wavelengths shocking and controlling my unprepared body after living isolated in nature for so long?

Eventually, I get to where I'm going. Hastily, I wipe my face to ensure there's no crumbs. My friends are hosting a potluck. Suddenly, my stomach's in agony from being so full. I don't eat anything at the gathering. When asked why, I blush and weakly whisper that I ate on the way here. I leave out that I ate the whole way. A voice inside my head wonders if someone followed me through the city, if everyone knows what I just did. Very anxious, I try to act normal as I mingle with the other guests. I'm ashamed of all the food I just shovelled into my body. And it hurts. I just literally ate a week's worth of food. I consider sticking my hand down my throat and trying to get it out, but there's people all around. I decide that I'm small enough, and am headed to a long yoga retreat anyway, so I decide to let it digest. I just have to make sure that whatever the fuck just happened never happens again.

Thirty-Eight

I catch my Christmas morning red-eye and arrive in Baja beneath a noonday sun in a big, bright, blue sky. The warmth makes its way into my sad bones and tries to resurrect my soul. From the airport, I take a two-hour bus ride to Todos Santos, the town nearest the yoga school. I am surprised to find that there are no hostels here. So much for clicking the first thing I saw, and doing no further research whatsoever. I guess old habits are hard to kick. I go to the most basic looking hotel. While I'm bartering for a room, the phone behind the counter rings. When the clerk returns from answering it, he tells me I can have a room for a discounted rate. I have the sense that someone, somehow, knew I was bartering, phoned the concierge, and offered to pay the difference. He smiles as he telepathically refuses to reveal my mystery philanthropist.

But even the haggled rate is more than I can afford, so I phone the yoga centre the next morning and ask if I can set up my tent a couple days early. They say yes, no questions asked. A cab from town delivers me to the Yoga School. It's beautiful. There's a private beach, across from an old growth cacti desert. There's a veggie garden, and a couple yoga pavilions at the centre of it all. Ravens glide in the sky above. I haven't seen any people yet, so I pitch my tent, then go to one of the empty pavilions. With the place to myself, I throw myself into yoga and exercise for hours, trying to work off the Vancouver binge. Once none of my muscles can handle any more movement, I head to the beach. As I settle on the sand, a long-necked Canada Goose flies by. I observe the thought that leaving the north during winter is natural, even necessary. The birds figured this out a long time ago.

At night, two of the teachers of the sixteen-day course invite me to have dinner with them. I'm doing the twenty-six-day course, so they won't be my teachers, but I'm grateful for the lovely company. The conversation flows like a warm, gentle waterfall.

"What's your philosophy for life?" asks Sage. He looks like Lynx's twin, so much so that I have to bite my tongue a few times as I'm about to say Lynx's name. I shake off the uncanny resemblance and answer Sage's question with the first thing that comes to mind.

"To have fun and to not hurt anyone along the way."

Karma, the other teacher, says she wants to experience as much as possible. I really relate to that, too, see it in my own calling. Our conversation turns to the big black birds wheeling overhead.

Turns out they're vultures, not ravens. We all agree that they have a nice presence. Most people don't like vultures because they're associated with death. For them, death marks a tragedy, the end of an existence, and the vulture symbolizes that to them. But the three of us, for whom death seems more of a curious transition — an adventure even — agree that the presence of the carrion creatures is, actually, quite soothing. We sit in a brief, comfortable silence, staring at the sky. But conversation is too pleasant and natural with Sage and Karma to stay in silence. The teachers invite me to come along to a Dharma Talk in town the next morning.

"Who's the speaker?" I ask.

"Robert K Hall," Sage replies, with a twinkle in his eyes. In less than forty-eight hours I've been vortexed back to a blissful realm full of magical synchronicities.

"I had no idea he lived here." I tell them about the meditation course I did in Bodhgaya, about how I was moved to record his teachings in my journal. It's back: The feeling that I'm exactly where I'm supposed to be. It's confirmed: Life is bliss when you jump into the path of following your dreams and ignore the fear around those dreams. The fucked-up shit on Hornby is galaxies away. Rainbow's better than fine, wherever she is, and whatever form she's in.

Our conversation turns to astrology and all the kinds we know a bit about: Western, Vedic, Chinese, Tibetan, Mayan... Like me, Sage is a dragon in Chinese astrology. "Woah!" I say, surprising myself with enthusiasm in my voice. I have read that two dragons together are the most invincible partnership in the Zodiac. I start to feel guilty because of the chemistry between Sage and I. It's as if I'm cheating on Nile. I abruptly announce that I'm tired and excuse myself to bed, ending the conversation then and there.

In the morning, the three of us drive down the highway, through the cacti, listening to dubstep remixes of Hindu chants. I feel as if I'm with old friends, and am beyond grateful to have realm hopped out of Hornby's merciless winter. We arrive at the Dharma talk. Robert K Hall is wearing a shirt with dragons on it. I ignore the fact that the Universe might be trying to nudge my path in a new direction. Nile is who I've made my commitment to. Being with him was so amazing at the start, surely, we could rekindle that initial chemistry.

The other yogis arrive. They look sickly pale after a few days among Mexicans and tanned gringos. Yogic philosophy says one shouldn't compare, compete, or judge. But I can't help but do just that. I haven't fully unlearned my culture programming, yet. I conclude I'm still fairly thin, despite the horrifying gorge in Vancouver. Deep down, I know I shouldn't care, but my physical appearance is becoming a mental obsession of mine.

Our days are extremely full. At moments I get moved enough by our practices to leap out of my shocked, sad, shattered state. Sometimes, I can emotionally detach myself from the romantic drama between my faraway family of friends. But, usually, when I think about Rainbow's close friends and family, the ones left behind, my light-heartedness gets bulldozed. Releasing the trauma of the last couple of months isn't as simple as hopping on a plane. I try to stay balanced and buoyant, but my heart has become an unruly ocean of storms and placid calm.

The main pavilion is prepared for us to ring in the New Year through dance. Normally, I can dance for hours as if they're minutes. I've practically gone entire festivals without sitting down. The music comes up, bass pounding, and I force my body to move. I'm unable to shake or shimmy out from under my storm cloud. Well before midnight, I retire to my tent, dejected. The next day, I wake up with worry that I cursed my year because I didn't stay awake to welcome and root it with positive intention. My mind's anchored to weird places of worry and woe, dragged down by every uncertainty, unable to swim free.

My mindful yogic control over eating habits has vanished, gone to hide in some far-off cave, with the bulk of my joy. At every meal, I take more food than I need. My appetite cannot be appeased. I'm gaining weight so rapidly that, every day,

I'm visibly bigger. My loathing for my body soon spreads to the rest of my being. Yet I continue overeating, sabotaging myself, dooming myself to a downward spiral of negative emotion.

Ironically, as the yoga course progresses, I become less and less at peace with myself. I try to keep up appearances in class, but I can hardly stand to see my own reflection. I feel myself unravelling, becoming more and more unstable.

There are some nice moments where I connect with the other students, learn more deeply about yoga, swim in the sea — and wow, am I ever opening my telepathic capabilities! More and more, I start to hear the voices of some of the other yogis in my head. Mostly just murmurs that fade out. Some of them compliment me. Some mock me...

Who gains weight at a yoga retreat? She thinks she's better than us. She's so pretty. Her voice is annoying, her "om's" are horrible. I wish I was that flexible.

On the last night, there's a beachfront bonfire. The flicker of the flames has no warming effect on me. I'm incredibly sad that the course is over, yet I leave my new friends and don't even bother to spend the last night with them. I'm just too tired and dead inside. Joy is found nowhere and in nobody.

The day after the course ends, there's five of us that are staying in Mexico to travel. Together, we go to a natural hot spring and hike in the hills surrounding. Maria, one of the young women from the course, invites me to join her in a nearby city where she's couch surfing, before her return home to Guadalajara. Despite the emotional rollercoaster that I'm riding, it's really nice to be travelling again. My Spanish is rusty, so it's a welcome distraction for my mind's energy. Maria and I stay at a young couple's house. The girl's really into yoga, too. We attend several classes together and spend the rest of our time hanging out with her group of friends. They are beautiful people, their vibe reminds me of my friends back on Hornby, before all the miserable secrets took their toll.

My last night in Baja, we dance the night away on the beach, then sit and watch the sunrise, huddled together for warmth. Conversation turns to how gratitude is the key to a happy life. I try to focus on the positive. I know I'm fortunate. Why is it so difficult to emotionally connect to that truth nowadays?

All too soon I'm on a plane.

Thirty-Nine

It takes a lot of convincing to get Nile to meet me at the airport. On the phone, he's reluctant to come all the way to the city to journey back with me, like it's not worth the hassle. It feels like he's climbing out of love with me. My love for him is also waning, but it's scary to see he shares the sentiment. But, when his big brown cosy sweater and blue toque appear in the crowd at the Arrivals terminal, I become giddy. He says, "I forgot how beautiful you are," and holds me tightly in his arms for a long time. I see and feel shimmers of light around us as we make love in the back seat of his car.

 The first night back on Hornby, as Nile and I lay asleep beside each other, I have a vivid dream. I saw Lila, surrounded by snow, channelling its chill into my heart with her hands. In the morning, I turn the image over and over in my mind, trying to interpret the dream. I conclude that something fishy happened, and she's trying to hide it by sending me deluding energy.

 When I see Lila in the flesh, I decide I've been ridiculous, crazy even. Seeing her I just remember that I love our friendship. We talk and laugh like we usually do, an intimate and hilarious flow. We stop at the concert hall, peek in at the jazz band playing inside, then leave to continue catching up. Our conversation turns toward her sex life. She's been busy while I was away. She laughs as she lists off the people she slept with. She wanted to experience promiscuity after years of being in committed relationships. At first that seems fine, I just listen and laugh with her. But my brain chirps in — what about the people whose partners cheated on them with her? She has her faults, but I shrug them off, her better qualities mostly outshine them. I've missed her. My life is so much less lonely with her in it.

    Since I've been back, it's become obvious that Nile is less smitten with me. He's becoming more and more distant. Every day he's staying up and waking up hours later than me, demonstrates that he cares less about spending time together. It also makes me worry and wonder if he's seeing someone else. Since when? Where? On our couch while I sleep? Who? Lila? Freya? Freya wouldn't. Lila would! Someone older and more experienced? Is he falling in love with someone else? Is having sex with me now some insincere duty? Is it because I'm not as thin any more? Is this all in my head? Is it clearly right in front of my face? Feeling like my love is being unfaithful hurts far more than I would have imagined. I used to theorize that monogamy is just an expression of a possessive ego. But this is tearing me to pieces. Doesn't he care about the pain this is causing me?

    Nala returns from Africa. Over dinner the next evening, Nala tells Freya and I that Skylar cheated on her while she was away. The night Nala left, Lila showed up on his porch with a bottle of tequila and flirtatious arm caresses. Funny how she failed to mention Skylar to me on her list of winter hook-ups. Nala breaks down while the three of us sit together at the table. She says she's hurt, furious, and humiliated. She's decided to move off the island, that she's in the midst of a transitional stage anyway, and this way it'll be easy to distance herself from her asshole loser, cokehead ex and her jerk ex best friend roommate. I'm sad that she's leaving, but at the same time I'm happy for her. Despite the shit circumstances, she seems really empowered at the moment. I tell Nala and Freya that I'm questioning whether or not Nile also had sex with Lila while I was away. They shake their heads. "I don't think Nile would do that." I'm not convinced. I don't have the karmic merit to be told the truth on this topic. Lila's very beautiful, spellbinding, and manipulative. She could have anyone she wants.

Nile and I go for a walk in the woods and bump into Lila. She bounds over to us. "Guess what?"

She's practically vibrating, hopping like a bunny. "What?" I say, trying to keep my voice gentle.

"I'm pregnant."

I turn to ice. Nile looks taken aback. Voice quivering slightly, he congratulates her and gives her a hesitant hug. I hear his voice in my head, praying he isn't the father. Once she realizes she isn't getting a hug from me, her eyes turn to slits, and she storms off. I turn to Nile, trying to hold back tears, and say, "It's possible you're going to have a baby." His eyes dart around and he gets defensive. He's a horrible liar. I let him coax me into delusion anyway. I don't want it to become real.

My demons get the better of me, and I can't help but believe that Lila and Nile slept together and are possibly still sleeping together. Lila's confession to me about the others was a smokescreen. Usually, I'm very trusting, but it's impossible to believe Nile when he denies it. I start to hear his and her voices inside my head. They're conferring in secret, deciding to leave me in the dark. I hear Lila's voice insulting me and pointing out all my flaws to Nile, my naivety, my lack of years… I've become a joke to them. This has come to be my reality. It's like a faucet has been cranked open; I've awakened more fully to heightened awareness through telepathy. I am blasted with visions of the two of them together from which I cannot distract myself. My heart is slowly breaking.

Weeks pass where I feel awful. I end things with Nile, tell him I probably could have accepted open, consensual polyamory. But even worse than secret polyamory, was the way he gaslighted my intuitions and my telepathic powers. How he blatantly lied to me. To make me distrust my inner knowing shatters my soul and is what hurts and disempowers me the most. My emotions are torturous. I place blame on him and Lila.

I drift around the island, do odd jobs when they're available, and house sit for various people as they vacation from Hornby's fishbowl isolation. I miss Nile so much. He hasn't made any effort to see me, further proof that he has someone else in his life. I crawl up a misery mountain, lost, not sure I'm going in the right direction, and with no idea how much harrow lies between the peak. Yoga is the only thing positive in my life. Some days I can't even muster the motivation to practice. I'm not feeling the uplifting revival that spring normally brings. I move into a caravan on an older couple's property.

I lose control again. Days pass where all I do is eat. I hover above my body and watch it eat a jar of peanut butter as if it was a bowl of soup. I try to cook rice… too slow… I wolf it down, half boiled. When all the food's gone, I lay in bed fantasizing about even more food. I should be far past satiated, but am crawling out of my skin, in hunger. I bike to the store, starving. Anxiety surges through me as I load a basket with pasta, cereal, chocolate, nuts. Why the fuck am I so hungry? I binge for days. Thoughts bounce back and forth from craving food, to horror at my ballooning body. In about a week I've gained twenty pounds. Hunger subsides a little, and I lay in bed too depressed and ashamed to go out into public.

I lay in bed for another week, lovesick. Palpable winds within my body, as if detached from my mind, move me. I surrender to the wind and let them carry me to Nile. It literally feels like an external force is controlling my body's motions and I'm just riding the wind and waves as they guide my vessel to his place. I walk up the driveway. He's smoking a cigarette in the sun, petting the cat. He's taken aback. Seconds later, he smiles, stands, and gives me a tight, long held and long yearned-for hug. Being in his presence makes me miss him so much more. A couple of awkward but glorious hours go by where we talk and play with the cat. I blurt out that I want to get back together. He pauses, looks numbly into my eyes, then kinda glances away, nodding yes.

He agrees. He does not seem overjoyed about it, probably because I've put on so much weight.

***

Summer solstice rolls around and a few close friends invite me to honour the solstice with a DMT ceremony. Our intentions with the psychedelic journey is to gain wisdom and to heal ourselves. We place the sacred white goop onto a pipe, with marijuana and tobacco as a cushion under it, enough DMT for the whole group. A bundle of sage is lit and we pass it around the circle, purifying ourselves for the expedition. I bubble with excitement. I've missed psychedelia, and feel like I could really benefit from its therapeutic powers at the moment. I am asked if I'd like to go first. I do.

I fly through stars and land on a faraway planet. A beautiful bright blue alien with an ostrich-like body and hummingbird wings gently flutters in front of me and stares into my soul with the largest and kindest eyes imaginable. She sends me vibrations of absolute, unconditional, eternal love, until I am filled with unconditional love and acceptance. myself. Then, suddenly, she blinks and flies away, back into the stars. I can feel Earth pulling me towards her. I don't want to go back. I want to stay in the cosmos. "We need you," Earth whispers. There's so much pain and suffering on Earth, I want to stay here, in the stars. "Please come back," Earth insists. I surrender and agree to return.

I feel my body on the ground. I open my eyes and see my beloved friends circled around me, in tears. "I'm so sorry! I love you!" They explain that I had turned blue, was convulsing, and that I urinated myself. My body literally almost died. They sat around me, om'd, and prayed for my life. In a surprised daze I tell them that my experience was ineffably blissful, lovely and free.

***

The DMT ceremony felt like it further unravelled the illusion of separateness. I can now feel peoples emotions and hear their thoughts, as crisply as I can my own. It's sometimes overwhelming. In my mind, other people's criticism and praise are now playing like a radio in my head that randomly crackles in and out of tune.

I start to spiral into what I don't have the wisdom to realize is literal insanity. People have set up multiple hidden cameras. I can feel it and hear their comments in my mind. I'm a mess and it's hilarious to them. Their laughter echoes through my head.

I've lost my two closest friends now: Nala to a move and Lila to betrayal. Nile and I settle over our old life together like vapour, haunt it like ghosts of our former selves. He doesn't treat me with the same affection he used to. Who could love what I've become? I yearn for Nile's attention when we're together. It's agony. It's so lonely being with him. But it's even harder to let go.

Summer's in full swing. The dead-end, underpaid, bullshit jobs are impossible to motivate myself to show up to, in this emotional state. I teach yoga twice a week. It takes all I have to smile and guide movement. I'm amazed I pull it off. I am dead and so far from the divine, inside. Faking it brings joy back into my life, if only briefly. In my mind's eye, I catch glimpses of my future self: mended, happy. But, as of late, everything is broken

Shambhala is next week. For the first time, I don't feel like going. My usual zest for summer fun just isn't present. I'm feeling really introverted. The only person I want to spend time with is Nile. But I feel like an annoyance to him. He's ambivalent about whether I'm worth his while. Maybe I'm depressed? That doesn't make sense, though. Life should feel good. Travelling has taught me that my circumstances are exceptionally fortunate. When did my emotions unhinge from that awareness? Aren't my head and heart line supposed to be unified?

Robyn and Freya bump into Nile and I. They've decided to make the journey to the festival and ask if we'd like to carpool with them. I shrug, tiredly. Nile's enthused. He looks straight into my eyes and says, "I don't want to go if it's not with you." His words fill me with a warmth that I haven't felt in months. I've always left Shambhala rejuvenated, and it only comes once a year. I agree to go, hoping with all of my heart that it will be medicine for our relationship.

The four of us set out for the long drive. Smiles are thin, and few in number. There's obvious tension between and within both couples. Freya and I share the back seat as the sun shines through the windows, unbefitting my morale.

We find a spot in the trees to set up camp as party people arrive in droves. So many of the females here are skinny this year. Far more than usual. They've heard of what I've been going through, and are all embarrassed and afraid to eat now, that's why. I'm a frightful example of what happens if you let yourself go.

Was it only last year that Nile and I spent the whole time at each other's side, beyond smitten? How do you feel so close with someone in such a short period of time? He's being aloof, as if we've been married decades too long. He frequently ditches me in the crowd, switches stages without inviting me, even when his favourite DJs are playing. My inner knowing screams that he's slipping away to cheat on me. This time, it's because I'm fat. The scale says I'm a healthy one hundred and twenty-five pounds. But I feel enormous and repulsive when I compare myself to how much smaller I was, just a few months ago.

I catch Nile on the sidelines of the crowd. We've hardly spent any time together all weekend. He notices me too and, reluctantly, we walk towards each other, like duelling gunmen in reverse. He opens his mouth to speak, but I beat him to it.

"You're cheating on me," I say, and then burst into tears.

This time he massages me as I cry instead of getting defensive and denying it. This is the much more painful of the two. I cry like I haven't cried in years. He still won't admit it with words. I don't even think he's sorry, just undecided as to whether he wants to keep dragging out this horrible mess between us. Tears pour as I realize how deeply and helplessly, I am attached to our love, or at least the memory of it. I rub the river from my eyes and notice Lynx across the dancefloor. The crowd swirls and blurs around him, but he's rocksteady, a stone in a river, staring at us, looking concerned. I turn away, overwhelmed by sad wonder, should I have just stayed with Lynx all this time? Eventually, my tears subside. No sadness was shed.

I curl up in foetal position for the entirety of the ride home. I crawl out of the car, lost, not knowing where to go, so I end up staying at Nile's.

After the sadness of Shambhala, I find the strength to fight the urges compelling me to eat. The strength surely comes from shame. At least I become small again. Thank God. Summer ends. The crowds leave. The island returns to quietude.

Forty

I need to get my head clear. I decide to partake in a seven-day meditation retreat at the centre where I taught yoga during the summer. Also in attendance are my friends Angela and Moss who've also traveled extensively through India, and a handful of off-islanders. We close our eyes, and gently settle into a mighty calmness. The retreat feels like a vacation for my psyche. The turbulent emotions are somehow put on pause.

Hmm… Enlightenment. Hmm… Just Be Enlightened…?

It's a conscious choice, ever present, not some elusive thing to be attained. Enlightenment is a simple, but selfless, decision. We know when our actions and speech are enlightened and we know when they are not. We feel the difference. It's Ahimsa (non-violence) towards others and towards oneself. It's altruism. It's humility. It's awareness of the ripples of the little choices we're faced with all the time. For instance, being conscious and intentional about what happens to the money you spend — whether it sponsors the anguish of our fellow man and our Mother Earth. It's taking care of yourself, such that you achieve a state most able to serve and inspire others towards their bliss. It's forgiveness. Forgiveness is evolution: the escape from ego, the conquering of hatred. It's accepting people for where they're at, not stooping to cruelty if one is mean towards you. It's being mindful of each action as it comes. It isn't complicated. We know when we're being enlightened and when we aren't. We all do.

Mindful. Heartfelt. Conscious. Constant.

It seems so easy and simple while I sit, disconnected from social circumstances. Maybe I should become a nun.

Nile and I are on and off again. I've been bobbing around the island, crashing couches and caring for the homes and pets of islanders when they go away. I'm gifted a generously paid five-week pet-sit that'll end come February. I wave good-bye to the owner of the house from her own porch as she drives off into the godforsaken grey drizzle, and then turn inside to get acquainted with the animals. Plume is your typical charmer, someone you instantly become fond of. She bats her beautiful round eyes at you while she strokes you with her head, whispering meows of appreciation. While Rufus, on the other hand, comes off as a tad annoying, a little loud, and overly eager. But I suppose I should let his exuberance in.

For the entirety of my five weeks in this house, I've forbidden myself from buying groceries, thus eliminating the option to eat. Part of me is telling myself that minimalism helps the environment. But really, it's coming from ego. I was programmed and raised in a superficial culture and just want to be thin so I feel desirable. Besides, it seems like a waste to not experience beauty in one's youth. I get back into accomplishing a two-hour yoga routine daily. Every day, I also go for at least one long walk with Rufus. And, three times a week, I bike across the island to work at a coffee shack. My fasting seems to have further unclogged my telepathic abilities. As I serve coffee to customers, I am now able to narrow in on people's thoughts at will.

One day, while walking through a trail in the forest, I meet a girl, and we stop to introduce ourselves. She's new to the island, recently arrived from travelling through Southeast Asia for several months. She has hand carved coconut spirals in her ears, the kind I wore after I stretched my ears with a lemon twig, back on the Andaman Islands. She is I. I ask her if she has any recommendations for places to travel to.

"Thailand's amazing."

She talks of an isolated beach called Nirvana. Heaven on Earth is where I'd like to be. Overwhelmed by the desire to leap from this insular island, I buy a one-way ticket to Thailand. I'm to depart the day after Plume and Rufus' mama returns. In the midst of a daily yoga practice, I'm hit with a revelation. It seems obvious, but also urgent to share with others. I fervently scribble it down to share with those watching through the hidden cameras that I'm ninety-five percent sure are set up in the house. I could see humanity and Earth actually healing if people took this to heart and heed. With the intention to heal the world, I announce it out loud whilst I transfer it onto paper in big, visible letters:

"We in the rich realm can choose to be angels. We literally have the power to answer the prayers of others. It's fair to assume that the people in places of famine and war are praying for food, shelter, and safety. It's our duty to acknowledge this reality and step into angelic responsibility.

Overpopulation is one of the most significant causes of environmental destruction. But we can regain equilibrium through adoption. There are millions of babies and children already born, but suffering. How dare we leave them in misery when we have the ability to give them happiness, health, and safety? All of humankind is a family. We've just been programmed to feel disconnected and separate from each other. Take in the children that are already alive, instead of bringing in more people who all demand resources and space from the planet. It is anti-evolutionary. There are many people, already here, that need us for salvation. Exceed your behavioural loop. Escape your social inertia. Humanity is currently caught in horrendous dysfunction. When one chooses to birth a baby instead of adopt, is it not from a desire to see your reflection in another? Does that not just come from a societally programmed alienation? Is it okay to bring a child into the world that you could not afford to provide for without supporting industries that have other, already born children trapped in slavery and war? We need to wake up from our stupor. We're better than that.

As soon as I finish scrawling down the channelled angel wisdom, I feel a blast of hatred shoot at me from every pregnant woman on the island. First from Lila, then all the others join in. I shout to the cameras broadcasting me, "You're just projecting your self-loathing onto me because these words make sense!" I feel more hatred blasted my way, hotter, sharper this time. I'm staggered. A teetering anxiety sets in as I become aware that friends, acquaintances, and even strangers, are starting to hate me.

I haven't seen Nile in weeks. Each time I cross the island to work, I think about visiting him, but I never do. I always go home after my shift — the dog needs to be taken for a walk, I tell myself. A week before I'm to leave for Thailand, I finally go to see him. Our eyes link, and a shy uncertainty settles into the space between us where a dead void used to be, and, before that, a blissful, devoted, passion. He tells me his sister's coming to Hornby tomorrow, and invites me to have dinner with them. I get confused. His attitude usually makes me feel like I'm not special to him anymore, yet he just asked for my inclusion in a moment with a dear and cherished person that he rarely gets to see. He too, still feels what we had. Our souls are magnetic towards one another, we were meant to share time together. That's why so many synchronicities happen when we're together. The goodbye phone call in the airport as I set out for India, finding the beedies at our first Shambhala, and so many others.

We have roasted veggies and nut loaf for dinner. I haven't had a proper meal in a month, it's okay to have one. I love spending time with Nile's family. I feel like I belong. His sister's lost a lot of weight, too. To my understanding, it's because I am being watched from cameras, not just on the island like I first suspected, but far-reaching satellite cameras are broadcasting me. In code, Nile's sister is trying to help me realize how important it is for me to be thin. No one is allowed to say it outright, or else it'll make my performance seem inauthentic. The more weight I lose, the more I will be perceived as pretty, and will be taking less resources from the Earth. The prettier I am, the more that I will be able to influence people to step into their angel nature and realize their full potential.

Telepathically, I receive the message of my duty. I am going to be broadcasted by satellites on my travels around the world. The past months of being filmed by hidden cameras on Hornby were to prepare me for this mission. I am relieved that everything finally makes sense and has purpose.

Nile offers me a ride to the airport. Again, I am very surprised that he suddenly wants to spend time with me. I accept his offer, still craving the fix of his love. At first, the nostalgia inside his car is nice, in that killing-me-softly sort of way. I suspect he's talking to me in code, too, trying to explain how I should act to help influence the world into a state of peace. It is against the rules to flat out say in clear language that I am being broadcasted all over the world. But the discreteness is frustrating me. I'm not sure if I'm deciphering the codes accurately. Why can't people just give me my script and tasks in direct, clear language? It would make the movie better if I had a concrete understanding of its purpose. In the middle of our ride my mood shifts and I can't help but be mad at him for cheating on me. My ego's not able to forgive him, which has me realize how unequipped I am to influence people to choose to evolve into angels. I can't be expected to lead others to become what I cannot even achieve myself.

Despite being mad, I simultaneously wish he was coming to Thailand with me. My emotions encompass all contradictions. I feel everything all at once. Separating from a soulmate is the harshest thing. Parting ways for worldly woes feels like such a shame and such a waste. But the mortal drama has a chokehold on me. By the time we pull into the airport parking lot I'm too hurt and angry to share a nice goodbye. With eyes of stone I coldly say, "Bye," turn, and walk away without looking back. Something inside me dies when I realize this could be the last time we'll ever see each other. Still, I do not look back. Whatever. Life will be very happy, very soon. I'll meet someone else, someone who wants to travel, someone who wants to live the same kind of life that I do.

My plan is to spend several years travelling. Not only for adventure, but also to volunteer work in places that need help. When funds dwindle, I will find paid work in Europe, Australia, anywhere will do. I am convinced that this is what I'm embarking on. Everything will work out to inspire peace and positivity. I have been chosen to heal humanity.

Practically everyone is rooting for me.

At a little less than one hundred pounds, I've never been more ready for the beach. It'll be easy to shake off my depression and cure my broken heart. I am a human symbol, chosen to model minimalism to advance awareness of environmental issues. I have been selected for the job of making
humanitarianism and environmentalism cool. They chose me because I'm telepathic, someone who is able to receive instruction without audible instruction, making the mission more impressive. They tell me that if I listen to the encoded requests and do a good job being a role model, I will be rewarded with incredible opportunities, opportunities beyond most people's wildest dreams. When I eat, or even if I drink too much water, the voices rally and I can feel the fury of the viewers shoot into my being, like guns into a bullet proof vest. There has never been so much riding on my journeys as there is now.

I'm pressed back into the plush of my seat by the momentum of the plane. The Earth falls away below me, gravity still weighing me down. I'm ready.

Forty-One

I land in Bangkok. I haven't had the internet, so I haven't done any research. But I feel safe. It's the middle of the day, and I'm broadcasting worldwide. The network wouldn't let anything happen to their starring talent. One of the many three-wheeled tuk-tuks buzzes me to Khao San Road, where most of the backpackers flock to. I meet a friendly traveller from Whistler. My friends from BC surely have secretly arranged for him to steer me to where I'm supposed to be for the first episode of the Thailand series. He's headed to the beach nicknamed Nirvana, the one the girl I met on Hornby also directed me towards. He invites me to hop on the back of his motorbike. I hear his voice in my head: People are waiting for you.

He insists I wear a helmet, but doesn't wear one himself. This is another confirmation that people are watching. I'm supposed to set a good example for the children. We rip noisily off down Khao San Road then onto the highway. I get confused and wonder if this a live public broadcast, filmed by satellites, or just hidden cameras that are going to re-cut the footage into a movie. It really isn't fair that it isn't being explained to me, or that I haven't given consent to this invasion of my privacy.

The city has long disappeared behind us. We weave through empty, palm-lined dirt roads that cough up dust as we grind our way through steep inclines and sharp turns. The guy controlling the motorcycle is obviously a professional driver. He has been assigned the job of ensuring I get to Nirvana. All I have to do is play my part, and I will be rewarded. I lean back and fake a smile. Soon enough I am actually enjoying myself.

Hours later, we finally descend to the white-sanded paradise. Nirvana is first-come, first-served.

The beachfront dorm has only eight beds, and they don't take reservations. The receptionist starts shaking her head. "No." Then, all of a sudden, narrows her eyes at me, catches herself, and says, "Yes, we have one bed left." She's recognized me. They've been waiting for me and have saved me a bed. For this scene in the movie, they're trying to make it look like some sort of synchronicity in my charmed wanderings. I try to make a show of being pleasantly surprised and wonder if this scene will be included in the movie. I ponder what the plot is, still unclear if it's solely satellite cameras filming. I don't see any cameras. I shake out of my thoughts to listen to the host as she tells me about the programs and classes that are offered here. She reaches the fasting program, her voice slows, and she stares intently into my eyes and starts to subtly nod. In my head, I hear her voice.

"You *need* to lose weight for what we have planned for you."

I unload my bag in the dorm, then go to make friends. The people here will probably be blissed out and friendly. We are in paradise, after all. There's a group sitting at a table with one empty chair. Surely, they're waiting for me. I go to take my seat. Conversation falls silent. I look at them and notice how outrageously beautiful they all are. Smooth, tanned skin, faces perfectly symmetrical, dressed in artful attire. They're obviously movie stars who've been waiting to make the film with me. I can tell they're disappointed, now that they're meeting me in the flesh. They wish that the people in charge had found a better star. Somewhere, someone murmurs, "Your 'It' girl sucks. Is this really the best you could do?"

I try to break the ice by expressing awe at the beauty of this place. They stonewall me, faces cold. I guess that goes with the profession. None of my co-stars want to be my friend. I leave them, increasingly anxious and insecure.

There's a party tonight. It was meant to be my welcome party, but no one wants me to go. I'm still not thin enough to fit the part. I'm not welcome at my own celebration. Depressed and stressed, I retire to bed. Does that at least reflect well on me as a role model? Finally, a semi-kind telepathic message.

You can dance in the daytime. Rest now.

I wake in the morning to pounding bass. The party's still going strong. Timidly, I make my way to the crowded dance floor and try to find my groove, but I can't. All eyes are on me. They know who I am. Their thoughts drown out the music, interject the rhythm, trip my feet up off the beat.

I thought you said she was a good dancer.

Her legs are fat.

Why didn't she party last night?

Because she's a loser.

Wow, she really sucks at dancing.

There is no way this girl's an Indigo Child.

I was told she's good at everything. But she sucks at everything!

A Buddha t-shirt at a rave? What a poser.

After a few minutes of stilted swaying, I leave, feeling extremely aware that I am an object of mass hatred.

Down on the beach, I see a woman sitting in the sand who

I recognize from the dorm. We sit and talk in the sun as it slowly comes to its zenith. Her warmth shocks me. She is my angel of empathy, when everyone else is closed towards me. Her company finally lets me tap into connection with my whereabouts; a pristine tropical beach under the glorious sun.

In the afternoon, I continue down the beach to an especially beautiful sandy stretch. There're a few people here, reclining in the warmth. One of them is lying alone, on a black sarong, in a black bathing suit, reading a black book called The Gargoyles. She seems strangely out of place. I wonder if she's depressed, something I can relate to and perhaps even help her with. The external pressure to be having the time of my life is making all of my negative emotions worse than they are already. I introduce myself, but have a hard time concentrating on the conversation. As soon as I start talking to her, beratement boils up in my head again.

Can't you see it's a trap?

Don't talk to her, she's clearly a downer, a loser, like you.

You have to choose the sparkly ones.

She tells me she works for a "Be Happy" School in Denmark. I get it now. It's a comedy, and I'm the fall guy. This woman in gothic attire is mocking me for striking up a conversation with someone who's obviously part of an over-the-top joke about my failure to inspire.

Or maybe... she's speaking in code? Maybe I'm supposed to teach people how to be happy. She must be one of the viewers who has no faith in my competence. She's passive-aggressively ridiculing me.

Whatever the plan might be, I'm not so sure I want it to unfurl. These people — the directors, the audience, the cast — are cruel and extremely shallow. I thought this was supposed to be about healing the Earth. It's all making less and less sense.

It's day three of living like a hermit and fasting at Nirvana. In the distance, I see someone wearing baggy red skirt-pants, and a loose blue t-shirt, almost the exact same outfit that I often wore on my trip in India. I walk closer to her, and, what's crazy is, it's Crystal, the British poet that I met on the beach during my first summer on Hornby. The uncanny outfit is her way of communicating to me, without breaking the standard of total discreteness that has been set in place; that I've been under surveillance for several years now. That is how she knows what I wore day after day a few years back. All part of the plan. She's trying to help? I go over to her to say hi.

She's mad at me. I can tell. We're having an ordinary conversation with our mouths, while simultaneously having a telepathic conversation about the real stuff. Our psychic exchange confirms that I am being watched and have failed to fulfil the instructions that were given. We talk for a few minutes and her voice, eyes, and attitude soften. She tells me that, before this trip, she spent a few months on another one of BC's Gulf Islands. She really connected with some of the people there — "like Sage." After she says Sage's name, she pauses and looks through me, eyes bright with anger. She's implicitly referring to my friend Sage, from the Yoga Teacher Training in Baja. Crystal's letting me know that he's mad at me, too. He's disappointed with me for not using this opportunity in the limelight to be the most inspiring I can possibly be. I'm not good enough to save the world through influence. I'm confused. I'm ashamed. Everyone hates me. Crystal smiles snidely and tells me she's leaving to continue her travels today. Originally, she must have come here to play in the celebration plot, but has changed her mind. I let her down.

She's done with me. Beat down from all the anger, I mumble goodbye and wish her happy travels. I start to dread the contrived coincidences to come. Being hated is far more painful when it comes from people that actually know me.

There's a Sufi dance lesson being held here. Excited to learn something new, I join the ten other students. Everyone twirls and spins like seed pods. The teacher invites us to lay on the ground once we become tired. At first, the room glows with calm focus until, suddenly, I am bombarded with the thoughts of the people surrounding me.

Oh great, now we have to pretend to be bad at this to make the stupid It girl look like she's better at everything.

I wish she wasn't here.

Everyone seems to give up quickly, and I am left the last person dancing.

Why did you come here? You aren't welcome, yet.

We're behind schedule. You need to lose weight for the movie.

I continue to spin, but idly now, blankly... What is the movie, anyway? Why is everyone being so vague on the details?

I walk down the beach and find another guesthouse. The ground is firmer beneath my feet here. The people send me smiles as I walk by, and even the mental chatter has mellowed out for the moment. Then a new voice drifts into me.

Don't be too hard on yourself. Take your time.

There's a dorm at this guesthouse half the price of the one at Nirvana. I ask if I can stay. They smile and nod yes, then tell me I can choose whichever empty bed I like. Each bed has a blue number painted on the wooden post that holds up its mosquito net. The number I choose is going to influence the plot of the movie. I can't decipher which number leads to which outcome, though. I start to panic and just pick bed eleven. It's too late to change when I realize I may have picked the fate of "Ill-Heaven."

I collect my things from Nirvana and carry them to the new guesthouse. As I leave, one of the kinder people that I can hear in my brain chirps in: It's rigged, Maya! You just have to do the work and you win!

I'm unsure what the prize is, or if I even want it. At this point, all I want is a calm brain, to be with kind people, and to travel Thailand in peace. I want to feel free.

At one of the tables in the guesthouse courtyard I take out my drawing pencils. But the pictures won't come. All of the vitriol that I've been blasted with has dammed up my creative flow. I can't trace a single line without becoming critical. Even though the hateful voices are absent for the moment, they've left an unshakeable impression on my thought patterns. I close my journal and a man nearby, fiftyish, strikes up conversation.

"Have you heard of Eckhart Tolle?" he asks.

"Yes. Are you him?" I reply.

He laughs a no, which catches me off-guard, since I've been hearing so much about a mystery reward. The company of a renowned thinker would certainly have explained the ironic, self-important airs of the people at Nirvana. Instead, he tells me to think about the concept of the "Power of Now." I haven't read the book, but I get his game. He's implying that I'm not doing what I'm supposed to be doing right now. Now, I have a mission. Now, I have opportunities. The opportunities won't last forever and will only be realized if I utilize the Now.

There is no time to waste. This plan is not my own design, but it is for the greater good, and I should still fulfil my duties, for others. I tell him I'll go meditate on it, and find a spot in the sun to do just that.

Within seconds of sitting down, I am buzzing with energy, too much to contain. A voice — this time different, impersonal —enters my mind, and tells me that people from all over the world are sending me energy, long distance, reiki style. Wealthy spiritualists want to prove that magic is real, and they've chosen me to demonstrate this. This is why I'm being filmed and followed by satellites. The voice tells me that I should feel honoured. I'm vibrating right down to my bones. I jump in the ocean and swim with the warm and wild waves. For the first time since I've been here, I feel like I'm pleasing the audience and have the approval of the people in charge of my show. Swimming pacifies the tormentors in my head. Their words are mostly of encouragement now.

This is what you're supposed to be doing. Good job.

You really need to lose weight. Continue.

Even so, when I get out of the water, I break. For the first time since arriving in Thailand, five days ago, I decide that it's okay to eat. Aren't I supposed to be setting a good example, anyhow? I order myself a fruit plate from the guest house's basic restaurant. A palpably awkward silence follows my request. I explain myself to the audience of now quiet tormentors and say, "Chill out, it's just fruit, it won't make me fat. And it's local and vegan, so I'm not stressing the environment or hurting anyone." Eyes dart away, and a few people storm out of the restaurant. The watermelon, pineapple, and mango chunks disappear into my mouth one by one. I was starving, but the pleasure is short-lived. Now everyone is even angrier at me.

Forget it, we'll find another It girl. You're impossible.

This feels not so much like being fired as being set free. Relieved, I decide to continue my travels. "So, this means you're all going to leave me alone, right?" I project out of my head. Hallelujah! Onward with life, then!

I bump into Tara, the angelically kind girl from the dorm at Nirvana. She says she's eager to explore as well, and suggests travelling north together to visit the Sukhothai ruins.

Forty-Two

On the road I become surly as Tara asks me questions about the life I left in Canada. She knows all about me already, everyone does! This is false. Why can't people just outwardly admit they've been watching?

Head hanging out an open bus window, drinking in the tropical breeze, with a new friend at my side, brings no joy. I can't tame my sour mood. Once we arrive in Sukhothai, I ask Tara if she wants to have dinner. She pauses, taken aback by the idea, then smiles nervously and agrees to go find somewhere to eat. As I chew my papaya salad, I notice she refuses to meet my gaze. She must know that I was instructed to not eat. Confused, I mutter, "I thought they were going to find another It girl." Whether by mouth or mind, it seems she heard me, because she puts her chopsticks down without finishing her meal.

Before the papaya salad is finished, I, too, have put down my chopsticks, too full of guilt to keep eating. For reasons I don't understand, I vow to try to obey every command. But what if it's hunger that is to blame for my dismal attitude? Seconds after vowing to listen, it occurs to me that the people ordering me around and shaming me are domineering fascists, uninvited and unjustified in their power over me. And, they lie! How could this possibly be about Healing the Earth? It's cruel and nonsensical. Now I become mad at Tara, and at everyone else, mad at them for not asking my permission to film me. I stop believing that there's a reward. If this broadcast had a kind intention, then I would be treated kindly. And look at me! I'm small enough by now.

This is just getting ridiculous. I'm starving!

Tara and I part ways. She doesn't want to continue travelling with me. I don't have to ask why. With me there is no privacy, and I'm grumpy as fuck to boot.

Forty-Three

I wind up at a crowded hostel in a nearby city. Nobody wants to talk to me. They all know who I am, and they're mocking me for not listening to the instructions that will lead me to the mystery reward. I feel like everyone sees me as an ungrateful jerk that refused the chance of a lifetime. I can hear them sneering,

Poor princess, we didn't ask her permission to make her one the luckiest people on Earth.

During brief periods of inner silence, save for my own thoughts, I realize more and more how little sense this all makes. I have been obeying their demands. I've fasted, gone travelling. I've cracked the codes where they appear and held myself up to their ideals. They abuse me while proclaiming that they're blessing me. They nominated me, commandeered my life, and now they guilt-trip me for not meeting their standards of perfection. They want me to model human excellence to the rest of the world, but their ideals are brutal and intolerant. The spotlight they project on me seems to scare everyone else away. I'm never alone, yet constantly isolated.

A formless voice interrupts my thoughts and announces that I'm hell bound if I don't follow the instructions;

Don't eat, do lots of yoga, and exercise like crazy.

Once they're satisfied by my results, I will be rewarded.

These tasks should be easy, and enjoyable to accomplish.

I can't tell who's saying what any more. My mind's

becoming ever more scattered. I then hear the voice of an intruder.

Do something interesting. You're boring to watch. You want to get paid, don't you?

Finally, in my mind I hear a foreign voice and am offered a partial explanation. They've invented a long-distance telepathy phone. I'm their guinea pig. They're tracking my movements through GPS satellites, which they use to beam down audible messages as well. That makes sense, I think. I can work with that. This new information brings with it a wave of relief, and the fussing in my mind briefly abates.

I arrange a four-day hike that finishes with a raft trip down a river to please the viewers and show them some of Thailand's landscape. Joining me are three girls from BC, a guy from Europe, a young couple from Japan, and our guide. It is explained to me through the telepathy apparatus that I'm either going to have to go back to BC, permanently, or travel the world for years. How I act on this four-day tour will determine my fate. The first day goes well. I don't eat and I run back and forward along the trail while the group walks. I have so much energy. It must be from the long-distance reiki philanthropists are paying for. When I'm active my brain's bombarded:

Go Maya!
Wow!
We love you!
You can do this!

I want to please them. I want the positive comments to continue to rain down. Even more than the prospect of a lifetime abroad, kind words of encouragement light a fire in me. That night, I find an area to the side of our camp and exercise for several hours, push-ups, crunches, jumping jacks, ignoring the group as they relax around the firepit. I focus on completion of the first task; adequate weight loss.

The group calls it a night and retreats into the sleeping hut. I stay awake, still working out, by moonlight. Out of nowhere, my energy evaporates and I am overwhelmed by exhaustion. Still outside, I sink to the dirt and close my eyes and, while collapsing into sleep, a bright green dragon-looking spirit jolts into my chest. I'm powerless to stop it. From within me, it blows green, gaseous fire and hisses, "We Hate You," and then the dragon form disintegrates as it slithers into my cells. Surely, Thai shamen have just cursed me and injected a demon into my body. They were fed up with me for not obeying my orders quickly enough. They loathe me for not complying one hundred percent when I had the opportunity to help them, Earth and other earthlings. Sleep soon brings blunt relief from my fear, shame, and misery.

Morning light comes, and the others tiredly trickle out from the sleeping hut. I wake with the prayer that I'll be able to do what needs to be done. Morning is oddly pleasant, until lunch is handed out by the guide. Everything contorts. A pad thai wrapped in banana leaves is handed to me. I devour the meal. The guide hands me a second one, and it, too, is quickly devoured. Holy fuck! I'm possessed! The dragon demon that flew inside me last night is puppeting me. Despite not being the one in control, I'm still filled with remorse. I walk up some rocks to a waterfall, to be with its serenity and try to shake off the guilt of my regretful, sinful, full stomach.

As I stand above the shimmering cascade, I hear the voices of distant friends. They've somehow gained access to the satellite relay and are watching and able to communicate to me now.

We love you Maya, don't jump!

I wasn't considering jumping, until being given the idea. Nonetheless, after so many insults and orders, it's very strange, and very soothing, to hear my friends' voices. To learn that there are a handful of people in the world who don't yet hate me.

We ride elephants. I don't want to ride an elephant, but a voice tells me it would be rude to decline. Is it the demon that's trying to convince me to not listen to my heart? The gentle giants are strangely sedate. They are guided down narrow dirt paths through the forest, day after day, by the men who've tamed them. On the creature's back, I am bombarded with more criticism, from many different voices. Some of the voices I'm starting to recognize, but can't put a face to.

Buddha wouldn't do this.

She's such a loser.

You're just another ignorant tourist. She only thinks of herself.

There are mass refugee camps, appalling pollution, wars, and genocides going on. You've been given an opportunity to show people what's happening on Earth... and you spend your time riding elephants?!

We hate you.

On the last day, our group splits into two rafts. The GPS telepathy laser informs me that this is the moment when the viewers vote on what my outcome will be. The guide looks at me. He rolls his eyes, and then they narrow. He practically bashes me with his paddle, motioning for me to get into the boat with the people from Japan and Europe, not the trio from BC. This means the voters want to watch me continue to travel.

It's rigged, we *had* so much faith in you. You don't deserve this.

It's becoming more and more clear that my relationship with the network is strictly one-way. I no longer understand what they want from me. But no matter how much I scream inside, I can't get them to leave me alone.

Forty-Four

I return to the city. I lose the ability to sleep. I want to sleep so badly, not because I'm tired, but just to have a break from all the abuse. My inner monologue has become a bad dream I can't pinch myself awake from. If only there was some way to change my circumstances. But I'm trapped. Too much money has been spent on this project, too much status staked on my failed performance. I've already told them I want my privacy returned. They don't care.

I buy a pair of shoes.

Your shoes are ugly!

You're supposed to be making humanitarianism cool.

You have to look good to make it cool, you fucking moron!

The explanation for why I'm being ordered around keeps changing. At first it was to prove magic is real. Then it was about making humanitarianism cool. Now it's a film that I'm responsible for making interesting and successful. "This doesn't make sense!" I exclaim, directed towards the controllers and faraway audience. Surrounding eyes on the street dart up at me, and suddenly I'm not being ignored. Still, no one smiles my way.

I hear the voice of a man, looming, taunting:

Are you willing to take the chance that this isn't about healing the Earth?"

With fear as my fuel, I resolve to continue to obey the

demands of the people behind the satellites.

The next two weeks I spend alone. I've become far too embarrassed of my actions to look anyone in the eye. All my time is now spent between stuffing myself with food against my will, likely from the dragon demon that possessed me, or running to the brink of collapse. As soon as I stop exercising, I am swept into more uncontrolled eating. I'm fully cursed. I try to explain to the filmmakers that I'm not feasting on purpose. Other spirits are entering me and moving my body, as if pirates have taken my vessel captive. When I sprint for long stretches, I start to hear kinder messages.

You can do it!

Save the World!

We forgive you!

One day, to demonstrate my shame and sorrow, I repent in the hostel's common area. I count one hundred and eight Sun Salutations, deep, dizzying, all-over body stretches, pushing myself to the brink of tears, before I'm filled with voices of kindness…

We forgive you.

Please keep trying.

We need you.

Next, I am blasted with a vision of an enormous refugee camp that is watching me on a large cloth screen. They are praying to me. Praying for me to help them. I must listen. When I think about it, I can't see the connection between my fatigue, and their redemption… but then, again, that looming voice…

Can you take that chance?

After another week, I break. Trying again is futile. It's impossible. "I give up!" I scream into the sky, crying. With every fibre of my being, I know that I'm possessed. I can't control myself. I explain this to the viewers while I sob. "People are voodooing me to eat. I'll never be able to accomplish what you want! I give up. I'm sorry. Find someone else before it's too late. I can't do it. I'm possessed."

I retreat to my dorm bed at the random hostel I'm staying at and try to sleep but it's impossible. It's not just the invisible audience any more: everyone is mad at me. Everyone. People all over the hostel are slamming doors, communicating in metaphors. So many doors are closing, so many opportunities. I don't care. I am broken. I can't do it. There are pigeons everywhere. They've been sent to mock me. Filthy, fallen doves. I can't handle being awake any longer. I buy some Valium and swallow four.

As soon as I wake, the scolding picks up where it left off.

Children are watching you, and what you do is take Valium and turn your back on helping the world?

"I can't do it; I don't want the job!" I cry, as I try to explain, again. "I would if I could, I'm possessed! You need to find someone else!"

They start letting Thai people use the telepathy mechanism.

We have a beautiful culture and landscape. You come here and all you do is eat. You're a poison on our country.

We hate you.

I am filled with shame. I feel evil. I must leave this place. I try one more time to explain myself. "I am cursed. A dragon spirit has possessed me. Forces beyond me are controlling my body." I go to the airport and purchase a ticket back to Vancouver. I am too mortified to stay. I am sorry Thailand. I am sorry Earth.

On my stopover in China, an Indian woman, wearing a sari and a bhindi, looks at me with deep compassion. Next, she goes into a McDonald's, and I see her walk out with a Big Mac. She's trying to tell me to forgive and accept myself. We all do things that aren't completely in line with our highest aspirations and ideals. She's still a Hindu, despite the occasional burger.

Forty-Five

I land in Vancouver and make my way to the Big Island's ferry. The ferries at this time of year are usually pretty empty, yet this crossing is crowded. Nearly everyone is young and beautiful, stunningly so. This is a movie scene, it has to be. Why else would the ferry be filled with such an improbable amount of drop-dead gorgeous people? I can't figure out if they're here to ridicule me or to inspire me. It's probably both. So then, why am I still being followed and broadcasted? I left Thailand in appalling form, this movie shoot must be over by now. The dragon curse is manipulating me to be a wicked, wretched monster. I am just watching my body go through the motions and listening to the thoughts of others flowing through my brain, invading and taking over what was once my private headspace, my sanctuary, my fortress of calm that I never imagined could be overthrown.

I get off the ferry on Vancouver Island with no option but to hitch-hike. Night has fallen. It's pouring rain and cold. But I am too ashamed to call any of my friends. I hike through the wind, the sky roaring in anger at me. A man named Bob picks me up on the shoulder of the highway. The clock reads 8:18.

Bob... 8:18...

Two palindromes, the same backwards and forwards. Thus, they must signify: The Eternal Now. The eternal Present. Bob is creepy and perverted, not the kind of person that picks up hitch-hikers simply out of the kindness of their hearts. My suspicions are quickly confirmed. He reaches over and rubs my knee. I push his hand aside as politely as I can, like brushing away a tarantula, not wanting to anger him. He doesn't resist. But I fear he'll try again, maybe more aggressively.

It is now. Welcome to hell.

The Hornby ferries don't run this late at night. Bob is going to Courtenay and drops me off downtown. I bump into Vince. He gives me a big hug. Seconds later it all comes back to me — I heartlessly berated him when we briefly lived together my first autumn after South America. He's acting nice. He's been watching. He came here to meet me, to remind the world that it's impossible that I could be a saviour because of how mean I was to him. It's obvious now: they've been watching and recording me for years. Vince is elated because I've made such a fool of myself. That's why he's smiling. It's mockery. He came to find me here, via the footage, so everyone remembers how horrible I can be. I want to express my remorse for exploding at him years ago, but can't find the courage to voice it.

I don't know where to go. My old friends must all hate me by now. I'm responsible for wasting millions of dollars on a project that could have significantly helped others. Instead of saving humanity during my exposure time, I over ate, drugged myself, and fled.

I spend a couple days running around town, trying to lose weight, hoping a friend, any friend, will come find me and take me away. Several recognizable faces drive by as I roam town with my backpack on. No one stops. My bad knee starts to crack from running under the weight of my backpack and my ugly, unacceptable, shoes. No one helps. Everyone hates me now. I've become an evil thing to them. It's not fair. My body and mind belong to the puppeteers.

I was supposed to save the World, to help the environment and to empower other cultures. This project was built on mountains of money donated by kind people, intended to revitalize mankind and our Earth Mother. All I did was make the world more fucked up than it already was. I stole hope from millions of our struggling fellow humans. Of course, none of my friends are coming to help me. Who would, after all of the lives that were left to suffer because of me? No one believes me when I scream out in broad daylight that I'm possessed. Tears stream down my face as I plea for empathy.

I buy a Greyhound ticket to whisk me across the country. As I take my seat aboard the bus, a command from a new and foreign voice enters my brain:

Stay awake for three days without eating or drinking, and all will be forgiven.

The bus tires slam against the metal ramp as we roll off the ferry boat into Horseshoe Bay. I'm relieved to have somewhere to be for a few days, even if it is just a seat on a bus. The signs lining the highway are speaking to me in coded messages that all seem to contradict each other. Numbers with names within names, meant to hint at imperatives that I don't understand. When a code feels cracked, I have no way of confirming that I've interpreted it correctly. For instance, "Nanaimo Ferry" means: Na, na I am O Fair Why? means that it is fair that I owe and am in debt to the people who've organized the broadcast. Soon, I start to ignore these bulletins, as spite against the people that have captured me.

I'm eating like crazy, again. Every time the bus stops, it's as if there's a restless, starving, screaming monster inside of me that can't be calmed or quelled. I keep buying more to eat, the kinds of foods I haven't eaten in years, candy bars, crap chips, typical vending machine fare, all mass-produced artificial junk food; poison. It's all that is available at the Greyhound stations we stop at. I try to stay awake at night, but it's too hard. The bus is dark and without distractions. A few times I fall asleep for minutes, only to spring awake in a panic. The people I sit next to vary in their telepathic mood between compassion and cruelty. My inner territory is even less familiar than what's passing by outside — but at least on the bus ride, I have the choice to get off. The satellite tormentors refuse to leave me alone, no matter how many times I desperately ask.

After three days, with less than three hours of combined sleep, I step off the bus into Canada's capital city of Ottawa. My legs and back are just too cramped from all of the sitting. I find a hostel among the brick-laid streets downtown and pay for a dormitory bed. I sink into the cheap mattress with a sigh and listen for the voices in the quiet. Even though I'm no longer anywhere exotic, the satellites are still stalking and broadcasting me. At this point I'm pretty sure that it's a twenty-four seven international livestream. My ratings continue to drop as I blow a year's worth of travel savings on mass amounts of shit food that I don't even want to eat. Yet that's become all I do. No matter how much I want to stop, I sit there, dissociatively watching my hands shovel food into a mouth no longer mine. I need to get back into my body's driving seat. I need an exorcism!

Mortified by my behaviour, I decide to check into a hotel so I don't have to deal with the shame of being around other travellers. Ninety bucks a night — my savings are really taking a hit now. But I just can't bear to look anyone in the eye. The clerk gives me a key and I lock myself in the room and bury my head under the bed covers, wishing I could find some peace. Instead, I lay in bed, tortured by voices inside my head that don't belong to me. I hold the pillows into my ears to stifle them, but they speak from within. My body's in agony from being stuffed with so much food, so I summon the courage to go outside to run off the pain. Again.

As soon as I finish my circuit, I am pulled straight into the nearest restaurant, as if I were a magnet, and it a cold, steel, fridge. Sitting down, I see the man who I'm pretty sure played Wormtail in the Harry Potter movies. He's eating with an obese woman, as if to send me the message that what happened is okay. We lock eyes and his kindness flows into me. He knows who I am, and he's attempting to comfort me. Yet anxiety overrules. All this does is, yet again, confirm that I'm being watched twenty-four seven by satellites, *Truman Show*-style.

Days of hiding away in my hotel room before, by some miracle, waves of calm begin to wash over me. The sudden stillness is like bumping into an old friend long since vanished, and thought dead. Through this window of peace, I decide I can cope with being around other people. I leave the hotel that I've been hiding in, mostly because I can't actually afford to stay there. Head hung low, I check back in at the hostel front desk, not brave enough to dart my eyes up from the ground.

The torture starts up again, full-blown this time. For a few days, the tormentors toggle between intense loathing and crippling pity. Hopeless to dispel the demons possessing me and to get the broadcast to stop, I go to the store and buy two packs of herbal sleeping pills.

From my bed in an empty dorm room, I start to explain myself aloud, to the invisible audience.

"I give up. I'm sorry…" Tears start to roll down my cheeks as I try to explain.

"There are spirits possessing me and moving me. There's no chance in hell I'll be able to complete the tasks demanded of me. I just want to be left alone, in peace. I'm sorry. I'm just not able." This is my pathetic goodbye to the World, perhaps the seeds of my next rebirth. It'll likely be a negative rebirth. I don't care. Anything to bring an end to this.

I gulp down the pills with tap water. Then, in the peculiar calm that follows, I start to ponder what's to come. I've heard different theories on dying. Some Buddhists believe that the energy one holds in the moment they leave their life is the most influential factor in how their next life will begin. This is why I chose herbal sleeping pills. I'm hoping to gently dream my way through death, softly, softly. I shake with grief while I pray for a gentle transition to a nice next reality. There are other theories. For instance, a Buddhist scientist once told me that karma and chaos theory are pretty much the same thing. Some karmic seeds blow through breezes and find soil, sunshine, and water. Others just blow into dust on the wind. Many religions say that a sinful heart goes to hell. For the cynics, there's nothing after life, nothing. Or maybe, we all come into Earth innocent, and return to wherever, innocent. I have no idea, but I'm about to find out. Who knew death would be so docile and welcome?

Twice in the night I wake up groggy from my induced sleep, with the overwhelming need to defecate. Using the walls as support I stumble to the washroom, then fill the toilet bowl with a mountain of brown sludge, barely conscious. I wonder if having an emptier, thus more pure body will be a positive thing for the beginning of my next incarnation — if that is, in fact, where I'm headed. I wobble my way back to bed where I instantly collapse back into a deep, dark, empty, sleep.

The next thing I am aware of is sprinting up and down a hallway in the hostel. I'm trying to leave, but I can't. The doors are all locked, the windows bolted shut. Guess they thought it would be funny to trap me inside. I manage to crack open one window. I scream for help to the people below. No one responds. Then, suddenly, the windows grow higher and farther from the street and the people below. Still, no one looks up to acknowledge me. Am I lost in limbo? Have I shifted into a different dimension where none of the Earth dwellers can hear or see me?

There's a room at the end of the hall that I hadn't noticed, despite running up and down the hall countless times, trying to escape. It just appeared from nowhere. It's dark. Some pasty-faced dude is playing video-games. I recognize him as an acquaintance from the most recent week-long meditation retreat that I did on Hornby. I ask for his help. He completely ignores me, then starts shovelling potato chips into his mouth while continuing to game.

I'm alone. I'm a ghost. I shriek. The world around me remains undisturbed. I shriek again. Then it dawns deeper; I am invisible and inaudible; I am dead. I've killed my body and my ghost is trapped in the hostel where I died. Or maybe they're just ignoring me out of spite, thinking I was only pretending to be possessed as an excuse to turn my back on humanity. I start to hear friends and people I admire taking great pleasure in watching this, taking great pleasure in the joke that I've become. Fits of cruel laughter echo through my thoughts, haunting me. Eventually, the hall shifts and there's a staircase that leads me outside. I'm running again, carried by my feet.

An ambulance pulls up beside me, lights flashing. A man in uniform steps out and timidly approaches me. I get it. I'm supposed to play the part for a movie scene. I'm so fucking mad at them for broadcasting me twenty-four seven without my permission and demanding me to submit, I tell them to leave me alone.

"I don't feel like acting out some movie scene so that you people can make a business out of it. I am not injured or sick, I don't need to get into an ambulance, I don't need to go to the hospital, and I don't have to do what you say any more! Leave me alone!"

Another paramedic appears. They're strong. They grip me above my elbows and force me into the back of the ambulance. This scene doesn't make any sense, I have no injuries. They strap me to the stretcher. As we drive away, I realize that I have a memory gap between leaving the hostel after the wall melted into a door. Where did the ambulance come from? How did I get here? I thought nobody could see or hear me. They take me to Emergency. People are speaking in French; I think I am, too. We've crossed the provincial border into Quebec. The controllers and wicked wizards possessing me brought my body here so that they can do fake translations of this scene into English subtitles that suit their plot. They just won't relent.

Forty-Six

My night is spent sitting bolt upright in one of the many beds of a hospital's emergency room. The woman in the bed next to me stays up all night, too. Telepathically, she explains that she's Adia, a friend and meditation mentor of mine from Hornby. She's teleported her soul into this woman's body, and is spirit sharing it, so that she can help guide me through the pieces of the puzzle out of here. If I don't escape, I will be experimented on by the doctors.

"Vicious spirits have been inhabiting and manipulating my body," I explain to her, using telepathy. "How can I block them from entering me?"

You mustn't eat, drink, or sleep for three days and three nights. "But it's the others that make me eat and drink!"

Keep trying. Never give up. No matter what is going on — Never. Give. Up.

Hours pass. I jolt my eyes open in a panic every time my eyelids start to sag. A nurse brings me some water in the wee hours of the morning. It's a test. I will keep my mouth shut, and bend my body away, but the opposite takes place. In trembling hands, I watch the cup rise to meet my lips and tip the water in. Now voices are bombing my head again, telling me that the seventy-two-hour austerity clock has just restarted. I steel my resolve once again.

The clock slowly grinds to dawn, then midmorning. A middle-aged woman in blue horn-rimmed glasses, a smart dress suit, and a red silk scarf, approaches my bed and introduces herself, clipboard in hand. She goes on to ask me a series of questions. I find this ridiculous. She, and everyone else, already know everything there is to know about me. They've been watching me for years. I entertain her questions anyway. For the sake of the plot, the psychiatrist diagnoses me as bipolar and tells me what I'm experiencing are symptoms of a psychotic episode. She says none of what I'm hearing is real. It's all a product of illness.

I wish I could believe her. But my experience of being recorded is so obviously real. After refusing to answer more of the psychiatrist's inane questions, I am transferred to the hospital's psychiatric unit. This makes more sense to me; psychiatric hospitals are interesting enough to make a movie out of. I guess the people in charge don't actually care about showing positive and inspiring examples. Or maybe the initially well-meaning broadcast was sold to people whose bottom line is to make money from entertainment of any form, with no regard to how I feel about all this. Regardless, I have been captured on more than camera now. This hospital is my cage.

The first chance I get, I ask to take a bath. I lock the door behind me, tear apart a disposable plastic razor, and try to slit my wrist. The blade isn't strong enough to fully open my veins. But it spills enough blood for me to lose my permission to leave the psych ward unattended.

I'm put on a cocktail of anti-psychotic medication. A week goes by; the meds don't change anything. This just proves to me that I'm not sick. I actually am being broadcasted and controlled by forces beyond me, otherwise the medication would have had an effect. As another attempt to "alleviate the psychosis," I've been put on electroshock therapy as well. It's horrible. They strap me to a bed so no limbs are broken in the spasms that can occur from having electrical currents jolted through my brain. The anaesthesia that they inject into my arm at the beginning of each treatment is excruciating. After it's over, I wake up groggy, head aching, memory crumbly and vague for hours afterward.

The meds and electroshock therapy combined have many side-effects. I have become extremely lethargic and numb. I shuffle and droop like a soulless zombie. My soul died when I took the sleeping pills. The only difference seems to be that, now, I sleep at night. I've also become overweight, like actual, scale-confirming, overweight. It's uncomfortable, but I'm too depressed to care. A part of me is hoping that they'll stop filming me now that I've become an ugly, evil clown. I take up chain smoking hoping that they'll ban me. Following that logic, I hack off my hair too. If I'm hideous enough, they'll have to cancel me.

Weeks go by. The nightmare continues. One day I look in the mirror and hardly recognize myself: my long, beautiful hair now a hack job, my exotic clothes worn on a slim body, now replaced by a mute teal hospital gown over a blimp. Self-mutilation scabs dot my arms where my smooth, glowing tan would have been. I was very pretty a few months ago. The kind of pretty where strangers would stop me on the street just to make sure I realized how beautiful I was. That was another life. I am hideous now. My appearance embodies how I feel on the inside. People must be compelled to stop watching by now. Or maybe they are revelling in laughter at how awful I look; the pathetic, rejected, broken contestant.

Tracy, one of the other patients, looks strikingly like a

woman I know who works for a company that brings sustainable clean water solutions to communities in countries where it is most needed. I decide she is representing the humanitarian acquaintance, as a kind of agent. Tracy's very kind towards me. This comes as a surprise, after the constant bombardment of insults from my tormentors. We share a table for breakfast and she declines sugar packets for her coffee. She goes on to tell me about the unethical ways sugar is brought to us.

"You care about those sorts of things, don't you?" she asks. "Yes."

"Good," she says, gently. A kind, soft, energy enters me.

Just do the little things for a while.

This phrase imbues me with unconditional love. It's been a long time since I've felt anything remotely like it.

My cousin, Yasmine, lives nearby, and has started to visit me regularly. I hung out with her a few times when I lived in Montreal; she studied there for years. Now, she's just returned from studying in France, and humbly tells me she was near the top of her class. She wants to find work ending female genital mutilation in Africa. She smiles at me as she tells me this. I get so confused about how she isn't mad at me; I could have really helped others too. Maybe she is one of the few that truly believe I'm possessed. Probably; she knew me before. On one of our walks around the hospital grounds, she offers me her old iPod. Most of the music isn't to my taste, but it helps to drown out some of the tormenting voices that I'm still hearing.

Weeks go by in the same starchy hospital gowns, reeking in them, too embarrassed to shower in front of the invisible, leering audience. I only shower when the nurses force me to.

The voices gradually become more compassionate and

less frequent. They're going to find someone strong, pretty, someone more apt to save the world. Some of the voices have started making jokes, as if to try to cheer me up...

Here's your reWARD!

She's out to lunch!

She certainly has expanded!

I don't know whether to laugh or cry. As they slowly relent, they leave the scars to dry, then swoop back to pick at the scabs. I'm a wreck. My mind is foggy and heavy, and so is my body. My spirit is broken. Yoga's impossible now; I can barely concentrate or muster the energy to get out of bed. I hate what remains of myself. It's of no consolation that my actions weren't my own. I still feel like I'm possessed, but if these demons don't leave me, then I guess I need to accept that they are a part of who and what I am now. I have become apathetic to my trauma, to everything. It's just too painful.

I'm put through a dozen electroshock treatments over the course of several weeks. Everything's been blurry. The mornings after I have electroshock treatments are the worst. It's like waking from a night of copious drinking. My head throbs and weighs sore and heavy on my neck. There're always unsettling holes when I try to mentally retrace my steps. It doesn't matter how hard I try to place what happened between point A and point C — I'm walking somewhere, and then it's a blank, and then I'm somewhere else. As if I'd passed out. I'm told not to worry, that that's normal when one undergoes shock therapy. The last round of electroshock is finally complete, and my psychiatrist says I can transfer to a hospital in BC if I want to. I promptly do so.

A few old friends come and visit me in the hospital on Vancouver Island. Upon seeing each other we burst into tears.

I have been so disconnected from anyone or anything that reminds me of happy times. Everything feels different now. I'm a bloated zombie, dead inside. I'm deeply polluted by the medication, the overindulgence of toxic "food," and the vibrational poison that is hospital living, constantly surrounded by sick people. I'm horrified with the state I'm in, yet too numb to be embarrassed by it. I remember how I felt when I left BC for Thailand, full of hope to travel the world. Excited, vibrant, free… my friends must be taken aback to see me like this.

I've transformed from a fluttering pixie into the Incredible Hulk. Seeing them reminds me of happy times. It only reminds me, though. Those states are completely ungraspable now.

My friends are… being nice to me? It's flabbergasting. Surely, they must know I failed my humanitarian mission. Some of the voices tell me that my friends are pretending to care so they can mock me and hurt me more as soon as I decide to trust in their kindness. I don't know what to believe. I've started trying to tell myself that all the mean stuff I'm hearing isn't real, feebly wishing that it actually is psychosis. It is so nice to see kind people.

July rolls around after a few more weeks in the hospital, and I'm finally discharged.

According to them, I've made enough progress in recovery. If I stay on my medication, I will continue to recover. What bullshit! I've been captured, restrained, drugged, and tortured. This is clearly contrived against me. I'm a science experiment.

Forty-Seven

I decide to return to Hornby Island. My old friend Yoshi drives down the island to pick me up from the hospital and offers me the spare room in his cabin. As we trundle off the ferry onto Hornby I duck and hide under the seat. The thought of being seen by people who know me is more than I can handle. They've all laughed at me so much since I left for Thailand. I could hear them revelling in delight, keeling over with laughter as they watched my body play the puppet at the whims of other spirits. Despite my cowardice, Yoshi smiles at me, says that it's okay to pace myself, that I don't have to be social until I feel ready. I can't tell if he's enjoying making a fool out of me, or if his kindness is sincere.

It's nice to be out of the hospital, but it is also terrifying. I'm shaken up, nowhere near returned to my former self. I can't decipher whether or not my experiences are real or delusional, nor where the divide between the two might lie. I'm yo-yoing between the possibilities, philosophizing in a dissociative manner. Maybe I actually am mentally ill. The doctors are telling me I'm sick, but it all feels so real. They could just as well be pretending that it's a mental illness for the sake of the movie. How could they do such a thing without my consent? Some of the voices tell me I don't have the right to be angry, that my anger is selfish, because being filmed opens opportunities far beyond most people's reach… I can't tell the difference. I can't rely on my own brain.

You can't trust yourself.

Those doctors are right about you, you know.

Reality is elusive. I find all this beyond unsettling. I'm filled with fear, despair, and shame. Shambhala festival rolls around and Yoshi wants to go. Spending a few days alone in the cabin brings me to an unbearably heightened state of anxiety. I'm getting mental imagery blasts of a throng of disguised men forming a circle around me, they slowly close in, swinging fists and baseball bats. People watching want to harm me. I'm sort of safe because I'm being broadcasted. Right? Wait a minute though… that hasn't always protected me in the past.

A friend stops by to check on me. She has an extra ticket for Shambhala. She's trying to protect me? I decide to drive to the festival with her and her partner. As intensely embarrassing as it will be to go out in public, it is nowhere near as dreadful as trying to cope with the anxiety of being a sitting duck all alone, listening to the tormentors. I suppose I have to rip the band aid off at some point. I used to be brave. Maybe my courage can be revived. Or maybe I'm just running from a greater fear. It doesn't matter. I've given up on attempting to understand things. It's pointless to try. It's futile and naive.

With the sand between my toes, under the glow of the psytrance stage, I start to remember who I was before the shattering suffocation started. No one points. No one stares. No one even seems to notice me. Have I really been alone all this time? Trapped in sick delusion? Maybe. Some of my thoughts are even positive and sensical against the backdrop of rhythm and melodies. I do my best to cope and try to accept that I am not being broadcasted. This doesn't come easy.

There's evidence to support both theories. I decide that being ugly is a good thing, it's humbling. How shallow I was! Nearly everyone I meet is kind to me. For the first time, I actually start to believe that my possession wasn't relayed around the world. Otherwise, people wouldn't be treating me so nicely.

Or, maybe, they're just trying to turn the show into something uplifting again. Maybe they just want a chance to become celebrities. Maybe they're holding onto hope that this could still benefit Earth, with or without my consent. Maybe I actually am mentally ill. Maybe I am not doomed to a life with no privacy or respect. Maybe there is a way to escape. Maybe.

May bee you're a bumbling humble bee?

Huh?

The friends that I'm getting a ride back with want to leave a day early. I kind of want to stay but lack the courage to do so on my own. Being at a festival, surrounded by hundreds of people who don't care about me, is the best I've felt in months. My shame and anxiety have momentarily dissipated. It's glorious to feel insignificant and anonymous. These moments are treasured as I surf through the typhoon of the tormentors. A part of me is wondering if my friends want to leave early due to whispers of a protest against me, auditions for the next It girl. I am not allowed to witness the protest because of their non-disclosure sanctions against me. We end up leaving early, together. It must be because they're trying to keep me in the dark about the protest.

On the drive back there are four of us, one of whom I just met. She's friendly to the others, but cold and pretentious towards me. It's obvious that she followed my show and has decided that she loathes me. The other two are being nice but curt with me, like I'm a bothersome child. They once showered me with love. They're barely lukewarm now. I can hardly blame them.

We stop at a hot spring. The thought of exposing my blubbery body makes me queasy, but I manage to tap into self-compassion. Staring into the gently uncoiling ribbons of steam rising from the surface of the pool, I remind myself that I'm only superficially critical towards myself, that that's probably the same for most people. And, even if that isn't the case, it's ridiculous to care what others might think. I peel off my clothes, then dunk into the hot spring as quickly as I can, less exposed and awkward in the balmy water. Nobody retches, nobody screams. I still feel uncomfortable, but my higher-self reminds me that that's not actually important. I used to pray for humility out of some egotistic deluded aspiration to be a more idyllic person. I guess, in its twisted way, my wish was partly granted.

When we get back to Hornby, I spend weeks on the couch, blinds drawn, glued to the television. I have no energy. I'm wiped out from my medication, and still shell-shocked from the whole ordeal at the hospital and the events leading up to it. Yoshi's patient with me most of the time, but whenever I try to talk about the broadcast, he rolls his eyes, throws his hands in the air and walks away. He's tired of the same conversation, telling me what I'm angry about isn't real. "I don't want to hear about it!" I'm still wracked with constant anxiety, and riddled with telepathic, GPS-laser blasted riddles. As sunshine fades into the months of fall, my tormentors rally, orbiting around my skull, refusing to let me be.

Yoshi's been cooking a lot, something he's always been quite lazy about. Nearly every evening he makes dinner for the two of us, under the pretence that he's suddenly found joy in preparing food. But I know the real reason. He's trying to keep me fat. He wants me to remain in a state of discomfort. He knows that the medication I'm on increases my appetite, and he's using it against me. Yoshi wants nothing more than to perpetuate my humiliation. That is why he invited me to live with him. I have nowhere else to go, and he knows it.

My tormentors have ignored my insistence that they vacate. So here I am, spending the majority of most days in the groove my lifeless body has indented in the couch. The tormentors carry on with their invasion, inside and outside of me. They permeate the TV broadcast schedule. Admittedly, TV's way more interesting when the characters talk to you. I find sympathetic voices in programs that would have never interested me before. The aliens from *Third Rock from the Sun* have given me hope that I can frustrate the tormentors enough to abandon me altogether. None of this seems plausible, yet it really is happening. At this point, my best course is simply to do nothing at all.

The space where my spirit should be remains vacant. My phone doesn't ring any more. Somewhere, a clock ticks the time away. Every second is a second closer to my death, which will, hopefully, come soon. I wish it were possible to slough off this torturous mentality, to leap out of it. But the meds don't help, rest hasn't helped, and, well, I just don't have the capacity to do anything more for myself. I've become an annoying burden with nothing positive to offer. Worse than that, my existence is actively creating suffering for others. Yoshi avoids being home as much as he can. He used to love hermiting in his house. I'm just too insufferable. Occasionally, friends stop by. They always act kindly, but I know that it's mockery. I fantasize about dying all the time.

I've continued chain smoking in an attempt to beckon death out from the future.

More weeks pass, more cigarettes, more television, more voices talking, talking, talking.

This is the Tall King: "Talk talk tick talk tick talk. Tic toc tic toc tic talk."

Reality is rudderless. Joy's become pain, because it's all in the past. It occurs to me that the good things in my life were carefully staged, just to deepen my suffering, to give me a taste of what could have been, and to mourn its loss. My suffering is necessary for the entertainment of the cruel elite. Death feels like the only escape. God is dead to me now. More and more, I'm fantasizing about how to bring an end to my life, how to swim into the beautiful, big, black nothingness that welcomes people once their bodies stop breathing.

My whole world sits between the couch and the indecipherable murmur of occult signals from the TV set. They're making fun of me.

That's entertainment! We make fun!

Ooh, how selfish you are to just laze around!

Fucking hypocrites. Though they don't shoot to kill, the tormentors haven't ceased fire. They've laid siege on my inner monologue. They berate all my thoughts and actions, like a cancer of the mind.

Then, one evening, as I kill time on Google, I research theories on being watched. A few clicks in, a new potential explanation for what is happening to me comes into my awareness. How could I not have realized it! This makes so much sense!

What I'm experiencing isn't yogic telepathy powers, but

it isn't mental illness either. I have an electronic microchip implanted in me. I find a website that explains Micro Neurophonic Implants. Then another website explaining them. Then another. Supposedly, these implants are used to remotely transmit signal patterns directly into the brain. They can generate auditory perceptions, subliminal messages, powerful emotions, even physical sensations and movements. They're known about in parts of the conspiracy theory community, but most doctors refuse to acknowledge their existence. My heart rises. This is it! This is what is happening! And there's nothing I can do about it! The more this all makes sense, the more trapped and hopeless I start to feel. I slam the laptop shut as tears start to run down my face, falling onto the stained shirt I've been wearing for a week straight. Yoshi walks into the living room. I see him hesitate for a split second, sense him wanting to turn around like he hadn't noticed that I'm bawling my eyes out. He sighs, and asks me what's wrong.

"What the fuck! They send me subliminal messages and movements! I'm practically a fucking robot!"

Yoshi clenches at the air in exasperation, then leaves me alone with my tears. He's worn through his patience with my misery. Maybe he knows about Micro Neurophonic Implants already.

Maybe he's scared to console me in case they'd want to inject one into him too.

Late one night, as winter's numbness really settles in, making everything worse, I sit around and observe my thoughts. I notice that I'm unable to feel emotion. Without emotion in the first place, I can't actually connect to the desire to feel something. Then, in thoughts, not in sentiments, I decide that I want to feel something. Anything. Driven by curiosity, I go to the kitchen to choose my knife. A small, serrated steak knife seems like the most efficient for my experiment. With my tool, I return to the couch, roll up the legs of my sweatpants, then swiftly slice myself four times. Two on each calf. Seeing the bright red blood trickle down my legs shows evidence that I'm alive and maybe not a robot. It doesn't hurt. As I watch it flow, I become mesmerized, and don't notice Yoshi when he enters the room. He freaks out, forces me into his car, and rushes me to the hospital on Vancouver Island.

Forty-Eight

My psychiatrist taps his pen, thoughtfully. I've just explained to him that I have an MNP, a Micro Neurophonic Implant, that I'm a science experiment. He responds that this is impossible. I read that this would happen. I conclude that my doctor is either wilfully engaged in the experiment, under blackmail and forced into silence, or he is brainwashed by the powers that be, and truly believes that MNPs do not exist.

"Then why haven't the pills worked? And the shock therapy?"

"We'll adjust your prescription. Take care of yourself, Maya," he says, seeing me out the door.

They switch my medication to some other thing I can't pronounce the name of. My depression actually lifts a little, enough for me to find the motivation to start burning myself with cigarettes on my permitted fifteen-minute walks around the hospital grounds. I can't decide if it's a mind over matter practice, or just the dumb desire to feel something. Either way, it's a good sign. A light somewhere inside me is flickering back to life...

I spend five days drinking coffee out of Styrofoam cups, while I draw on cardstock I found in the psych unit's art supplies. They don't let us use regular mugs. Supposedly, those are dangerous, yet unsupervised smoke breaks somehow aren't. The result of those caffeine fuelled days is a handmade deck of tarot-like oracle cards, all original designs of mine. I even laminate them after I finish, so they can shuffle smoothly together in my hands. I've been told that divination cards are most powerful and accurate if you make them yourself. I do basic Past-Present-Future readings for two of the other patients and one of the nurses. They all say my reading made sense, genuine surprise visible in their eyes. After I explain her cards, one of them even tells me that she sees her situation differently now, that there is hope. For the first time in months, I feel good about myself.

A month goes by sluggishly, with brief reprieves from the monotony offered by the interesting folk filling the other beds of the psych ward. There's one man who thinks that he's a noble knight, not a homeless schizophrenic. He spikes his Styrofoam coffees with whiskey when he can and will be glad to jollily toast his knighthood with you. There's another girl that likes to draw too, and we share our self-taught tips. We, the mental outsiders of the world, take care of each other here. We are kind and accepting to one another when nobody else is. And there's the drugs. Everyone's mood improves when they doll out the calm pills. But, all in all, living in a hospital is pretty fucking boring.

As curfew approaches the night before my discharge, I realize it's impossible that Yoshi would want me to move back in with him. Out of consideration for others, I decide to not return to Hornby. Nobody wants me there. I'm an energy vampire, an emotional dead end. Might as well save everyone from the burden that I am. I walk to a pharmacy a few blocks away and buy three bottles of extra strength Tylenol — three hundred pills in all. Back at my room in the hospital I pour pills into my hand by the bottleful. Some of the little red pieces spill from my hand and click-clack to the tiled floor like vending-machine candy. I choke them down with water and repeat this until the last bottle is empty. Within less than a minute I am overwhelmed by nausea. I run to the bathroom and projectile vomit a gravy of pills, aiming for the toilet but spewing orange sludge all over the surrounding walls and floor. This is by far the most foul-tasting thing that I've ever experienced: an acrid, corrosive chalkiness coats my tongue. Eons worse than Ayahuasca. It hurts so much that I start using my hand to purge up the rest from my trembling body. It comes out very easily, my body completely rejecting the mountain of pills. After ten or so minutes of expelling sludge, I wipe the bathroom clean with armfuls of toilet paper, then stagger to bed and collapse into sleep. I kinda thought I'd swallow them, pass out, and, by the time anyone would think to wake me, I'd have been long dead.

I rouse from bed, extremely disappointed to be alive. Yoshi's here to pick me up. He gives me a hug, weak enough not to mask his disappointment at my release. As we walk out of the hospital lobby, I see Lynx's stepdad. I'm too horrified of what I am to say hello. I hope I look different enough for him to not recognize me, and, in thinking this, I suddenly realize that a part of me believes that I might not actually be being broadcasted. Maybe all is not lost after all.

Forty-Nine

I continue to take the new medication I was prescribed at the hospital. Less and less often voices bully me about turning out to not be a Buddha. I still feel soul killing remorse over this, and decide I am unworthy of yoga or meditation. Until, one day, my familiar, old, pre-psychotic mind chirps in, as if back from hibernation: Just because I'm not the goal doesn't mean I shouldn't be allowed to practice. In fact, that's a great reason to practice! I vocalize this realization, directing it at the people watching and criticizing me. Saying this out loud actually seems to silence the taunting — at least, when it comes to the Buddha stuff.

I start doing yoga again. I'm very out of shape and still suffering from the shock of extreme dehydration, from all the attempts to not eat, drink, or sleep for three days. It takes real willpower. I remember a yoga teacher who once said, "When yoga is most difficult to do — that is when it is most necessary." Within some two weeks of daily yoga, I can hold effortless headstands, bridges, and bows again. This partial revival comes with faint smiles, more fragile than porcelain. I'm less psychotic?

My self-esteem crawls back. I start going out in public. I go for bike rides alone and bump into familiar faces. I talk to them and they talk back warmly. They're nice. Such simple, human things. Maybe what I experienced actually was the result of mental illness. My diet returns to healthy foods.

Fruits, veggies, rice and beans. I try to treat my body with love and respect again, instead of constant apathetic overindulgence. I feel like I'm coming back to life.

As I begin to return to my old self and pick up my health-conscious lifestyle again, I decide to stop taking my medication because of the nasty side-effects; lethargy, water retention, increased appetite, and so on. And they're unnatural, probably toxic. But most of all, I feel like I don't really need the meds anymore, as I'm feeling well-ish again. The pills have served their purpose, so I abandon them. The little orange bottle rattles with pills as it bounces off the lid of the trashcan. Won't be needing those any more. And, all too soon… we're back…

It's a neurophone, not bipolar disorder. They laugh cruelly as they boom different voices into my brain.

Look… we'll make your arm twitch. My arm twitches a second later.

Hahahahaha...

Micro Neurophonic Implant Robot Girl!

Hahahahahaha…

Yoshi stresses that he wants me to take my medication. The sick part of me believes he's only saying this to appease the people who are watching. Telepathically he's agreeing with me that the meds are causing more harm than good. I don't admit that they're already long gone, thrown out with last week's garbage.

My resurrection was short lived. I become very ill again, an insufferable blob glued to the couch. I pity Yoshi for having to put up with the burden that I am. That thought strobes through my mind, commingling with all the other familiar rabble nestling back into its home.

Demands for a three-day fasting vigil have started up again. Once I do this I will be rewarded immensely. How many times do they have to tell me? On and off for a few weeks I start trying to stay awake without eating or drinking. Most of the time I cave within the first thirty-six hours, either through a mood swing or realizing that it could be insanity itself that's asking me to do this. I have no problems staying awake; drinking and eating prove my weakness. I make it to fortyish hours a few times, each time a little harder as thirst, hunger, and exhaustion take their toll.

I go to see a doctor about blood that's started showing up in my stool. While waiting in the office, I notice a syringe lying on top of the yellow toxic waste disposal box. I grab it and put it in my purse, I don't even care if it's clean. That night I try to kill myself by injecting bleach into my veins. I can only push out about a centimetre of peroxide from the needle before my arm starts to burn and seize up in agony. I do this a few times in a row, figure that ought to do it, then fall asleep. The next day I wake up surprised and, again, disappointed, to find myself alive. I then try to inject air into my veins several times, never with success. Out of frustration I crack the syringe in two, and instantly regret the destruction of a potential suicide tool. I have returned to an emotional hellscape. I am being kept alive as a tortured science experiment.

I feel guilty for existing. Yoshi is too kind to say it, but I can tell he's fed-up with living with me. He barely looks me in the eye any more. His smiles are strained, few, and far between. I can feel his regret for naively trying to help me. I can feel him forget who I was before I fell ill. Or, maybe, he's realized that person is dead, too corrupt to salvage. I have no spirit or sparkle to offer. I can feel that none of my friends want me around any more. Like a tremor through the Earth, I am unlovable.

One sunny day in early spring, Yoshi and I actually leave the house, and go for a walk through the forest. I tell him I need to leave, because it's not fair to him to have to put up with me. I'm unfixable. He doesn't protest. Him agreeing should hurt, but it's nothing compared to the insults on rotation through the neurophone. I must leave. It's now an acknowledged truth: I am unwanted.

I decide to wander via the WWOOF (Willing Workers on Organic Farms) foundation for a little while. Or, maybe, a long while. I don't know. Maybe working outside will be good for my morale. I need to start moving my body, too. A tiny ember of stupid hope ignites inside of me.

Fifty

I step off of a bus into a typically small and shabby station, then walk down a street, past rows of worn storefronts. I've arranged to volunteer on a small hobby farm in the interior of BC. I emailed several farms, and booked with the first one that replied, assuming that no one else would want me.

I find the sombre downtown plaza, take an empty bench and start to people-watch. Rubber boots and raincoats, worn from use, scutter past, most people avoiding eye contact with one another. I take notice of a frail woman and a young boy with tangled, unruly, dirty hair. They appear to be asking for directions or something. When the woman notices me watching, she abruptly walks towards me, practically dragging her tired child along behind her. They're both dressed in tatters. She points at the running shoes I have strung to the top of my backpack and asks if she can have them. I interpret this as her asking me if I want to exchange situations with her. She's resorted to metaphor because openly admitting to my celebrity remains strictly forbidden and would result in grave punishment. I untie the sneakers from my bag and hand them over without a moment's hesitation.

"Miss, being watched and judged twenty-four seven might not seem difficult to you, but yes, I will gladly trade shoes."

She looks surprised. To prove my sincerity, I offer my iPod and its charger to her son as well. His eyes bug out a little before he hesitantly reaches forward to accept it. Less is more? But, will letting go of these material possessions free me? Is this actually selfish of me? Is she going to walk a mile in my shoes now, and I hers? I shake the thoughts from my head and return to the mother and child. The boy beams, clutching the music player in his little hands, and gives me a well-practiced thank you. His wide-eyed smile makes me like myself for the first time in months. As I watch the beggars walk away, I wonder if we did, in fact, just trade circumstances.

I locate a bunged-up payphone stall, and punch the number from my pocket into the cold and sticky metal keys. A jolly voice answers right away, and my host George tells me he'll come collect me from the plaza in the better part of an hour. I return to the same bench as before, under storm clouds that are rolling in overhead. A man in a fancy suit sits down on the bench beside mine and lights up a cigarette while he unfolds a newspaper.

"Excuse me, could I trouble you for a cigarette?"

He hands me three, winks, and says, "Pay it forward."

"I think I just paid it behind," I say. He looks at me quizzically, as if I'm delirious, and absorbs himself in the newspaper.

Flame sparks from my lighter. I pull gently on the cigarette, and that breezy dizziness fills the front of my head. It's been days since I've smoked. I fold up the butt and score a goal on a nearby trash can. I fidget to stay warm for a few minutes, then light another. As I'm rubbing out the final embers of the third cigarette into the pavement, a voice asks, "Hi there, are you Maya?"

"That's me!" I reply with a smile, strangely elated, buzzed on tobacco and the cusp of new adventures.

George, in cowboy hat and trim grey beard, stands before me. He tells me he's grateful to have some help as I follow his broad hat through the streets to his rusty green pickup truck. "Hop in!" I clamber into the cab. The whole interior is coated in a soft layer of dust. George cranks the engine to a sputter and asks me what kind of food and beer we should pick up while we're in town. His kindness is baffling. I thought everyone hated me. Maybe changing stages means that a fresh movie is being made. Or, did I literally trade paths with the woman who took my shoes? Is this the dawn that follows a long nightmare? His kindness can't be sincere though. Can it? I chalk it up to pity as a fine drizzle starts to fall on the fields and ranches, we cruise past.

When we run out of small talk, George twists the radio's volume knob to the right and fills the truck with twangy country music. I bite my tongue and shake my head as I pretend, I don't mind the whiney music.

During my grand tour of the hobby farm, the sky clears and the sun beams down on George, I, and the two clumsy baby goats frolicking alongside us. He walks me through the sprouting veggie patch. Kale's the only thing thriving at the moment. All the beds are covered in a thick blanket of damp weeds. We cross the property to the large fenced-in chicken coop.

"Cluck, cluck, cluck," George squeaks, in a high-pitched voice, as he shows me the ramshackle hutch where the food pellets are kept. Hens in hues of teak and amber fuss about their wire-mesh enclosure in aimless excitement. "Every morning they get about half a bucket of feed sprinkled around the coop. The big golden one's my favourite. Her name's Turkey. You can name the others if you like. Since you're the first farm-hand of the season, you get to stay in the spare room. The others will have to tent when they arrive."

We walk towards a tiny old brick house, past half a dozen pear saplings. He opens the door to the muddiest mud room I've ever been in. It is built up like melted candle wax in places. I shake my boots off of my feet and follow George to my room. "It ain't much, but it's cosier than a tent." The walls are a faded blue. Most of the space is taken by a twin bed with mismatched blankets, and the empty bookshelf across from them. He smiles at me again.

"Make yourself at home. Help yourself to anything in the kitchen. Coffee's ready around eight a.m. We'll get to work after."

In the morning, I drag myself out of bed, wanting to ensure I don't sleep in on my first day. I throw on a pair of old jean shorts and a thrift store t-shirt then make my way to the small, cluttered kitchen. George is dull-eyed, pouring water into the coffee maker.

"Sleep all right, Maya?"

"Better than I have in quite some time," I tell him, surprised by that truth.

We bring our mugs to the veranda and chat as we listen to birds sing. I down two mugs of strong, black coffee and ask where he'd like me to start. "If you could feed the chickens, weed the far veggie patch, then plant the carrots and beets in it, that'd be mighty appreciated. After that, come in for breakfast. I'll whip us up some omelettes. I make a mean green omelette."

The day passes with ease. We have a leisurely breakfast, chat about this and that. I learn that there's no Mrs. George. She passed three years ago.

"And let me tell you, Maya, since then I sure do love meeting all the different folk that come through here. Sure, is nice to get someone with experience, though. Some people show up here not knowing a dandelion from sorrel," he chuckles. I nod while I try to imagine how it would feel to lose your closest and longest companion. Then I realize that I don't even know what it'd feel like to have a partner for decades, to synchronize life paths and dreams together. To stay by each other through the highest highs and the lowest lows.

"I'm sorry for your loss."

"Ain't that life, though. It gets easier. Just gotta keep myself busy and get out and about so I don't get too lonesome."

There's a long, speechless pause. Unable to find appropriate words of consolation, I ask him what's the next task for the day.

"Woodshed needs a paint job. I've got loads of leftover, uh... auburn, and teal, paint. You pick which colour you think'd look best. After that you can call it a day. No need to overdo it."

In the evening he invites me to a local gathering. I agree to come along, despite the anxiety that going out in public tends to give me. We hop in the truck and trundle down a dirt road a few miles, then pull into the community hall. Inside, there's about thirty people, smiling, mingling, all seeming to know one another. I try to swallow my timidity as George introduces me to everyone. "Everyone, this is Maya. Maya, this is everyone." Eyes surround me. Piercing, glittering eyes. Being the centre of attention makes my heart pound. The voices redeploy for the first time since I left hornby.

What is she doing here?

I forgot about that ridiculous show!

I want peace and quiet in this community!

It's like they're more mad at the tormentors that hijacked my life then they are at me. I deepen my breath, hold my ground, and, astonishingly, the voices actually fade away. A jam starts up. A couple of guitars, a xylophone, a few hand drums. Most people break start to dance. I join in, mostly to avoid social interactions. Everyone I do end up talking to is warm, some even give me welcome hugs. The people here range from twentyish to fiftyish, and all seem to be gardeners, artists, do-it-yourself societal dropouts. My people, you might say.

It feels good to be working outdoors. My depression halts here and there, but is usually present, like a gargantuan, black storm cloud, taunting its power. Some days I work a lot and some days I just sit around after a few hours. George seems okay with this. He never pushes me to work when I'm not in the mood to. Some afternoons, we sit on the porch and drink beer, chatting until the sun goes down. I really lucked out on farms, considering I just picked the first one that replied to me. At the time, I had assumed no one else would respond. Who could possibly want me?

One afternoon, while George and I are kneeling in the wet, soil planting beans, he abruptly asks me if I'm mentally ill. I freeze. Nobody's ever asked me this before. Will he kick me out? I tell him I was diagnosed as bipolar, then later as schizoaffective type bipolar. I search his eyes for judgment, but find none. He just listens calmly as I confide in him my diagnosis.

A new farmer arrives for the season and almost instantly sparks up a 'nice to meet you' doobie. A minute after passing it, my mind rapidly reaches a simmer, then boils over with voices of fierce urgency, so many at once that I can't even distinguish them. They are one roar, a wave of voices. I leave the guys and go and lay down in bed, waiting for the miserable storm to pass. Then it breaks, and I can make out the words. It is being explained to me that I'm a robot. The original me died during a suicide attempt. The soul I can remember having has departed this incarnation. Using the microchip that they implanted in me, they revived my body, all of its organs, even my now-soulless brain. I have become an android. It seems unlikely...

We'll show you!

All of a sudden, my arm gets... moved, raised up into the air, then spins around without my intention.

See? You're a robot. We control you now. Look, we'll go make you eat!

My body, against my wanting, lifts itself up and saunters into the kitchen. I'm a marionette machine. It feels the same as what happened in Thailand. I've lost control of myself to the tormentors, they're able to manipulate every muscle of my body. They flex my left arm up to the cupboard, pull it open and grab some tortilla chips. I try to pull my hand away, but it doesn't obey. It's like I'm watching television.

Haha, you're a robot.

I get roboted back to my room and lay in bed, terrified. Check it out, try and move...

Go on, move your arm!

I push with all my concentration to make my brain send the signal to move my arm. It doesn't move. It no longer belongs to me. I'm paralyzed, terrified, and surrounded again by a chorus of wicked voices that I cannot silence.

Haha! You can't, Robitch!

Fifty-One

I'm roboted to move to another farm. I wish I could stay, but it's not up to me anymore. I make my way to town to meet a woman whose WWOOF listing says she's building an ecovillage. As I step off the bus, a tanned woman with dark brown hair that falls to her waist walks over, smiles, and says, "Welcome, sister," then hugs me. Like the last place, she instantly treats me like a dear old friend. Once we get my bags unloaded and take our seats in her van, she looks into my eyes and asks me how I'm doing. Maybe the viewers' fervour has settled, now that it's been unveiled that my miscreant actions and words were electronic and against my will. We get to Lola's property, her ecovillage is barely in the conception stage. She introduces me to the only other volunteer, Mario, a middle-aged masseuse trying to purify his soul for the 2012 galactic shift.

He's also very kind to me, which is strange and confusing. How could people possibly like me?

In the evening, I sit outside and breath in the freshly mowed field where Lola intends on building her village of clay-and-straw cobb homes. As the sky dims into twilight, I see two spirits slowly drift across the property. They are shaped like humans, but are formed from static, instead of solid, and float along a few inches above the ground, weightlessly. They cast a gentle glow, and disturb nothing as they glide across the property. I don't question this phenomenon at all, just let myself enjoy the calm that they emanate. I turn in as the air cools, knowing I should rise early tomorrow morning.

At dawn, I'm roboted to meditate in the brick courtyard, weeds crowding through every gap like tiny fingers, while I wait for Lola and Mario to rise. I don't protest this subordination, it's actually quite pleasant. I needed a reboot. Lola and Mario appear from the main house and join me. After tea and smoothies, Lola asks me where I'd like to start.

"Would you like it if I weeded the courtyard?"

"If that's the kind of thing you're in the mood for, that would be wonderful!" She goes on to insist that I follow the rhythm of my energy levels, and to use the tasks as mindfulness practices. By noon, the cracks in the courtyard are all smooth and dark. In the afternoon, I walk the three adopted street dogs down backcountry roads. Afterwards, I do gentle yoga in the field where I saw the incorporeal beings last night.

On the evening of the New Moon, Lola and I linger at the patio table long after dinner ends, talking softly by candlelight. As night's shadow falls in, I start to see the faces of various other wise women I've known appear across her face, morphing and trading places with each other. Sitting there in the tea-coloured glow of the flames, it seems I am visited by every powerful, inspiring woman I've ever known. Mentors from Hornby, gurus from travels, distant friends that I admire. The shadowy masks of these women play across Lola's face, and their energy radiates from her. All of the women that came through her are kind avatars of feminine strength. They are all sending me love. I'm immersed in their affection, rejuvenated by it. Even though I might be a robot, the world has tinted rose for this moment. Perhaps doing my best to stay in the present moment will be my salvation.

Some days are difficult. Some are joyous and satisfying. The dirt in my nails, the stillness in the air, and the shared effort to make the world a peaceful place feels so good after months of sedentary depression. My emotions are stabilizing and my body is returning to health? I'm breathing calmly again?

One day, Mario and I walk the dogs together. We arrive at the river, unleash the dogs so they can swim. We sit down beside the water for our first deep conversation. I am shocked by the direction of his words. Until now, all I knew about him is that he's here to spiritually cleanse and elevate himself in positivity to prepare for the 2012 astral shift. And what does he do, but start dissing Lola. I don't care to join in on the negativity, and, gratefully, I'm not roboted into doing so.

"She thinks she's an angel!" he says, exasperated.

"I used to think I was an angel."

"Really? What do you think you are now?" Mario asks.

"A robot."

He has a surprisingly subdued reaction. He must have already known. Conversation keeps flowing like the water beside us. Soon we're laughing like little kids, as we puzzle out our hypocrisies and dreams.

One evening, while the planets are alleged to be doing something rare and significant, I sit outside under the stars. As I cast my eyes toward a hedge about ten feet ahead, it starts to come alive. Suddenly, the leaves start to morph, sort of spin-melt, one by one. While I'm mesmerized by their swirl, Lola comes over to me.

"Did you take peyote?" I promptly ask, wondering if the explanation given to me — that I'm absorbing her peyote experience — is true.

"No," she replies gently, as if that was a completely normal question to ask.

"The bushes are dancing," I say.

She sits beside me and we talk for a little while. We share a nice silence, then another long dialogue, late into the night. I am grateful for her openness, the way she doesn't seem to judge. Maybe she is an angel. She tells me she saw a spirit on the property today. I tell her I saw two the night I arrived, but none today. The leaves around us are still frolicking in fractals. I re-mention the lightshow to her. She's still seeing them how they usually appear, almost motionless. She asks me if I want to see my body's energy lines. I do.

We walk over to Raven, her rusty old van, and Lola flicks on the high beams into the black night.

"Put your hands in front of the light," she says. I see them right away, lines of blue light coming out of my fingertips, motes of pollen swirling in the beams. "Yours is blue," she says, confirming that what I'm seeing is real. Or, well, at least a shared vision. I suppose that's what reality is though: the most common, agreed upon, illusion.

We keep talking, until, once again, her face starts to shift between the faces of all the wise women that I've known and admired. It's as if they're trying to let me know that I'm safe with Lola.

A few days later, I continue on to the next farm, wondering if I'm being roboted, or simply carrying on because that's what I tend to do. So, I'm a nomadic pilgrim cyborg? The thought is so bizarre that I actually have to laugh, rather than contemplate in horror.

Fifty-Two

From a window seat on a bus headed to a city I've never been to, I stare out the window at the rock walls lining the highway. The surface of the stone ripples over with hundreds of faces, thousands of eyes, countless spirits looking back at me, seeing through me, being one with me. It's the Earth, her spirit, composed of pieces of countless other timeless souls. They are trying to communicate with me, to reconnect me to source essence. Earth feels my actions. Earth hears my thoughts. She cries with me, she rejoices with me. The elements, the creatures, that which I am made of, are trying to re-harmonize with me. I feel Earth's voice whisper inside of me, "You have to heal. We need you."

I get off the bus in the city I set out for. I have a little bit of money that Lola graciously gifted to me as I was leaving her place. If I'm frugal, I will be able to wander freely for a little while. It is time to let Earth's spirit guide me.

Walking the fresh streets, I slow down to look at some of the trees along the way. Their bark does the same thing that the rock did. When I stop to look at it, first it is still, then its bark coalesces into a whirling mosaic of faces looking back at me. The faces are friendly and calm. They're ancient, all-knowing, and all-loving. When I look up from the trunks, everything else appears as per the usual, agreed-upon illusion: motionless and solid. The trees are trying to communicate something, specifically. I can't quite unpack the message.

A sacred hush has fallen over the street. I guess because, well, everything is sacred? As I watch, faces rise and fall, birth and die in and out of each other, I'm reminded that all is one and all is infinite, and all is in a constant dance and evolution. Life is a flow, ever changing. Perhaps their message is to not cling to the past or dwell in the imagined future. I've so missed this feeling, this satiating connection to divinity. Eventually, I stop staring into the trees and continue to walk around the city. Refreshed, I smile at all the people I come in contact with. They smile back at me.

Maybe I am a robot, though I don't feel like one at the moment. Or, at very least, I'm a sentient robot. Maybe I am being watched by satellites. Maybe the people watching do send me energy that alters my feelings and actions. Maybe I'm going through psychosis. Maybe I've opened myself up to uncharted realms, without proper guidance. Maybe it's a combination of some, or all, of those theories. Or, maybe, it's something entirely different, a phenomenon that I haven't even conceived or considered yet. I yoyo between which philosophy feels most true. I yearn to understand, yet to decide that I could possibly understand what reality is seems outrageously naive. At moments I actually feel like my pre-shattered self, the one that was numb and in shock, the me that felt like it had died and misplaced its soul. Sometimes, it's as if different spirits are simultaneously battling for control of my body, they argue and pull me out of harmony. If that's what's happening, I suppose, in a way, We are One.

Fifty-Three

I drift to Vancouver and set up camp on a beach that's about a fifteen-minute walk from the city's centre. It's warm here. I tell myself that it is safe to sleep on the sand under a primitive driftwood roof because I'm being watched. But when I stop to analyse that reasoning, it occurs to me that I'm in denial. The people broadcasting me don't give a damn about my wellbeing. Haven't I been under their watch for years? Haven't they always sat idle, laughing and revelling in my suffering? Was I not being watched that night in Bolivia, when the crooked narco assaulted me? Didn't they put me through needless electroshock therapy? Was it not because of them that I became an object of mass hatred and humiliation? To trust in the protection of their gaze is foolish.

Tumultuous anxiety reclaims me. Many days go by where I panhandle in the morning, then head for the liquor store, then drink myself numb while I stare blankly into the sea. The voices only I seem to hear have swelled to an overwhelming crescendo. They've become self-possessed, and argue amongst each other, in addition to simply bullying me. Sometimes, I just sit and listen to them converse and brawl with each other. I've started to refer to this as "listening to the radio." I decide to leave my beach camp due to the fear and misery that has been escalating with every day that passes.

In downtown Vancouver, planless, and practically penniless, I sneak onto the Sky Train and blast through black tunnels and glassy cityscapes at high speed, just ride around, back and forth, killing time. When Transit Security enters the trains to check tickets, I hop off and slide into the crowd.

Exhausted, I find an arbitrary park. Birds lullaby me as I collapse into sleep under them. The birds' song is still in the air when, in the early evening sky, someone gently stirs me awake and hands me a twenty. I stay awake all night in a nearby cafe, slowly sipping bottomless refill coffees and drawing on napkins.

I feel the pull of nature and the sanity that it sometimes brings. I set out for the Sea-To-Sky highway at the cliff-braced outskirts of Vancouver. My ascent of the steep road starts on foot. If I walk the whole way, I'll be able to accomplish staying awake for three days without eating or drinking. I commit my entire self to this attempt, although for whom, I am no longer certain. A few hours into my pursuit, an old blue station wagon trundles past, slows down, then pulls to a stop along the shoulder of the highway ahead of me. An arm emerges from the driver's window and waves me over. Curious. It's not like I'm hitchhiking. As I approach the car, a smiling face pokes out the window. It takes me half a second to recognise the driver, a vaguely familiar acquaintance from high school. He offers me a ride. This encounter is compelling proof that I'm being followed, watched, broadcasted. He knew where I was and came to find me.

"No thanks," I say, and keep walking, determined to complete my vigil. He seems disappointed, even hurt, at my dismissal. Confused, I shake it off. He must have been either trying to interrupt my vigil, or he came to find me to make sure that I know that I'm still being broadcasted. But I'm determined to succeed this time, to abstain from food, water, and sleep for 72 hours. I'm going to earn my passage back into a bliss realm.

Hours later, it switches, again. What I'm being instructed

to do does not make sense. The logic of my mission has become as breathless as I have. The voices are just messing with me, they must be. Doing anything for seventy-two hours is impossible when one has multiple robot controllers vying to subvert them. I halt my march, jam out my thumb, and am quickly picked up by an elder living on a First Nations reserve about halfway between here and Whistler. I ask to be dropped off at a lake — any lake — and I am. We sit and talk for a while, then I set out into the forest trail that leads to the lake.

Once it feels like I am the right distance away from humanity on each side of the trail, I drop my bag, sit down on a log, and burst into tears. Great, heaving sobs of pain. Yet these tears are not my own. It's the Earth that is crying through me. Then, all of a sudden, I am roboted to leave the forest and continue walking up the highway. The traffic is violent and obnoxious, not the hike I had in mind. I stick out my thumb again. Someone headed to the Whistler Village picks me up and takes me straight there.

I take a nap on a bench, until I am woken by someone who wants to give me money, again. This adds to my certainty that I am under watch. I don't look like a typical homeless person, and I'm not even asking, but people keep giving me money. They know I need it. My show is more interesting when I have cash. Heavily depressed and mad at myself for giving up on trying to stay awake, I spend the money on whiskey. Night is falling. The liquor will keep me warm. So different from the last time I was here, at the yoga conference.

I'm miserable. I'm aimless. I'm cold, exhausted, and utterly confused. Broken, I go to the walk-in clinic and ask to be taken to the nearest psychward. Back to North Vancouver I go.

Fifty-Four

I'm already fit, a lean and strong one hundred and twenty pounds. But I want to be little again. I spend the first two days on cardio reps, running, and yoga all day, all while abstaining from food. I want to look good. Maybe, then I'll feel good, too. After a few days, and seven pounds less, the robot controllers strike again. I'm piloted to the psychward's kitchen where there is a ready supply of juice, muffins, and sandwiches for us patients. I eat and eat and eat. The robot controllers are rolling in the aisles laughing. Their cruel cackling echoes through my head. They call me disgusting for what they're roboting me to do. More than anything, I wish they would leave me alone.

After a few days of automatic consumption, I enter another fitness frenzy. I hear one of the nurses say to my doctor, "She switched."

We've flicked the switch.

Haha! Robitch!

I watch my body be taken to the kitchen and start eating oily bran muffins. So many muffins. I make a sign in protest for the people watching to have sympathy for me, and walk up and down the ward brandishing it. "Robots have feelings too!"

One of the other patients reads the sign, and says, "Well, okay!" I feel her compassion, even though I'm a robot. One of the nurses points her fingers at me and coldly tells me to take off my sign. She doesn't care that I feel. I am not on the same level as true human beings.

One of the other patients looks vaguely like Snape from the Harry Potter movies. I decide that he is, in fact, Severus Snape, that cameras make people look slightly different. Movies are created by satellites watching people, and cutting and pasting the footage together in scenes. That's why the people in them are called "stars." They're filmed from satellites flying around with the stars in the sky. Snape's totally nice. "They portrayed you so unfairly," I thought-share with him. I wonder how many other tormented movie slaves there are.

Bright yellow sunshine streams in through the common room windows. I want to be free, it's summer! I request a lawyer to try to get me discharged. Our case folds. My doctor's report on me reads: "Her physical and mental state would deteriorate if we let her go."

I become marginally better and exaggerate my wellness to my doctor. After a couple of weeks of my insistence, the staff comply and release me to a homeless shelter across the city. As I'm collecting my few belongings, I realize that being in the hospital wasn't so bad, other than the sheer boredom. There were some cool people here. Everyone's kind, no one judges or bullies. A quiet, enclosed environment was probably exactly what I needed — and still need. Little do I know that, in just a few short days, looking back on the North Van hospital will come to seem like a paradise lost.

Fifty-Five

Upon arrival at the sinister grey building, just beyond the suburbs, the staff spray everyone's bags with harsh chemicals to control bedbug infestations. As they open my backpack to sterilize it, I stare at the organic fair trade coffee beans that I've been carrying around to chew on, for the times when I needed energy to stay awake for safety. It's treated as heavily as everything else inside, sizzling with spray. I don't belong here. Or rather, I wish I didn't belong here. Realm hopping isn't fun any more.

The people here are mostly haggard old drug addicts and alcoholics. A lot of the old men hit on me, and keep creeping after I bluntly voice my disinterest. There's a dullness in their eyes, a vacancy I cannot stand to be around. I want to die. The shelter has another refuge in a more vibrant part of the city. Maybe being there could lessen my utter lack of desire for life. I request a transfer and, after a few days on a waitlist, the call comes through.

It's close to downtown. The nice downtown, with clean sidewalks and busy shops and people that smile; not the impoverished, drug-addled, dead-end downtown. Like the last place, it's mostly men dwelling here. Old, dirty, most of them intoxicated. There's a large, cot-lined dormitory in the basement that houses them. On the second floor are tiny, shared rooms for the females, two or three women in each. We have to be out of our rooms during the day. Breakfast, lunch, and dinner are served in a rudimentary dining hall. The food's all donated, and is usually expired and stale. There's a common room adjoining the eating area, with a TV and hard metal benches with plastic "cushions" that are rarely unoccupied, and always damp with chemical spray. We are shouted awake if we try to sleep on them because, already, there are not enough seats to go around.

A scrawny, gap-toothed man tyrannizes the channel dial. It's set to football at all times. I hate football. He screams at anyone who tries to change channels, spit dripping from his disgusting face. When he looks me in the eye, my soul feels dirty. Most people have given up fighting with the old asshole to change stations. There's a little outdoor smoking area in the back that's hidden from the road and the renovated brick buildings beyond. That about sums it up.

The people here are in rough shape. Full-blown addicts with nothing left to live for, and the severely ill; down on their luck, abandoned, shunned, all alone. Needless to say, all parties are impoverished and forlorn. I hear them telepathically trash-talking me. They know all about my life. I've travelled the world. I'm a princess. The naive, stupid, snobby princess. "Princess" resounds in my mind, dripping with disdain. Even here, rapidly approaching rock-bottom, I am resented.

I share a room with two other women. Breanne is about forty, fresh out of rehab, and on heavy methadone. All of the shuddersome men here get easy winks and smiles from her. But she's ice-cold towards me, except when she wants a cigarette. One morning, I'm doing sit-ups on my hard bed. When room-lockout time comes, we go downstairs. She walks over to a group of men waiting in the breakfast line and loudly says, "She has an eating disorder," to the crowd. Heads turn and stare at me with their blank, bleary eyes. She's just a junior high bully, trapped in a decaying middle-aged body.

People are on edge here, and petty fights frequently break out in the dorms and hallways. They snap at each other like dogs fighting over scraps. Poverty is like a contagion of anger. I've returned to numbness. I want absolutely nothing to do with this realm.

I don't reach out to any of my old friends that live in the city. I've isolated myself for too long, those bridges have all gone up in flames. They've probably all heard that I fell ill by now. Maybe they're afraid of me. Mental illness has a horrible stigma. It's been so long since I've connected with any of them that I doubt they'd even care. I'm just a memory, a sad story, something interesting to talk about, as they do nothing but pretend they still care about me. I who, sadly, is no longer fit for friendship. Besides, I was a miserable bitch during the months before I went full-fledged insane anyway, snapping in deluded anger at the slightest offense. Not unlike the seething people around me at the shelter. And now, here I am, years later, still crazy, a vapid soul among even further gone zombies. Who could possibly want me around?

I still love all the people that I was friends with before I lost my mind. I miss them unbearably. I miss myself. I can't let go of my past, when I was surrounded by so many good people and when life was hopeful and sort of made sense, and was full of opportunities, options, choices. I'm surrounded by people here — bitter, damaged, vindictive people — but I hermit myself. I'd rather be completely alone than participate in their callous spiral.

I used to be optimistic. I've lost the energy to hope for a better future. It's foolish, stupid. It would only set me up for more disappointment. Look at where I am. I'm never going to climb out of this pit. It's too deep. Now, a good day is one with breaks in the auditory audience, moments where no one is looking down at me in my pit, sneering as they toss stones for a laugh, while I wallow helplessly.

I spend a lot of my time distracted, "listening to the radio." I hate the fucking radio. There are a few okay moments, the rare kind voice in my head trying to make light of things with feeble jokes. But, for the vast majority, life is suffering. It's fully possible that I will continue to live in anguish and squalor, and even worse. Poverty and insanity, together, form a vortex of social antigravity. I'm surrounded by older people that have been trapped in gloom for most of their lives.

Unlike me, these people didn't suddenly become homeless yesterday. They've been stuck here for years. This shelter must be like a nice vacation for them. I cannot guess where this path will lead, but I'm afraid to move any farther forward. I don't deserve this. Does anyone?

The shelter staff force me to take the prescribed antipsychotics. Medication is doled out daily in little paper cups, under watchful eyes, to ensure we swallow it. Despite obediently taking the pills, I am still tormented by an ongoing diatribe of cruel taunts. Whatever compassion I had left for myself has been annihilated. I can't hear it through all the hateful noise.

One of the few young guys staying at the shelter asks me if I want to come look at a house that's advertising rooms for rent. I tag along for the slim chance to get away, doubtful that anyone

would accept me as a tenant. I have no references, I'm unemployed, and I live in a homeless shelter. We find the address that he's scribbled onto a torn scrap of paper. The green calm of the other lawns on the block ends here. Trash festers on the brown, reedy grass: beer cans, gas station coffee cups, pulled-apart plastic bags. We walk up the porch steps where a pile of soggy newspapers leaches into the rotting wood, and ring the doorbell.

A middle-aged woman in stained sweatpants opens the door. She doesn't even ask our names, just walks us to the two vacant rooms in the large, rundown house. There are five rooms in total, each costing four hundred dollars a month. They're rooms. I can say that much about them. The two men living here are conspicuously disinterested in meeting us. They barely glance in our direction. After the landlady, who turns out to be the only woman, has lazily shown us the shabby rooms, she immediately asks if we'll take them, as if she's as desperate as us.

Having no alternative, I ignore the red flags. The woman signs both of our disability rent forms within five minutes of being here, no questions asked. In a couple of weeks, November is going to roll around, and I am going to move in. As I bus back to the shelter, I get queasy wondering why they were so incautious to find tenants, still ignoring my intuition as it tries to holler above the voices, insisting that I not move into that place with those people.

I should be in a good mood, I just found somewhere to live. But I already know it's going to be bad. I'm ignoring the obvious, blocking out what I don't want to think about. Yet being back at the shelter makes it hard to conclude that it would be a mistake to leave. Poverty has made everyone here rut-minded, angry, and mean. Each day I hate being here more than the last. The days leading up to my departure cannot go by fast enough.

It's welfare check day, and everyone has money for the first time in weeks. I open the bathroom door and walk in on two women smoking something white and gooey from a dirty glass pipe.

"Can I try?" just comes out of my mouth.

"You've never smoked rock?"

"No."

They pass me the crack pipe and show me how to smoke it. Steel wool jabs into the tip so the crack doesn't fall through when it melts and burns under the flame. I inhale the spiralling smoke through the other end.

Bam. Stress and misery blast away. The voices shut up. I suddenly appreciate my company. I feel relaxed, content, and alert.

"I want more." Brittany, who's pushing twenty-five but looks forty, takes my hand and brings me to the common room. She lets go and walks across the room to the fat toothless pervert by the television set, points at me, and cackles, "She likes rock!" He tells me to come with him. I wave at Brittany to come with us, afraid of being alone with this man. We go to the street and he gives me a bright little pebble of paste to smoke.

For the first time in so long there's silence inside my mind. No voices, no insults, just silence. Everything is sparkling, the breeze is fresh and delightful, my mind is calm and crystal clear. I'm composed, serenely awake. Move over, medication. This stuff actually works.

"I want more," I let him know, as soon as the peak high begins to waver.

He crams more in the pipe and passes it to me. As I pull

the smoke into my lungs, he starts groping me. Rough, abused hands doing rough, abusive things. It's nasty being touched by him, but easy enough to kinda just ignore it through the high. I take another hoot. A few more guys from the shelter come and form a circle around us.

"How much rock would it take to let me fuck you?" one of the younger ones asks.

"A lot," I say with a confident and playful smile that must be influenced by the crack.

He produces a white rock the size of my thumbnail and I take several gigantic hoots. It mists and smoulders inside the pipe, smoke whirls and separates off of the densely-packed chemicals. It unfurls up into the flat, grey sky, riveting me. I barely notice having sex with him, out in the alley, in front of the others. By the time I do, he's already come in me, it's over. Like it didn't even happen.

"Wow!" I giggle in surprise, wiping the cum trickling down my thighs with my skirt, then reach for the pipe again. I don't want this feeling to end. I'm in awe… it's marvellous to have a mind free of voices, chatter, and constant beratement. Nothing else exists in this high. It feels miraculous. Everything's silent and sparkly. Maybe I'll die. This would be a lovely way to die. Maybe there's a cloud in heaven waiting for me, where I could lay my head down and rest on it's clean fluffiness. That'd be nice.

The shelter staff hear about the crack incident and kick me out. "It's not fair! Pretty much everyone else is obviously getting high too!" I protest. One of the younger, less destroyed men, walks over and whispers that it's for my safety. "The other women want to beat you up." I'm not sure if I believe him. I guess it doesn't really matter. They send me back to the other shelter in the dull part of town, but it's only a couple of days until I can move into the room I rented. At the other shelter, I get some men to procure more crack for me. They're unsurprisingly eager to provide. I'm not ready to return to the way I normally feel.

Fifty-Six

My new roommates make my skin crawl. They're cold-blooded, narcissistic, demonic. They come into my room when I'm not home. I'll return and find the things in my dresser drawers rummaged through, my clothes scattered on the floor. The worst is coming home to find the few objects of worship that I have left, arranged on a shelf in a crude but sacred altar, scattered and stolen. My prayers themselves have been vandalized. It makes me shiver to my core. After a week of begging, the robot controllers finally allow my body to buy a padlock.

I can tell from the chemical smell that two of my roommates are regularly smoking drugs, as well as openly taking GHB. Sometimes they offer me some. I'm so dead inside that usually, I take what they offer. The landlady woman and her partner scream and fight at all hours of the day. She scares me as much as the men do, massive, volatile, and callous as she is. These people are mean-spirited children walking around in intoxicated adult bodies, no different from the shelter folk. My already blown mind reels. My world has become a spooky wasteland. What the fuck am I doing here? I wish the controllers would let me leave.

Since I was discharged from the hospital, I keep thinking I've hit rock bottom, but the descent into fiery hell deepens. I've been pushed off a cliff. As I plummet, I crash into boulders and trees, bashing my bloody, wounded limbs. I can't believe I was dumb enough to numb myself out on a crack bender. My brain is a broken vase. That this could all be laid at the feet of mental illness has actually become the most encouraging possibility. Then there'd be some potential remedy, an escape door. But the pills were useless to me. I am, can only be, a helpless cyborg science experiment.

One night, I lock myself in my room, wishing I could escape this house and the people that inhabit it. I lay in bed, listening to the radio, my body paralysed again. I'm trying to move my limbs, but can't reach them. This brings their attention back on me.

Robitch. You're trapped here.

"Let me kill myself!" I plead to the robot controllers, quivering through the tears. They refuse. I am helpless to liberate myself from this torture.

The various controllers direct my movements and words differently. Multiple Programmer Disorder would be an appropriate name. The robot controllers fight over which new experiments to force me through next. I watch it all, through my eyeball cameras, unable to reach the off button.

You're in the Realm of the Hungry Ghosts. The next time you get the opportunity to escape samsara, you'd best take it.

"That doesn't even make sense... I'm a fucking robot! How is it my decision?" Or are you being moved by ghosts and spirits?

Are the spirits and ghosts trying to make you feel dead because they're suffering? Nothing is permanent.

Remember this.

Because the robot controllers won't let me kill myself, I scour my war-torn brain for solace. A rare kind moment flies in from out of the abyss and the radio DJ reminds me that just because something feels real, doesn't make it true. I think back to the palm readers in India who told me to remember through difficult times that I chose a life where I wanted to learn a lot, and that the truly grand parts of my life, I'd have to wait for. It's not very comforting, but it's all I have to cling to. Death won't return my calls.

The controllers finally let me leave. Or, at least, they stop preventing me from doing so. I purchase a bus ticket to Fernie, a small ski town in the interior. I've never been there, just heard nice things about it, years ago, from friends that I am probably now dead to. It's a spontaneous destination.

I flee Vancouver, traumatized from these past few weeks... months... years... On the bus ride, I pray for a fresh start. That seems all that's left to me now, is prayer. It's not much. I'm not so sure I still believe in God. This world is just too cruel. God would be kinder. I'm fleeing danger, but have no guarantee of exiting this downward spiral, come my arrival at my destination. This is just another makeshift move, another something else. It's practically hopeless. My doom has spread as wide as the sea, and I'm a wreck in it, splintered across its rocky shores. Fantasizing about dying has become a constant backdrop of my thoughts. I wish that the robot controllers would let me take my insufferable life.

Fifty-Seven

I reach Fernie, locate its lone hostel, and ask if they have any vacancies at the monthly rate. The clerks reply with friendly smiles. But, when it comes time to pay from my empty pocket, I have to get the owners of the hostel to sign a Social Assistance form that would cover my rent. When I confide my bipolar disorder, the stigma is palpable. Smiles vanish, postures tighten. Eye contact is lost, and the manager's hand wavers before she moves to sign the form, as if scouring her brain for an excuse to refuse me. When they hand me my dorm key, their tone of voice is beyond awkward. It's hostile.

I walk around town, head hung low. I don't raise my eyes till I reach the old wood and steel railroad passing through. I fantasize about throwing myself into an oncoming freight train, or, better yet, just standing there, staring down the oncoming pillar of sheer locomotion, all black smoke and white light and raw momentum, about how wonderful it would be to splatter my body and end this nightmare. Like the train I swallowed on ayahuasca, that blasted me back to Earth's embrace.

We're only keeping you alive to torture you, you know. Go ahead... just try to walk over to the train tracks...

I try to get up from where I'm sitting. My brain strains like a sore muscle but can't conduct my body to move onto the tracks. The robot controllers send me a chorus of cruel laughter. Some of the voices I hear laughing are familiar, old friends who loathe me now. Some belong to familiar strangers who have been watching for years. It goes on, I'm being kept alive by the dark sciences, tortured in the name of entertainment.

More and more since I was released from the hospital, I've been using alcohol as a coping mechanism. Whiskey, wine, beer. Anything will do. Nowadays, the only way I can fall asleep is if I'm stone drunk. There's a little bar at the hostel. Word quickly got out that I have mental health issues. The other tenants, who are mostly international party kids, gossip openly about me. I hear them warn others against me. Faces at the bar stools seek me out while they speak. But conversation with people in the normal Earth realm has a silencing effect on the voices inside my head. Even when the people are being rude and prejudiced, which has been the case for the most part, just sitting with them is a miraculous break from the hell that has been flowing in and out of my botbrain.

The regulars at the hostel's bar continue to bully and isolate me. There's one bartender who always refuses me service, gives bullshit reasons like, "You've had too much to drink," when I haven't had anything to drink, yet. Someone must have overheard me explaining my disability housing assistance situation to the hostel owner, about my should-be-private struggles, because everyone knows. Lots of people go out of their way to make it clear that I'm unwelcome. They're nice to everyone but me. I try to put myself in their shoes, but can't find a justifiable reason for their hatred. Why is it that I'm a freak that doesn't deserve kindness? If I had a tumour, or the flu, they'd probably have compassion for the pained innocence of illness.

One afternoon, as I lay in the foetal position in my dorm

bed, someone walking down the hall sneers, "Go away! You belong in a mental institution!" I guess crazy people are the lepers of our time. I don't need assholes in my life anyway, I tell myself. But I desperately desire just one true friend. The discrimination hurts, but I'm generally able to let it roll off of me. This is still way better than the house I've just left. It could be worse. I have bigger problems than being bullied and ostracized. I'll take a stranger's abuse over the voices in my head any day of the week. You know what? I'm just gonna smile at them and see what happens. I don't know what else to do but treat them how I'd like to be treated. If I'm just some disposable test subject, I might as well run my own experiments on the world.

I find a job working in the ski hill's cafeteria. My days of exclusively working at ethical businesses for appreciative people in nourishing environments are long gone. Disability checks are barely enough to keep me afloat. I'm more than willing to ignore my moral compass if it means pulling myself out of poverty and isolation. Aside from the extra money, there's another perk: a season pass for the mountain. Nonetheless, flipping burgers is repugnant. I can't distinguish embarrassment from humility any more.

Think of all the people of the world.

I suppose, relative to the people in impoverished, war-stricken countries, I still fall into the category of privileged, lucky, but it's impossible to emotionally connect with being blessed. Self-hatred deepens as I realize that I'm just another entitled western brat.

Whenever I'm not at work, I'm drinking. I've gotten quite good at it. It helps to quell the pain, to numb the humiliation of being broadcasted. Using the bathroom while being broadcasted and taunted by perverted, faraway voices is something one could never adapt to. Liquor is my medicine. It enables me to pass out at night, though it's always a brief sleep. Phantoms have started to come to me while I lay in the dark. When I manage to fall asleep, I'm inevitably woken by ghosts brushing up against me, mumbling in indecipherable tongues. It's a new kind of terror.

The snobby dude working the hostel's reception tells me there is no vacancy next month. Minutes later, as I string up my boots in the lobby, I hear him book new arrivals in for next month. This stings. Despite all the open discrimination from others staying here, I want to stay. I *need* to stay. Between beers, I try to not fret to much about becoming homeless again.

One night, as I lay in bed, I feel the shadows of three separate beings surround me. Their bodies are entirely invisible, but I can feel the pressure of them pushing up against me, like a creepy, slow-motion, soundless mosh pit that I'm trapped in the centre of. Their individual breathing patterns pulse through me in scattered rhythms. When I get out of bed, they follow me. It's hard to breathe through their throng. I freak out and call nine-one-one, clinging to the faint possibility that this is all an illness that can be remedied. Or, at the very least, tranquilized with Ativan to blur out the ghosts. An ambulance comes. I explain to the paramedics that I'm on the brink of a panic attack caused from the ghosts that are surrounding me. The two of them exchange a bleary glance on faces as young as mine.

"The hospital's an hour away. Just relax."

"You know, ghosts aren't real," the other follows.

"They're pretty real when you can feel them," I respond.

Their attitude is of total indifference, an apathetic void.

On the odd night when I actually fall asleep, I am visited by the same nightmare. There is no longer an escape into dreamland. It starts out no different from where I am and what I do when I'm awake during the day. Then, I wake up in a panicked sweat, spooked from bloodcurdling ghosts circling in on me. When I wake, they depart to my relief, only to return again. Believing I've woken up is only momentary; then the nightmare repeats itself. I wake, thinking I've escaped it. But no, I'm still here, still preyed upon in my sleep. When I finally do rise from slumber, I am left to question whether or not I'm still dreaming. Maybe I'm in a coma. Maybe one of my suicide attempts led to this looping purgatory.

I hate my job at the ski hill. I smash the pink and red cow meat into pucks on a sizzling flat top, then serve it up, charred and tortured, to be eaten by heartless snobs. The other cooks and servers are all chatty with each other, but cold towards me. On my first day, someone noticed the scars on my arm.

"She cuts!" he yelled out.

Someone actually laughed. Now the two of them call me Eddie Schizo Hands. To cope, I return to the meditation that I learned at the ashram in India. Just letting all the external sounds float through the ether that is my brain, with no reaction, no clinging, and no labelling. I'm pretty detached nowadays. Dissociation is effortless.

Being here is adding complexity to my already twisted mind. If all the young hedonists of this microcosm have arrived here, to the Realm of Travel Partiers, in virtue of glowing past karma, why are most of them so ignorant and cruel? Shouldn't they have a kind essence, a cosmic depth? Why are the karmically bankrupt allowed in this favourable realm?

One afternoon, I sit on an increasingly snow-covered picnic table, ignoring my shivering body as I listen to the radio. All of the robot controllers are present. For a while, they're just chilling with each other, but then they start to argue. I leap out of my radio trance to go find a drink. It's too much to just sit there. I wish I could choose the station, control the volume, and reach the off switch.

The clock's ticking. I need to find somewhere else to live or I am going to be homeless again. Homelessness in a Canadian winter is not an option. The paramedics made it clear that the people in charge of broadcasting me are done with hospitals. Psych wards have become a bore for the viewers.

One day, after work, I make my way to the exit of the lower parking lot to hitch a ride down the mountain and back into town. I meet two hipster guys drinking beers by the side of the road while they stick their thumbs out at the trickle of passing cars. They smile at me and hand me a cold one. We chat until a truck pulls over, then all hop in. Connecting and conversing with people in such a normal and natural way is peculiar and strange. It's been so long. Once back in town, the guys suggest going to the hostel's pub.

"They've cut me off," I say, straight-faced. The guys laugh at this like it's brilliant and suggest heading to a different bar. Over our first pitcher, I ask them if they know of anywhere with rooms to rent. Liam, one of the guys, says he's looking for a roomie. It's a small miracle, finding a place with someone who treats me like a valid human being. But my skin has thickened. I know not to trust that his kindness will last. We play pool, chat, and laugh for hours, downing several more pitchers of beer. I end up going back to Liam's place with him on the pretence of scoping out his spare room. Drunken sex ensues. I move in the next morning.

Hooking up probably wasn't the wisest thing to do with a new roommate, but it's too late to undo what happened.

My hallucinations are starting to cool off. The ghosts and tormentors are surfacing more quietly, and less often. I can only wonder at what is suppressing them. Maybe the toxic people and places I've left behind were more cause than outcome of my terrible visions.

Liam and I become fast friends. It's a relief to be living with someone who drinks as much as I do. It's easier, it's more fun, like a game. I'm having a genuinely difficult time being sober. We've slept together a few more times, just drunkenly, casually, mindlessly. We aren't a couple, but I suppose we're more than friends. We haven't talked about it.

At night, the bar remains my home. Every night. Any bar. Some of the people that were mean to me at work have warmed up to the freak show. They smile and ask how I'm doing when we bump into each other. Although less, I still hear the commentary of people who are watching me, but the character of what is said has become predominantly kind. The peace is precious. But it's likely just the eye of another storm.

I've lost weight, too. Finally! It's been weeks now of just booze and skiing, with not much eating in between. I'm starting to like the body I'm in. Except my arm, that hideous appendage, mottled with self-inflicted wounds left over from my various bouts of depression. I wish I could scrub out the scars.

As routine settles around me, I realize that here I am, once again at the far end of a deep, dark, and damaging tunnel through life. I have a decent place to live. I have a lover… ish. I have a job that lifts me out of extreme poverty. I'm looking good. My life seems to be in psychic springtime, blooming and returning to beauty. Life is nowhere near its past pinnacles, but I appreciate the simple things so deeply now, after living in their lack. Warm, comfortable shelter, friendly company, access to food and drink when I desire it. These all fill me with gratitude now, even flabbergasting awe. Perhaps it's true that overcoming hardship are critical factors to one's happiness. Everything else, the material externalities, they're an empty rat trap.

Early one morning, after yet another sleepless night, I shuttle up to the base of the hill. I glide my way over to the chairlift to catch the first tracks in the powder that dumped down last night. At the peak, I paddle my ski poles to the wildly steep north face of the summit. The borrowed skis are sticky in the snow. I'll have to bring them in for a wax when I get to the bottom. I set off down an empty run, zig and zag over its many moguls. About halfway down, I curve my feet left to turn away from the thick trees lining the run. My skis wedge in under a foot of powder, slamming me into the snow.

I scream as white-hot agony burns through my left leg. I try to move it, but it won't bend. The snow's too thick for me to reach and unclip my boot. Chill roars as the minutes crawl by. I sob out little clouds of steam as I wonder how long I'll be out here, all alone. I could slowly freeze to death. That would be okay. Or… the more likely outcome… I could get frostbite, lose a limb, and life could become even worse.

A bright green jacket whizzes through the trees up above. I wave a pole in the air and yell for help. They set out towards me. Through chattering teeth, I tell him that I can't bend my leg, or even twist my body towards my foot to remove the ski. Buddy unstraps his boots from his board, and digs out my leg, freeing my foot. I'm still unable to move my searing knee. He calls the ski patrol and waits with me for what feels like hours.

The men arrive. One of them grabs my foot while the other two make small talk with me. I hear a howl from the depths of hell escape my throat as the man holding my boot pulls on it, snapping my leg straight so that I'll be able to lie in their toboggan. They lift me in, then strap tarps and blankets over my body and face, like I'm inside a coffin. I hear them warn me that the ride down's going to hurt. It does. Every bump rattles my broken knee, blasting shockwaves of excruciating pain through my whole body. A torrent of tears streams from my eyes beneath the dark tarp casket.

I wait with nothing to do but think as I lay in the starchy hospital bed. I was stupid enough to think that life could actually shift to decent again. Am I still that dumb and gullible? Everything hurts more from momentarily stepping out of my numbness. There's a theory that the more hardship one experiences in life, the greater the happiness they are able to access, that the spectrum goes to the same depth in both directions. A rubber band of karma... What a crock of shit! Suffering is not a recipe for joy. Joy is the absence of hardship. I think about the others living here. I envy them, all of them. Their lives all seem so easy. They've spent their adulthoods partying, travelling, and playing their way through their shallow, privileged lives. Yes, shallow! As in, not having the depth of despair. Fuck all the philosophies that suffering makes one better. Suffering's absence is what happiness is. Pain is torture, not a wellspring of bliss.

They knock me out, put a metal rod in my leg, and sternly tell me not to put pressure on my knee for a few months. With a brace and crutches, I hobble down to the lobby. I haven't taken the painkillers they offered me because I don't trust western medicine. To me, medicine that contains toxic substances is paradoxical. Alcohol will suffice. Liam picks me up and drives me back to our place. I stagger into a holistic store and, with the little money I have, buy some red clover and stinging nettle to help strengthen my bones.

I am determined not to spiral back into a deeper depression. I have had enough suffering. I can't repeat last winter, sitting indoors, half welcome, mostly alone, miserable, left to wander the wasteland that is my mind. I'm not going to put myself into that pressure cooker of psychotic isolation again. I get in touch with old friends who are now scattered around BC. They all say I'm welcome to come visit them, that they're looking forward to seeing me. Their warmness surprises me. Why didn't I reach out before now? Am I not being watched and despised for disobeying all the orders that the tormentors commanded of me? Or is this simply a trap so they can further ridicule me?

Liam gives me a stinky hungover hug and wishes me a good life. Backpack strapped, I slowly slide to the highway on one foot, carefully picking my way through the ice and snow. I stick my thumb out and, in less than two minutes, a van pulls to the side of the road. Its door swings open and the three men inside tell me to hop in. I'm not dead yet. I step inside toward whatever awaits.

Fifty-Eight

My ride mates are three friendly, middle-age men heading home after a week of work in the mines near Fernie. They're heading near where Nala now lives, and offer to drive me all the way, seeing as I'm on crutches. Hitchhiking as a lone, lame, female is gonna be a breeze. The men are all kind, and I feel completely safe. So safe that I doze into a sleepy boredom as we make our way through BC's snow covered interior. I get dropped off at a cafe in the small community Nala lives outside of, and she comes to meet me.

Nala. Someone I know. Someone who knows me, who knew me before my life became a hurricane. Flashbulb. Reality warp. Realm-hop.

Hanging out with Nala is warm and familiar. For a moment, it feels like it was just yesterday that we were a close constant in each other's lives. We catch one another up on what we've done in the last few years. Hours roll by and our conversation shifts to reminiscing about the fishbowl island we once loved. We laugh through the pain of unresolved hurt and anger while we talk about Hornby.

Being in new forests, among kind folk, is literally medicinal. I'm probably not being watched. Why else would everything feel so normal right now? Maybe my prayer to be miraculously healed after breaking my knee was answered, in a roundabout kind of way. I'm probably not a robot. I feel like maybe I am what I used to think I was, before this insanity:

just some sentient girl, gloriously insignificant. I'm tempted to go into detail about the mental struggles I've been experiencing, but it would probably just freak everyone out and have them turn away from me. I don't fully understand why things feel so conventional again, but it's lovely. It's as if I was drowning and, at the last second, pulled out of the stormy waters, gasping to fill my lungs with warm, sunny prana. But my lungs are bruised, it's not clear the air will sustain them.

Hitchhiking around Nala's community, I meet a man that happens to have homemade comfrey herb poultices in the cab of his truck. He gives me a few and instructs me to wrap my knee in it, that the bones will heal faster. I give it a try and can feel it soothing my bones. It tingles as the fragments reknit. Natural medicine feels healthy, true, and magical. Western medicine feels like a violent hypocrisy.

Everyone I encounter is welcoming. What is happening? Am I dreaming? Is there a live audience, waiting on the edge of its seat for the punchline?

Of course, the respite fades. Soon, I'm hearing people say all sorts of mean things again. Maybe they actually are auditory hallucinations. That's what makes the most sense at the moment. Maybe I'm still crazy. Or a robot being experimented on. I don't know. Do I even need to try to define it? Understanding what is happening wouldn't actually make it any less terrible or give me any control on the situation.

I want to ask Nala if she knows about what I've been going through. I'm wondering if she knows how cruel people had been to me in Fernie. It feels like she does. That's why she's being so nice.

After about a week I start to feel my strain on Nala's tiny home. Some of her friends are road tripping through the town where Cody and his new partner now live. I get a ride with them. The road is stunning, snow-capped trees and frozen rivers. Everyone is calm. We eat nuts, chips, dried fruit and chocolate all day as we drive through the wilderness. Are they making fun of me? Or are they acting from pity because I went several weeks subsisting on beer? It's probably kindness. Or, maybe, I'm being egotistical and narcissistic. The excessive feasting probably has nothing to do with me. My mind chases its tail like this, round and round. I cannot silence these ponderings.

Fifty-Nine

Cody meets me in downtown Vernon, and we drive to the outskirts, to his small house, nestled between orchards. We catch up, and my heart returns to simpler times. How easy my world was, back then. Because his brother, Aubrey, died from schizophrenia, I feel I'm with a friend who would never desert me because of the stigma of mental illness.

Cody's partner Ara is at work for the night. We have a few ciders at their cosy country home. As evening fades, I find us moving closer together on the couch. It's so nice to be with someone I love. Someone who loves me. It doesn't matter that the form of love is friendship. It is bliss to share an evening of closeness. Conversation peters out. Our eyes wander towards each other. We fall into kisses and cuddles. But, before much longer, we come to our senses. Cody jolts upright and heads to his bed — the one he shares with Ara. As I lay silent, staring at the living room ceiling, regret creeps in. Sleepless, I suffocate myself with hatred for the adultery. They've gotta be in an open relationship, that's why it felt okay, that's why he initiated it, I conclude, but know that I'm probably lying to myself.

In the morning, we have breakfast and act just like we always have, good friends since way back when. Right before Ara comes home, Cody casts down his eyes and asks me to not say anything about what happened last night.

Wow. I have become what I hate. This is no tormentor.

This time, I recognize the voice talking to me as my own. I'm a jerk, not worthy of friendship. I used to think that cheating was something that I wouldn't ever do…

But that's exactly what I did. I stormed into a happy household, got comfortable, and promptly shattered an established trust. I hate myself more than I did before. I finally forgive Nile for cheating. I understand the weakness now, the ease of infidelity. It was just so nice to be in the moment with someone who knew me before I was a shattered, irreparable mess. It was wonderful to pretend that I hadn't left behind who I used to be and the life I once had; to pretend that I'm still desirable, still loveable.

Ara jangles through the backdoor and gives me a big, oblivious hug. Guilt festers inside of me. Maybe I deserve all the torture that I've been going through, like a pre-emptive punishment. I used to think I was a good person. I try to act natural, conceal my shame, knowing it's wrong.

She's being so nice to me. It shouldn't matter that Cody and I kissed. More heart denial as I roll through the days as their unworthy guest.

I get in touch with a lady from my yoga teacher training who lives nearby. I experience powerful telepathy over our tea together. The whole time we are talking, a second, more intimate conversation takes place between our thoughts. I wonder if she's experiencing the same thing. She's an advanced yogi, so her third eye is probably more open than most people's. As our teacups cool, her voice comes into my brain saying she's bored of catching up with me. I oblige her, and hurry our meeting to its end. She gives me a ride back to Cody and Ara's place and, within the long hug of a warm goodbye, I realize there is not a drop of reluctance in her. We could have spoken more, I could've told her everything. But that window has shut. The parades of mixed mental messages have annihilated my self-esteem.

A mellow week of slow, hobbling dog walks, upper body yoga sessions, and home-cooked meals floats by. But, with each passing day, I am more anxious about whether or not I am still welcome. I can tell that Cody and Ara are becoming less enthused to have me around. Surely, they miss having their home to themselves. Especially Ara, who knows me less, and has no deep attachments towards me. Thin smiles mask her annoyance with Cody's hobo friend taking up the couch. My telepathy escalates in intensity, filling my head with toxic thoughts. I make a point to be out of the house more. I start finding outings to go on so they can have some alone time. They turn down my invitations to the cinema, art shows, the library, confirming that I've overstayed my welcome. Over Sunday morning coffee in their garden, I tell them a joke I heard not long ago.

"What does a hippie say when you ask them to get off of your couch?"

"Nah ma stay."

Silence. I resist tears. I want to stay forever, with these nice people, who know me, and don't judge me, and lead stable lives. I lock my self-hatred, deep in my vault of sorrow, as I seem to do so swiftly with my pain nowadays. It's such a hurtful, shattering thing to do to someone. I'm unworthy of friendship, and Ara must sense it. I'm a mess that's just messing other peoples' lives up.

I announce that I've decided to leave tomorrow morning. On the surface, we're all still on okay terms. Cody says that I'm welcome back, any time. Their smiles must be of relief at my departure, and their return to privacy. I'm pretty sure they're just being kind because they pity me for being mentally ill, not because they actually want me around. But really, who could actually want me around nowadays?

Sixty

Between hitches, I visualise safe and kind drivers at my side, and allow myself to trust that they will manifest. They do. Cars are quick to pull over to the shoulder of the road. I wonder if it's out of respect, kindness, or pity. I don't ask. Each ride is brief, most of them with friendly young men, and one from an elderly couple worried about my safety. Aside from the dude who fed me chocolate chip cookies as a ploy for me to accept Jesus Christ as my personal saviour in our twenty minutes together, the rides are pleasant, even fun. Hitching is effortless when you're injured, young, alone, and female. I've yet to be left on the side of the road for more than five minutes at a time.

A chain of wayward hitches eventually lands me in Vancouver. I stay with some acquaintances from Hornby that Cody got in touch with when I told him I had no plan for what to do next on my vagabonding. We haven't seen each other in years. They seem so healthy. Being in Vancouver with nice people who haven't seen me since before hell possessed me makes the last few years feel like an awful, unreal, nightmare. I do my best to hide my unwell mind and finances, as if I'm still the charmed, carefree, person that they knew years ago on the tiny island community that we called home. They're busy with school, so leave me a spare key to come and go from their apartment. I cook dinners which we share over wine in the evenings. Another lush oasis in the desert of my life, quenching my thirst, just barely enough to keep going.

My two stints in Vancouver don't fit together at all. From homelessness, to psychwards, to prostituting myself for hard drugs, to living with people that terrified me to the core. And now this: Peace, comfort, and nostalgia. I don't stay in the city long. I want to avoid cropping up another overstayed welcome. I wish I had somewhere positive to go, that I was more than a lost and stranded burden.

Sixty-One

The wind takes me. I hitch-hike back to the interior, and arbitrarily end up in Nelson, the city my ride happened to be heading to. I hobble around for a few minutes. The town pulses with funky fun. I've passed through here on my way to and from Shambhala festival several times, but never stayed longer than an hour or two. Artists and musicians fill the streets, even though it isn't festival time. The heart of the festival beats here, even in winter. The town sits in a valley with lots of crystals in the surrounding mountains. That crystal resonance may be the reason why the atmosphere is so elevated here.

"Hey, Maya!"

I rock back and forth on my crutches to turn around. Another tiny miracle, Tayler, a friend of a friend, has recognized me. He brushes long blonde hair from his dreamy, lash-laden brown eyes. When I tell him I'm just tramping around with my thumb and a bum knee, he doesn't hesitate to offer me a place to stay, and invites me to a gathering with him later tonight. He takes my backpack, and together we slowly hoof our way to his house. He shows me the couch I can sleep on, then brings out some homemade wine and sits down with me so we can get to know each other. Within our first glass, I develop a crush. He must have heard about my going insane through the grapevine, yet he's relaxed around me. He has a girlfriend anyway. On night two, he blindsides me with a sort of half-cuddle around the shoulders. I freeze, solid, remembering the guilt and self-loathing after kissing Cody. I can't change the damage I quietly inflicted on their bond of trust. But I can at least abstain from doing something like that again.

In town, I see a brochure for a spiritual retreat centre not too far from here. I get in contact with the owners and arrange to do a work stay in exchange for room and board. The owners of the centre are kind enough to accept a worker that's on crutches. Centering myself in nature with conscious people seems like exactly the medicine I need. It always is. Plus, it'll force me to take a break from drinking. And I won't have to impose my presence on friends, or friends of friends. With cautious optimism, I make my way through the wilderness to the isolated centre.

Sixty-Two

There was a landslide here not long ago. My hitch and I wind our way up a dirt road carved into the mountainside. We pass the section where the flood of trees and rocks came crashing down, leaving a sudden and horrid gash on the peaceful forest surrounding us. The community here has less than one hundred people. Everyone knows everyone, and everyone knew those who were killed in the slide. Devastation hangs heavy in the air.

It's the off season for spiritual retreats. There is only one other guest here at the moment. He and I will share the few duties that remain in the absence of clients. I'm invited to just relax for the afternoon. So, I crutch-walk down the road to the defiled clearing where the landslide fell.

I hunker down into the raw, stripped hollow, into Mother Earth's torn wound, and close my eyes. In that dark, a pure and mighty pain finds her long-lost voice. First sobs and shakes, then wailing screams escape my throat, echoing off the maimed cliffside as I pound my fists into the dirt. The pain of the shattered land provokes my emotions, but my thoughts are with the past few years of my life. The loss of trust in reality. The loss of friendship. The loss of destiny. Time wasted and youth stolen. Morality decayed. The prison-spiral of poverty. The drugs. The pain. The rage. The unshakable guilt of knowing that most people on this planet are in far worse situations than I, while I've made myself useless to help anyone. I shout myself runny and raw. The air leaps from my lungs. I feel it in my sternum, it hurts like I need it to.

Eventually, my tears subside to gasps, the smouldering coals of sorrow spent. I am just a tiny creature again, held in Earth's womb as it collects itself to birth life again. Recalling my teachings, remembering the impermanence of all things, I disassociate from the pain, try to forget the cruel, ignorant people that I've crossed paths with. I feel empty. But yet, here I still am, alive, my mind still split, my outer world still bleak and frightening. I haven't realm-hopped. Just released some pain. Probably in vain. Odds are the future holds plenty more suffering for me. Happiness is such a fragile thing, frightening, even. I know its other side. Feeling a cathartic cleansing, but far from free I get up and crutch back to the centre.

I curl up in bed with a dusty book about all the different forms and ways love can be defined. Love feels so abstract and distant right now, untouchable, like the planets and stars. I start to sneeze, so I close the book and retreat into my own thoughts. I pull out my journal and scribe down what love is to me, then drift off to sleep, red-eyed. In the morning, I decide to leave. Working on crutches was unrealistic, and I realized I want to be with the people I love.

Sixty-Three

Spring arrives, and the bravest part of me lets in a bit of its glow and splendour. Joy is terrifying once you've experienced deep sorrow intimately. The long, sunny days remind me of simpler times, when my world was a kaleidoscope of exciting and beautiful adventures, when I felt free as the birds in the sky. So many gleaming smiles with fellow dream-walkers, sharing in sublime synchronicities. Was that it? Has my life peaked out? Probably.

The crystals that hug the valley magnetize me back to Nelson. The people and vibration here nourish me and make me feel less broken. I spend a couple weeks sleeping on the floors of new friends, making art, dancing, and celebrating life with people that are open to me. I know staying here would be positive, but my mind gets in the way. Rationale says that, if I return to Hornby, I can hop back into my old summer jobs, reconnect with friends, put money aside, and perhaps even travel come winter. I let that logic of guaranteed work decide my course and leave.

Once in Vancouver, I make my way to the ferry terminal. I have only a handful of coins to my name, so I fashion a cardboard sign — "Spare Change for Faerie" — and start humming and attempting to beatbox in front of the ticket queue. With the bemused smiles of strangers come quarters, loonies, and toonies, nearly enough to pay my way across the Georgia Strait. But, as I'm counting change, a tired-looking ferry worker tells me I'm not allowed to busk here. Drat. I go outside and a couple approach me, asking if I made enough for a ticket. "Almost," I say. They graciously hand me a twenty, and tell me to buy myself some food on the crossing.

The bridge rises, the horn toots, and the wind begins to blow. Hoping to ride out the wave of kindness that got me here, I wander the deck, and ask other passengers if they have a spare seat in their car. I meet a strung-out hipster who's driving through the town where Angela and Moss now live. My ride and I talk and laugh the whole passage to Vancouver Island. I silently pray that my life has been re-charmed, but this boon has barely risen before I start to become nervous. Is returning to Hornby a bad idea? I'm stubbornly attached to what it once was, so I keep the plan.

Big hug hello with Angela and Moss. It feels like the good ol' times could be resurrected. They, too, have transitioned off the globe-trotter's path, and are settling into careers and the sedentary lifestyle that tends to come with them. Turning back to this page of my past warms me. I decide that, perhaps, going back to Hornby could actually be a good decision. Now, I can't wait to see my other friends, too! But Angela and Moss are probably treating me better than most would. They're closer to enlightenment than most people I know or have met, thus pure kindness and open mindedness naturally comes to them. I guess I'll just have to wait and see how my return to the closest place I have to a home unfurls.

Sixty-Four

As I step foot off the Hornby ferry, I take a deep gulp of the familiar crisp and salty air, then embark on a grand tour of the island. I skip my way along, knocking on the doors of old friends. The first four places I go, nobody's home. So, I trail-hike to my favourite beach for an open-eye meditation. Staring at the crashing waves, I try to tame thoughts of worry, excitement, and expectation. As evening commences, I make my way back to another old friend's house. The faces I meet are painted with surprise. There's no big hugs or, "Ohmygodhiiis," or anything else to that effect. They offer me their couch with reluctance, and say that I can stay for a couple nights, but I need to find somewhere else to live. After, they promptly go to bed, with no desire to catch up or re-engage whatsoever.

The next day, I borrow a bicycle and visit all my beloved friends. Each of them meets me with hesitation or indifference. My heart and lungs cave in with this reality check. The people I was excited to see — the people I hold most dear in the world — they don't care that I'm back. They don't even seem to like me any more. None of them are glad to see me, or care to spend time with me. My presence is met with either apathy or avoidance. Is this because I now have the label of schizoaffective type bipolar?

It's been years since I was myself. For the duration of my madness, I was disconnected from my friends here, and at least a couple of years have passed since I was actually close with the people I still consider to be my best friends, my tribe, my soulmates, my family. It's clear that they've all let go of me, like I'm a poisonous lost cause. It even seems like some of them actively don't want me here. I feel — no, I know, I am being shown — I am unwanted. I am unlovable.

I find a mouldering, rundown cabin to rent on a quiet side of the island. Each passing day makes me feel more alone in the Universe. The beauty of each walk, forest bike ride, and beach bask breaks me, bit by bit. Such terrible beauty. More and more, I am shown that this is not my home any more. My employers at my old jobs that I had planned to return to are all treating me differently. They were like loving aunts and uncles at one time. Now, they've gone cold, as if they're racking their brains for a valid excuse to not rehire me. Because I'm crazy.

Hornby Island was my home, my constant. I didn't think my heart could break past the point that it already has, but fresh new fractures are splitting out from the deep old ones, as if it crumbles more and more easily, each time I childishly glue it back together.

It was a mistake to come here, to think Hornby's world would stop spinning while I was away. I need to leave. I don't know where. But Hornby's repulsion towards me is unbearable. There is a Buddhist teaching that says: Non-attachment is generosity. I'm not sure if I quite get the concept, but I want to test it out. I want to understand. What else is there for me to do? I collect all of the possessions I have left in the world from a former friend who had been storing them for me.

Under the full moon, I gather twigs and branches and light a small fire on the beach. By handfuls, I toss in a lifetime of sentimental attachments. Photographs, pictures of my travels and old friends, all the good times. I glimpse the now young-looking faces of the high school tribe that I thought of as my family. Into the flickering flames they go. I see a picture of Lynx and I hiking through the Andes. Lynx, who was once the inseparable love of my life. Nicaragua, India, so many travels… something I thought I would be able to do forever. Just unattainable, bitter memories now. Pictures of happy times with Hornby friends… another family lost. They burn blue and green as they warp into white ash. My old journals are next into the fire, their spiralled metal spines pop and uncoil in the flames. I burn the deck of oracle cards that I had made at the hospital on Vancouver Island, laminate and all. Old drawings and paintings that I made or that were lovingly gifted to me. Every other clung-to mementos from over the years, joins the purging blaze. Once the last of the flammables are gone, I stare at the embers in stoic shock.

Alright, time to dive in and test the waters: Non-Attachment is generosity. All I have left is a small backpack of everything I might need for spiritual evolution and basic survival. I spend the night awake, tear-stained and sleepless. Dreamless. When the sun starts to bring light to the land, I go down to the edge of my driveway with all of my remaining stuff, and hitch a ride to the freestore. I leave it there in a milk crate, to be broken down by others and made into new and unknown things. It's just me and a backpack again. Except, this time, I don't have anything or anyone to return to.

In India, I was awestruck by the spiritual devotees who had renounced the material world. They practice abstention to reach moksha: Liberation from cyclical births and rebirths of suffering, from samsara. That song I sang years ago, at the end of my time in India, came true. I shall be a wandering ascetic.

I will live a life without possessions or property in order to attain union with the Absolute. This shall be my life now. I am a sadhu.

Goodbye, Hornby Island. Forever.

Sixty-Five

A hitch brings me to his destination, the Salt Spring Island ferry. Back to the mainland, via Salt Spring, I suppose. I sit and try to calm my nerves about being homeless, again. The man next to me looks up from his book and strikes up conversation. His name is Champo, and he's a Tibetan refugee. It's a powerful and positive omen. There is real purpose in what I'm doing. Maybe, somehow, my decision to drift actually will bring me, and possibly others, towards the direction of peace and wisdom, like Champo's culture is founded upon. He tells me he's in landscaping, and my heart leaps. My heart leaps for landscaping. Simple work, but it pays, and I know how to do it. A part of me wants to slink away from the walkabout at the prospect of an income stream and a friendly person's couch. But, as my question tastes the air, I tame my worry, and summon the courage to face the unknown. I don't tell him that I'm starting the path of renunciation. I worry saying it out loud would result in me talking myself out of it. The ferry docks and we say farewell.

Sixty-Six

Downtown Salt Spring, I see a poster advertising a discussion group hosted by a yoga centre this evening. My path to the centre is lined with serpentine arbutus trees and towering firs.

I arrive early, and sit down on a spotless sofa in the immaculate, large, sun-washed common room with some of the resident yogis. They all radiate the calm openness of people sincerely trying to embody divine peace. Talking with them is as soothing as leaping into a gentle river on a hot August afternoon.

A glowing, vital old woman gently interrupts the soft chatter to form a circle on the ground and open discussion with the whole group. Tonight's topic: Bhakti Yoga, the Yoga of Love and Surrender to God. How appropriate! Another omen that my quest has a destined purpose. Perhaps the path of a sadhu was a good route to choose. We are invited to make offerings to the altar in the centre of the circle. Seeing as we are talking about the Yoga of Love, I take the page from my current journal, the only one that wasn't cremated. I place what I wrote at the retreat centre by the landslide, into the altar.

Someone reads a few pages from a book. We sing call and response chants together. Then, the woman guiding us asks if we have anything we'd like to share. Seeing as this journey is about stepping into courage, I decide to swallow my shyness and read aloud to the group what I had written about love. My voice trembles slightly, and I can feel my face turn red as I speak.

"Love is a vibration, an action, a life purpose.
Love is the soul's most powerful medicine.
Love is the absence of greed.
Love is inspiring, energizing.
Love is our nature.
Love is a miracle.
Love is fun.
Love is a return to source.
Love is taking a pause in being healed.
Love is the best hug."

I muster the confidence to look up from my sheet to find warm smiles and eyes closed in attentiveness. I recall a teaching from a guru at my yoga teacher training in Mexico that quoted: "At any moment, we can choose love over fear." After a deep discourse on trying to grasp the ways of love, our discussion group ends. Someone gives me a ride back to the sleepy storefronts of the island's commercial district.

Night has fallen. I eye up which bench would be best to sleep on, and start to shiver as I am reminded how scary it is for a girl to sleep outside, alone. All too soon, I have realm-hopped. Life is terrifying again. At any moment I can choose love over fear? How does that apply now?

I ask a passer-by if she knows of a *cheap* place to stay. She directs me to a party house nearby that often hosts travellers. I find the old house with chipping, purple paint and knock on the door. Ken appears in the doorway to offer me a confused, but kind, welcome and a floor to sleep on. In the morning, I leave a drawing to thank them and make my way back to the ferry that'll portal me to the main continent and, hopefully, some magical, blissful, destiny.

Sixty-Seven

My hitch off the ferry dead-ends at the outskirts of the city where Ara and Cody live. Is this karma presenting me with the opportunity to right what I have wronged? For a second, I think about going to their place. What would I do? Knock on their door, tell Ara that Cody and I kissed, then ask if I can spend the night? That's pretty messed up. I'm supposed to be living in divine trust. How can I trust the Universe when I'm a liar? I mull it over as I stand, thumb out and ignored, at the shoulder of the blistering highway. For the first time, hours go by where no one stops to offer me a ride. Karma. I give up and hoof my way to the downtown area of Vernon. A man comes up to me as I sit cross legged on the sidewalk. Flatly, but warmly, he invites me to a restaurant. Over veggie burgers and fries, we talk some more. After footing the bill, he shows me the way to a women's shelter and returns to his privileged life.

The vibration here is sickly and grey. Illness, addiction, and anger fill the halls. The saddest stories belong to women taking only temporary respite from the abusive men they keep going back to. All's not lost. The shelter has a plastic tub of neglected art supplies buried in a backroom closet. I paint a mandala of planets with faces swirling in orbit around each other. I surprise myself by actually being satisfied with my work, even finding it beautiful. Maybe I can sell or trade art on my journey to cover my basic needs.

My trusty thumb takes me east along the highway. A sad

man in a fancy sports car pulls over to pick me up. He's drinking beer and pining the fresh loss of his girlfriend. I've barely pulled the door shut before he hands me a can. It feels so strange that it must be another movie scene.

I try to focus on the conversation with my jilted driver, but... we're back. I hear and feel messages in every detail. Two-track conversations at all times, between the ear track, and the head track. The spoken word alone has a dozen layers of encoded meaning that's hard to decipher. There's a lot of contradictions, too. Sometimes it's interesting, but, mostly, it's just exhausting and impossible to keep up with. I'm unable to pinpoint what's real and what's not. I'm bombarded with messages from the radio, unable to mute the volume or change stations.

In the next arbitrary town that I wind up in, I watch myself as I sit on a busy curb, trying to sell the canvas that I painted last week. The scurrying shoe-souls of countless strangers pass me by, until a derelict man buys it. This is obviously a movie scene. He is such an implausible customer.

With the forty bucks I made from the painting, I head to a health food store, clinging to the faint hope that psychosis is, in fact, what I am experiencing. I seek true medicine, desperate to put an end this torture. If a "medicine" can cause other ailments, then it isn't an authentic healing substance, just a ruse. So, I look to Nature to rediscover balance. I've read that Omega-3 fats are medicinal for the brain. I choose a 250 ml bottle of flax oil, apathetic that it costs almost half of the measly money I have.

In a nearby park, I down the entire bottle of oil. I close my eyes and am sent a vivid vision. Amma, an India spiritual leader, considered to be a saint, often called the Hugging Saint, appears to me. She's floating, glowing, smiling at me, and radiating love. The medicine is guiding me towards what I need to do to heal. Amma's going to be in Toronto at the end of June.

I already had the idea to make the pilgrimage to hug her. This vision clarifies that that's the right direction for me to proceed. I head to the highway backpack on back, thumb in the air. Destination: Toronto.

Sixty-Eight

There's ten days until Amma will be in Toronto. Wonderfully tame rides bring me to the edge of BC. My first night is spent awake on the stoop of a truck stop gas station. I drink awful coffee until the fluorescent buzz gives way to sunrise and the illusion of safety that comes with daylight. Around mid-afternoon I'm let off on the side of the highway just past Calgary, where, eventually a huge sixteen-wheeler pulls over. I climb into the passenger's seat, and wave hello to a middle-aged, East Indian man, named Kunal. He's headed for Winnipeg, the capital of the next province to the east. He insists he's grateful to have company for the long, monotonous drive ahead. He's done it a thousand times alone.

Night comes, and Kunal announces that he needs to stop to sleep, that there's a tiny town not far ahead. We get to the truck stop that has the village name on a billboard: Indian Head.

Really? "Indian Head"? Is that the director giving me instructions on what to do? I can hear the laughter from the hidden observers in my head. Okay, this is totally a movie. I'm a degree removed from the situation, as if I'm just another observer. Then Kunal places a hand on my knee and asks if he should get a room for us in the grimy motel that lines the huge, empty parking lot. Reality punches me in the face and winds me. This is for real.

"No," I say, trying to sound strong.

"I'll pay you."

I shake my head. "No."

"All right," he sighs. "Do you want to go have a beer at the diner?" I nod.

The diner turns out to be more of a dark, dingy bar than a restaurant. There's a couple of slot machines, a billiards table, and a dozen or so empty tables. Apart from the man decaying behind the bar, there are only two stern, must-be locals, playing pool and a couple of other truckers forking down greasy meals. The check-in counter for the hotel is in here, too.

Kunal buys us each a beer. Maybe I could summon the courage to hook if I got really drunk. I could use the money... Was that even my own thought? Kunal points to the slot machines and asks if I want to play. "Sure," I shrug. He puts our drinks on top of the machine, drops a loonie into the coin slot, and gestures for me to push the big, square, neon button. Fluorescent fruits flash from the screen and a river of coin rattles into the metal tray. I get three matching lines in a row, winning over fifty dollars in coins. I decide to quit while I'm ahead. Kunal insists I keep the money. It feels like this salvo of grubby prize coins is supposed to be his proposition for sex. I decline, nowhere near intoxicated enough to relax into this situation.

Last call follows our next two drinks. We cross the barren parking lot back to the cab of Kunal's semi. He keeps trying to put his arm around my shoulder. I keep brushing it away. As I step into the cab I say, "I'm not going to do anything with you," and take my seat on the passenger side. He lays in the cab's bed, behind the seats, and asks me to join him. In a voice as stern as I can muster, I repeat more clearly that I'm not going to sleep with him. As he continues to insist, his tone begins to shift. Each time it comes across a little more as a demand than an invitation. I'm scared. It's the middle of the night, the middle of nowhere, and no one knows where I am… if there's even anyone left who'd care. Even though Kunal's being pushy, I become paralysed by fear. I'm just as afraid to go outside onto the highway, alone, at this time of night. He repeats himself, from the bed behind the front seats, in an aggressive tone.

"Come here!"

"No!"

I get onto the floor, lock my door, and curl myself around the passenger's seat, my head in the middle of the two seats. Sternly, I say "Stop asking me, or I will leave you!" Amazingly, he drops it. He mutters something then falls silent. Minutes later his snores and farts fill the cab. I stay curled around the base of the seat for hours. Eventually the adrenaline subsides and I fall asleep.

I feel a tap on my shoulder. The sun is rising and Kunal announces that it's time to hit the road. He's all buddy-buddy again, as if last night didn't happen. Soon, we're talking and laughing like friends, instead of trapped in the roles of horny man and potential prostitute or rape victim. We pull into a gas station. "Cup of Chai?" asks Kunal, shifting the gear to park.

From a compartment, he produces a single propane hot plate, a few tea bags, a dash of loose spices, and plops them into a pot of simmering milk, warming the cab with the aroma of cinnamon and cloves. With steaming mugs in our hands, Kunal revs the engine. I buckle my seatbelt and we break gently into the chilly dawn.

Kunal asks if he can take my picture. I shrug. He probably just wants to sell it to the tabloids. He turns to me with his phone and clicks, the phone plays a fake camera sound. As he returns his attention to the road, he sees that the truck is drifting toward the left-hand ditch. He jerks the wheel back towards the centre of the highway, throwing the full weight of the trailer off of the tires. The truck comes with it, tilting over and then slamming onto its side. My seat belt suspends me sideways in the air.

Suddenly, vividly awake, I unclick and climb up and out the window, then jump down onto the pavement. Kunal climbs up through the compartment and jumps out of the cab. We stare at the accident in mute shock. Adrenaline surges through my body. We're both intact. The trailer lays on its side, blocking both eastbound lanes of the highway. A minute passes until a semi appears from the east, across the grassy strip that separates the two directions of the empty highway. Kunal flags it down and tells me to leave. He'll get in trouble if I am found with him.

"You're sure, you're okay?" I ask, noticing for the first time that his entire left elbow is webbed in blood.

"Yeah, I'm fine... GO!"

Why do you even care whether or not he's okay? Was that my thought? goes the next thought.

The other semi slows to a halt on the shoulder of the lifeless highway. The man on the passenger seat swings the door open for me to climb in. It's in the opposite direction of Amma, but I climb into the other truck at Kunal's insistence. I guess I'll just have to retrace my steps. Sometimes you need to step back before moving ahead? Maybe one day, I'll understand some of the clichés about wisdom.

I climb aboard and the truck revs onward. Dizzying vertigo fills me as I realize how precarious these beastly vehicles are. I slow my breath and try to calm myself. Turns out I'm cruising back to Calgary. The trucker chauffeuring me is young, friendly, and kind.

The streets that lead to Calgary's downtown core are congested and loud. My driver buys me lunch and offers his place for me to stay at. He's about to leave for another week-long work drive. I'm tempted to take him up on his offer of rest and shelter, but I decline. This is only a stepping stone. I'm going to see Amma! He then asks me where I want to get dropped off. I'm still too shaken up to be back on the highway, so I ask him to drop me off at a bus stop that I can get to downtown from.

The city buzzes in light and warmth. I meander the streets, momentarily destination free. I come across a few art galleries. I've made art at least as good as some of the thousand-dollar works on display. Maybe I do have a chance of becoming a successful something one day. Maybe my future isn't doomed. Maybe. I spend a couple of sleepless days wandering around Calgary, attempting to stay awake without eating or drinking. The radio is rambling on about the promised mystery award, again. I've made it into day three of the vigil.

The sunshine breaks. A storm of biblical proportions rolls in. A demon sent the storm. I've nearly accomplished three days and nights without rest, food, or water. The demon wants me to fail. Rainfall swells into a monsoon and I purse my lips to not let any water in. Night coats the city in darker wetness. The torrent intensifies. The street-sides have become fast-flowing streams. Rapid water courses over and across the sewer manholes. I spot an open bar and run for shelter, through the water that's now rising past my ankles.

The bar is massive, packed with people who must all have

cars, and coats. Everyone's dry. How luxurious! I take a seat at the lone remaining table, peel off my sodden backpack, shake off my pens and paper, and busy myself with drawing, in hopes that the bartenders won't notice that I'm not buying anything. Before long, a buff dude in chic clothes comes up to me and asks if he and his friends can share my table.

The stools around me fill with other swanky people wearing curious stares. One of the girls asks to look through my drawings. The table passes my journal around and everyone pretends to be wowed by my senseless doodles, though even their mere willingness to be kind is encouraging. One of the girls stares into one of my kaleidoscopic mindscapes for more than a minute. When I gift it to her, she asks me to sign it and I become confused, not sure what my name is now or what it will be if and when I become a successful artist.

One of the guys offers me a beer. Through sleep deprivation, I momentarily forget that I was about to reach seventy-two hours of abstinence. I swallow my first sip of cold beer and realize all is lost. I do my best to not to mourn the lost victory. It's just homelessness in torrential downfall, anyway. We talk and laugh through several rounds of drinks. By the time the bar closes we're all quite tipsy. I ask if one of them has a couch I can sleep on. "Of course!" Three of the guys are sharing an apartment that's only a few blocks from the bar. We wade there in high spirits.

The elevator takes us up to the seventeenth floor and I collapse onto the cold leather couch. As I close my eyes, I am filled with remorse about not seeing my sleepless days of fasting through. I'd only have had two hours left at this point. Two! I was so close! Devastated, I try to keep my eyes peeled open, but can't.

The apartment stirs awake to a power outage. From the window, we see that the city below is starting to flood. The cars outside are all submerged in a foot of swirling, silty water. Everyone takes storm selfies on the balcony. I pretend I'm not interested in taking photos, not wanting to admit how strange and poor I am, that I don't even have a phone. This brings me to the realization of how much easier it is for me to find hosts on my vagabonding, because I'm a young, pretty, girl. For a second, I'm grateful for at least that. Then I realize how less scary this would all be if I wasn't a young, pretty, girl, all alone in the world. Can I trust that the Universe will support me and keep me safe? There's only one way to find out.

The monsoon continues. One of the guys receives orders on his cell to evacuate the building. I wait while everyone else packs their things, cat included. With flashlights, we make the long descent down the darkened stairwell together and drive out of the city in a big, shiny, white pickup truck. I can't help but start to wonder if they are a team that found me at the bar to foil my three-day vigil at the cusp of completion? Was their kindness a ruse?

We cross a bridge over Calgary's downtown river. Grey-brown water overflows onto the yards and lots below. As we rise further out of the city centre, the flood thins and subsides. I ask my hosts to take me to the highway that heads east. The rain's still coming down in buckets, so they find me an overpass that I can shelter under while I wait with my thumb out. I thank them and hop out onto the road. They pull away, and I turn to face the oncoming traffic.

I stand at the sloshing roadside for a long time. I only have two outfits, and they're both soaked through. A small car finally pulls over. I am so grateful to be getting into a warm, dry vehicle. The young man driving is going east for a couple of hours. We leave the storm behind and a relaxed silence settles between us. I am content with this here and now. There is no sense in worrying about the future, nor pining over the past.

My next hitch is headed all the way to Montreal. We drive through the day and into the night to a constant thrum of mediocre psytrance music. At first my driver seems quite glad to help me. But slowly, I become more and more unsettled.

Outwardly, he's chill and kind. But I'm starting to hear all sorts of telepathic threats. People that want to harm me are attempting to teleport into his body so that they can control his actions. I come to fear him. He's someone else, now, not the same friendly dude he was at the beginning of the drive. He's being invaded. We reach a truck stop close to midnight, and I take the opportunity to flee. I run over to some truckers buying snacks and ask them for a ride. They're reluctant, but one says yes and takes me all the way to Winnipeg. My feet meet the outskirts of Winnipeg in the wee hours of morning. I'm now one province away from Ontario.

Getting out of Winnipeg takes hours. My thumb doesn't drop 'till I am picked up by a man driving to the East Coast. Right away I have the impression that he knows who I am. He's been watching me. I see an aura of darkness around him, a hollowness in his eyes. There are bugs splattered all over his windshield. I watch a butterfly flatten against our speed as it smears into the rest of the gore. He laughs, as if he took pleasure in its death.

He tells me he has sleep apnea. Seconds later, I fall asleep. My subconscious cries out: He's a robot controller!

I jolt awake, terrified, and promptly ask to be let out of the truck. I hop out in the middle of nowhere. As I'm about to shut the door, I am roboted to ask the controller for money. "Do you have any money?" just rolls out of my mouth without any forethought.

He smiles and gives me three twenty-dollar bills, adding, "I'll give you more if you give me a kiss." He's mean-spirited. I am loath to share breath with him, so I slam the door. As I'm leaving, I can swear I hear him say, "Goodbye, my Queen." Huh?!

I'm at the western edge of the gargantuan province that is Ontario. Toronto is still hundreds of kilometres to the southeast. The highway's quiet, mostly just the odd freight truck, here and there. I am such an idiot for hitch-hiking across the country alone. This is terrifying. I try to visualise a safe journey, but my mind is a tangle of foreign voices and images. My own sense is feeble among them.

Please God, Please Robot Controllers, Please Universe, Please Amma, Please Intuition… Please get me to Toronto safely.

Eventually, another trucker opens his door for me. We drive for a while, then he takes me out to dinner in a rundown highway town. The day is ending, and he says he needs to sleep. I decide to try to hitch through the night, afraid of what he may try to do if I spend the night in his truck.

The night brings the ghosts and spirits out. Just as their cold, windy bodies begin to close in around me in the blackness, I get picked up by another semi. The driver is young and friendly. So much so that I quickly relax enough to sleep.

I feel a hand shaking my shoulder. My driver announces we've made it. I'm in disbelief to be setting foot on the concrete of outer Toronto. I turn to wave goodbye, and voice another, thank you.

"You forgot something!" he calls out, waving me back over to his truck. He reaches out of the window, unfolds my right palm and places a bright red fifty-dollar bill in it. A city bus pulls up to the stop next to me and he says "Hurry, hurry! Enjoy your destination, Brave One!"

Sixty-Nine

I hop off the bus at a subway station and follow the steep steps underground to a seat on the first train that passes. I rumble cluelessly through deep tunnels for a little while, then squeeze through the train doors at an arbitrary stop and hike up the stairs past the milling nine-to-fivers, back into the sunlight. Carefree pedestrians fill the many coffee shops and bars. The atmosphere is easy and free, filled with the joy that summer brings.

    I wander the sunny streets in a daze. I just hitch-hiked across the country! I made it! I can barely believe it. Toronto pulses with life well past nightfall. I go dancing in a few different bars to celebrate my successful journey. Once the bars close, my little backpack and I wander the downtown neighbourhoods. Waiting until daylight to sleep seems like the safe, sensible thing to do. I spend the next few days and nights walking around like this, with breaks for coffee and journaling. The city is stimulating enough to keep my senses alert. In the afternoons, I take short naps in the safety of crowded parks, never needing more than a few hours of shut eye. Maybe I'm in a manic phase?

    Friday comes. Amma is here. At sunrise, I find a laundromat to wash my bag, blanket and clothes, everything but the shirt on my back. With some of the little packet of detergent that I got from the laundromat vending machine, I wash my hair in the sink. I want to bring my purest self to

Amma.

A bus takes me across the city to the hotel hosting the Hugging Saint. I am directed to a huge conference room, vibrant with giddy people lined up to share a moment with Amma. I rub my eyes as I take in the room. Amma's at the far end of the hall, sitting amongst a beloved crowd. She's in spotless white robes, with a smile of pure bliss, and a soft haze of sparkles orbiting around her big, beautiful, self. The wavelength of the room fills me with calm contentment. I close my eyes and breathe in full presence of the beautiful energy.

I slowly sway my way around the room. With some of the money my rides gave me, I buy a purple and white prayer scarf to use as a veil against the summer sun. I choose it for the colours of the two uppermost chakras: purple for the Third Eye, located between the eyebrows, and the centre of intuition, telepathy, and foresight; and white for the Crown Chakra, located at the head's summit, the connection to forces of life beyond oneself. The room sighs as Amma serves the last of a long line of people who were there to be embraced and receive her whispered words of love, spontaneously channelled for each disciple. She leaves the room for a break. I talk giddily with others about how full of love our hearts feel in Amma's presence. I am buoyant with peace.

When Amma returns to the room to offer more hugs to her love-drunk flock, I take my place in the long, gentle line that forms. As I inch towards her, an even mightier energy radiates over me, sharpening my awareness. My turn comes. She bows down from her chair, holds me in her embrace, and recites four words in my ear. I shall keep each and every one of those words to myself for the rest of my life. Amma hands me an apple and a chocolate, then gently turns to hug the next pilgrim.

I join the group of people meditating in her orbit and bask in the beautiful vibration. I don't stay for too long. It's only fair to share the space, so others, too, can heal their souls and their cells with her entrancing vibration. My mind is tranquil and whole, no longer a warzone of discombobulated, fragmented pieces. The sensation of peace is familiar, but it feels like it's been ligetimes since I've felt such splendour. It's been too long since I've felt peace like this. Later in the evening, I accidently fall asleep on a couch in the hotel lobby. Despite a sign forbidding this, I wake up from an undisturbed sleep, the deepest and most revitalizing of my life. I give a prayer, from and to Spirit, "Please bring me to also emanate a vibration of love that helps heal this planet." I put on my backpack, wrap my prayer scarf around my head, then float back into the city.

What now? My quest has been accomplished. What happens to pilgrims after their pilgrimage? I spend days in Toronto drawing, writing, and wandering. Sometimes I try to beatbox for money, but I'm horrible at it. It's rare that people stop to give alms and when they do, it's just measly coins. At night, I roam the empty concrete jungle like a lost animal avoiding predators. With each passing day, I feel more and more distant from the energy I felt when I was with Amma. Clear thought is like water which I thirst for.

One night, I become too exhausted to continue walking the five hours I've got left until sunrise. I walk to the fluorescent storefront of a twenty-four-hour convenience store. It's the only place still doing business at this hour. The sliding doors squeal as folks come and go, but having people around makes it feel like the safest option. I lay down on the pavement and interlace the straps of my backpack with my arms to keep it from being stolen. I put my tied-up arms and bag under my head for a pillow. Despite laying down on a dirty pavement, sleep comes instantly. In a vivid dream, I am brutally murdered right where I am sleeping. When I wake, I find an undone zipper on my backpack. A little pack of toiletries is missing. Because the bag was under my head the whole time, the missing items prove that I was moved and murdered in the night. That was no dream.

I have become a spirit that is invisible to others, one of the evening ghosts of my visions. I roam the city, confused about why I'm still on Earth. In a large park I pass mural of a beautiful being, half tree, half woman. She is blowing a kiss into whirling winds. Her hair is lush with gorgeous multi-colored autumn leaves that dance in the breeze behind her. A goddess of bloom and decay. I hear a voice: "Maya, your spirit was once this beautiful."

Tears cascade down my cheeks as I mourn all the good that died in me while I was still alive.

I continue through the park. Spontaneous song slips from my lips. Mostly just sounds, summoned from source vibration. Inspired notes morph into song. Mmm. Oh. Wu. Awe. The air feels like it's circulating in and out of my lungs simultaneously. Breathing in both directions at once is further proof that I am no longer of solid human form, but one with the air.

But, by the end of another night of aimless roaming, I've returned to uncertainty about whether I'm a robot, a ghostly spirit, or lost in a coma filled with nightmares. In spite of my epiphany, I've sunk back to the miserable mess that is all too familiar. The robot controllers keep switching the movie that they're roboting me to star in. There's simply a new movie added to the list, one where I am a ghost trapped among the living.

Days pass where I emotionally realm-hop several times throughout the day. Struggling through tsunamis and splashing in warm oases. I give up; I need no explanation for what I'm experiencing, or for what I am. Reality shifts constantly anyway. There's a deep sense of sanity in realizing that I don't understand anything. It's too exhausting to keep up with what I think is happening and what I believe myself to be. As soon as something feels absolute, another factor comes in and shifts what I thought I understood. I am all of it. Then I am none of it. When I am none of it, it's because I need to help save Nunavut. Then I am something incomplete. Sometimes it's frightening. The evil beings laugh at me after my moments of hope of saving the world and threaten to create more suffering with their power.

At moments I feel like I've attained nirvana, and nothing can hurt me. At other times, I plummet to the ground and return to being filled with despair, believing that I am but one of the many that is responsible and will be trapped in suffering, poverty, and filth for the rest of life. Am I doomed to be a miserable hobo? Am I an idiot for throwing myself into the path of a wandering renunciant?

Everything changes again. And again. And again. And again.

I have a few material possessions that I brought to have purpose on this journey. It's time to let them go. A deck of Wisdom from Other Realms fortune telling cards, jewellery made from guitar strings and collected plants, a selection of crystals from special people and special times, and all the art that I've drawn since becoming a renunciate. I walk around the city chanting, "Om Namo Narayanaya," while gifting the last of my things to the Earth, decorating the city with all the physical attachments I have remaining.

So here I am, chanting sounds that feel soulfully profound, too deep to be articulated and boxed into a language. I ceremoniously place the rest of my Wisdom Cards, one by one, in bushes, on window sills, in flower beds, on church steps, gifting them each with a prayer. I'm giving the Earth everything that I have, praying that all I have is enough to help Mama Earth, somehow. But I fear I am powerless.

I've been in Toronto for weeks now. The city is chewing me up. I've never been so filthy. I need sleep. It's rare to share a smile and a hello with another. One day, while I panhandle, someone hands me a pamphlet of youth shelters. The cut-off age is twenty-four — my age. The number boggles me. Am I actually still considered a youth? My life is so freaking weird and drastic. How is it that I've seen so much, died and been born again, and yet I'm still called youthful? I feel old, beaten, and jaded. I've lived so much, yet I've just been reminded that I'm young. What could be in store if this is only the beginning?

All right, hobo-bot. Time to hop to another realm.

As the sun wanes and the fear that comes with being homeless in the dark resurfaces, I decide to make my way to one of the shelters. I borrow the phone of a coffee shop and dial a few numbers from the pamphlet, until I find a shelter with available beds. With the last of my coins, I take a long subway ride across the city. As I walk briskly down a dark road towards the youth safehouse, the street lamps become weak and the hissing ghosts return with the darkness. They swarm behind and around me at the edge of my vision. I hurry to the shelter entrance as fast as I can, crawling out of my skin in discomfort. Inside, I'm given a room that's shared with another girl. Our room reeks of urine. I'm so exhausted, I don't even care. I pass out as soon as my head hits the plastic pillow.

The moment I wake up, my roommate gets in my face and screams, "I hate you." She points to a lock of dirty blonde hair that she cut from my head while I was sleeping. Surely she's mad because I blew her chance to appear in a movie by sleeping instead of hanging out with her. I take the lock of hair and bind it with a rubber band to one of the dreadlocks that's formed on my head. An embodiment of my journey.

After breakfast, I walk down to the park with one of the other kids staying at the shelter. "What's your name?" he asks.

"Maya," I say. "What's yours?"

"Sega."

He's obviously implying that he's "Dreamcast." He's charming enough to be Dreamcast, I think to myself, wondering if he can hear my thoughts. Most of us staying at the shelter walk down to the basketball court. I sit on the sidelines and draw the planets aligning.

I'm quite certain that everyone here already knows who I am. I'm famous. It's no big deal, though. Several of them have also been tormented by robot controllers. That's why the ghetto is called "the projects": it's an experiment. A bunch of them are star subjects, victims being broadcasted and experimented on, like me. That's why they're so kind. They can empathize with what I'm going through. They already understand it's no dream to be a movie star. Well, at least the trapped-by-satellites kind of movie star. Yeah, satellites up in the sky, with the stars, making big burning messes out of people. That's why celebrities are called stars.

Sega stops playing basketball and comes over to sit with me. He points at a cup and asks me what I see. "Is it a cup or is it something spiritual?"

"It's both. It's whatever way you choose to look at it and however you choose to use it. Defining it is what makes it something. Something separate from the air around and in it. Maybe."

I suppose there's now a philosophical film on the agenda.

I go on to watch myself stumble my way through trying to articulate metaphysical notions. "True reality is so far from what most people believe it to be. They define their experiences into narrow incomplete theories that they dogmatically believe to be whole and absolute, thus trap themselves into boxes and cages they've built around their knowledge. So many people see themselves as knowing, as comprehending. Ironically, this behaviour is stupid, the oposit of knowing and understanding. They label themselves clever because they've decided that they comprehend the world and how it works. But really, they are putting limits on what they can perceive and the potential of what they can learn and experience.

All is one. All is nothing if something isn't everything?

If you think you understand something 100%, you are limiting your potential.

I hope you don't understand. Do you hear the picture?

Words and language are inadequate, outdated tools. They aid the beginning of comprehension, but don't take us to the elusive finish line. But, thereafter, reality will change. Maybe. But that's okay. Maybe.

One of the other kids comes over to talk with us. My focus is turned from inside to outside, even though that's where my attention was anyway. But in a different sense, I guess?

As we talk with the other guy, his face starts to morph. Someone watching just hopped into this boy, transported themselves inside of him to spirit-share his body. That's the actual cause of memory gaps or spacing out, at least in some cases. Someone's spirit teleporting into the vessel of another and momentarily taking reign. After about ten seconds his face turns back to how it was before. I try to shake off my thoughts and return to our conversation. He was spacing out too, as someone else's spirit occupied his body.

I stay at the shelter another night. It's quite pacifying to hang out with other fucked up young folk, like at the hospital. In the morning, I'm roboted to leave. It's summer. It's time to get out of the city, to go to BC and take part in the festivals. I'm afraid to hitch-hike back west. My mind is occupied by so many forces that I've lost faith in my ability to focus enough to visualise, and thus manifest, a safe journey.

I find an internet cafe, log onto my neglected Facebook account. My cousin Yasmine is online. I tell her I'm penniless and stuck in Toronto. She offers to buy me a plane ticket to Vancouver, and a room in a hotel for tonight.

I find the hotel. The clerk scowls at my grubbiness. While he hands me the key he leans back and his nostrils tighten, as if he's afraid I'd pollute him. In the shower I wash weeks of grime off myself. Once I'm clean, I still feel like I don't belong. It's strange to all of a sudden be in a clean and private room. This realm is familiar yet surreal, like a vague memory of a past life that I'm haunting. I wrap myself in a towel and hand wash my clothes in the sink. It feels so strange to be clean. The smog and dirt of weeks on city streets and benches had seeped their way deep into my pores.

I'd assumed I'd be able to collapse into prolonged sleep. But when I turn out the lights, I hear the hissing. I see the wisps. Lights on, I spend most of the night awake on the couch, feeling like an imposter.

In the morning, a bus takes me to the airport.

Seventy

I walk out of the Vancouver airport and sneak onto the Skytrain. The train costs four bucks, more than I have to my name. I'm the only person on board. I start singing again. The acoustics bouncing up and down the empty train car resound as powerfully as an opera house theatre, my tonedeaf voice unworthy. Singing reminds me that I'm one with the air, a planet and different solar breezes are unfurling through me, spiralling around me, morphing in and out of each other. I'm a sentient galaxy, fully aware of its shooting stars. At one stop, a group of transit cops step onto the train. I keep singing. They don't even look at me. I get a free pass because it's a movie scene. I was supposed to sneak onto the train.

Outside the Commercial Broadway Station, I sit down, put my hat in front of me, and begin to sing, or at least try to sing, between all my cracks and flat notes. Within a half hour, I've made nearly twelve dollars. That's enough work for one day! I buy a few beers and make my way to a park. It's filled with hacky sack circles, friends throwing frisbees, and people just laying around, basking in the summer's warm light.

A few days go by where I'm pretty much experiencing the same thing I was in Toronto. Trying to surrender, as I surf the shifting shores of the great surreal.

In Chinatown, I notice a Buddhist temple and ring the bell outside the tall gate and am buzzed in off of the street. A woman meets me at the door. I slip off my shoes then follow her up the stairs. There's a large altar populated by glowing golden Buddhas, colourful paintings of paths through different realms, with offerings of flowers and food at their feet. Some of them look demonic. Probably because they've travelled through all the realms of samsara. I pray. I focus all of my energy and emotions into a soulful intention of becoming a Bodhisattva. A real Bodhisattva. To attain enlightenment, but consciously return to realms of suffering to help others also reach absolute peace, rather than choose to dwell in nirvana for the remainder of infinity. My mind quiets while I sit, taking a break from life, in the calm of the temple. It is so still here. Suddenly a voice from within interrupts.

You've outstayed your welcome.

Abruptly, I stand and leave to return to my melancholic vagabonding. A blind turn brings me into a Skytrain station surrounded by sickly, dirty pigeons. People walk through the fallen doves, rushed, apathetic. The pavement that is my bed is glazed in pigeon shit. I take seat in the middle of the storm of birds. I'm as filthy as they are. From the desire to help my sister birds, I start to speak to them. "Why do you come here? The city is hurting you!"

Tears start to stream down my cheeks. Everything about me is broken. I don't have the energy to endure infinity. Already, I regret my fresh prayer to become an enlightened saviour. Sitting amidst the birds I realize that, if I were to become a Bodhisattva, I'd have to continue realm-hopping until every last particle of existence reaches bliss. I don't want to endure anymore suffering. I look to the skies, tears in my eyes, terrified of that path, and scream, "I don't want to be a Bodhisattva!"

I stay in the epicentre of the displaced, dirty doves for

some time, and cry into the sidewalk, as if my tears could wash the cement pure. Someone comes and sits next to me and gently says, "You know, you actually know me." I don't even look up at him. Just stay, head lowered, focused on my misery. After a minute or two the person at my side gets up and leaves. Slowly, my tears subside, and I return to my bleak empty wandering, vacant of any destination.

I'm tripping out on my palm again. What does it mean? Why are the heart and head line not separate? As I stare at the large triangle taking up most of my palm and the second triangle inside its centre, for the first time I notice a third triangle. It's tiny, hidden deep in the centre of the second triangle. Three triangles... sacred trinity? I don't know if I'd be able to find a knowledgeable palm reader around here. Ancient eastern sciences tend to be scoffed at and disregarded until the western sciences catch up. Is it truly a special and sacred marking? Do I bear the marking of a grand destiny? Again, I think back to the words of palm readers.

"You are going to have a really good life, but you are going to have to wait."

"Your name will be known."

"When times are hard, remember you chose a life where you wanted to learn a lot."

I find true solace in recalling their words. Maybe there is a beautiful outcome to all the hell I've been through. It's too much to handle if I don't let myself believe life may turn out okay.

It's Shambhala festival time. It fills me with sadness that I am not there. I had years where life itself was a festival of bliss, a long summer. Now, I am homeless, impoverished, alone, inert. I am filled with dread for life. There are so many elderly homeless people, those who have plummeted down without ever getting back up. What if that is not only my present, but also my future? What if I'm unable to weave my way out of these circumstances? I almost wish I didn't have happy memories. The contrast is hardly bearable.

I walk through the maze of streets and wind up at the crossroads of Pain and Wastings. The corner of Main Street and East Hastings earned its name for being the poorest district of Canada. Most people on these blocks are homeless drug addicts. There's so much prostitution and crime here that nobody seems to care to fix it any more.

I kind of feel out of place, as I'm completely sober. But, at the same time I feel like I belong. I am one with the anguish. I am pain, and I am waste. It's almost comforting to be surrounded by lost souls. Maybe I've just gone numb, but places like this don't scare me anymore. Maybe I'm just too tired to feel emotion. I have disengaged from my circumstances. It seems like everything in life has passed me by, detached from me. Life is a dirty river I am floating down on a deteriorating raft.

Seventy-One

More hopeless wandering brings me to Victoria, across the water from Vancouver. For the hundredth time, I roam a city aimlessly. For the thousandth time, I'm being told that if I stay awake for three days, without eating or drinking, I will be rewarded. Through some combination of distrust in the controllers and being too exhausted to care, I decide to ignore them. I stumble upon a women's shelter and am given a private room. There's a hissing ghost in the room with me. Their charity was a ruse. They know that the room is haunted, and they purposely gave it to me.

In the first couple days of being in Victoria, I bump into several people I know. Or rather, once knew. It isn't synchronicity or coincidence, just confirmation that I'm being watched. My former friends and acquaintances crossed paths with me on purpose, to make sure that I know that I'm still on camera. Still, no one is at liberty to flat out say it with words. Seeing them makes me realize how far away and unreachable the life I had three years ago is. As if I was a different species, on a different planet. One person truly reaches out and offers me her couch for the night. I sense reluctance, so I decline. A night off won't save me anyway.

Being here is a heartbreaking reminder of who I used to be, of how life used to feel. Life was so happy and fortunate. I gallivanted around the world, marvelling at my luck and karma. My dreams would manifest as easily as I drew breath.

Remembering my past makes me more infuriated at the robot controllers. How dare they steal my motions and emotions.

Back on the city streets, I continue to bump into people who were once friends of mine, but now avoid eye contact. Later, I get kicked out of the homeless shelter for dyeing my hair in the shower and staining it purple.

I'm roboted to a Greyhound Station and, with the majority of my freshly reinstated disability check, I buy a ticket going to the East Coast. The thought of having three days to not worry about where to sit and sleep is a decadent relief.

Seventy-Two

I listen to the radio most of the way, only half-interested but unable to turn it off. After three sleepless days, rest finally visits me. I am roughly jostled awake in Moncton, New Brunswick, and am told to get off the bus. The driver doesn't seem particularly bothered that I've come further than I paid for. The controllers deliberately roboted me to sleep so they could intentionally take me to "Monk Town." The name itself is the director's way of instructing what I'm to do without breaking the suspension of disbelief. It is a continuation of the aspiring Buddha-on-spiritual-walkabout narrative.

Once I step off of the bus I am overwhelmed with dread. The East Coast is bitterly cold. I don't want to be a roaming renunciant any more, it was a naive and egotistical aspiration. I get on the next bus going back west, just wanting to bide time on a warm bus for as long as possible. The respite from not having to worry about shelter or warmth ends all too quickly. Half a day later, I wind up in Quebec City, completely out of money. What's my next fiasco?

Seventy-Three

I find myself on the cobbled streets of Old Quebec City. I was brought to this place for its timeless look. The new movie is set in the past. Pedestrians step aside to make way for elegant, horse-drawn carriages, as the clip-clopping of hooves echoes off the stone walls of eighteenth-century churches and homes.

I wander into a boutique to choose my outfit for the show, something appropriate for the era it's set in. I put on a full-length, turquoise velvet gown, a leather belt, a shiny necklace of copper chunks, and a big hat with an even bigger feather sticking out of its rim. With a freshly ring-encrusted hand, I wave the cashier over to the mirror and do a twirl for her in my new outfit. I tell her it's perfect, smile and wink, then do a one eighty and head for the door, and the fifteenth century world beyond it. With slight desperation, the cashier insists that I either pay or get changed. I am shocked by her response. Does she not want me to model her clothes? This is an opportunity for free advertising in a major motion picture! Deflated, I squirm back into my rags in the changeroom, then head back onto the cold, windy, streets, realizing that my role is still one of someone forlorn.

The brisk breezes keep one moving on the streets of Quebec City. My legs carry me places I don't notice any more. I walk past a grocery store, then watch myself swerve back and head for the entrance. They aren't laughing this time, aren't berating me, but I know it's the electronic voodoo, the sensation of wind entering my body again. I watch myself grab a small round of cheese and a half litre of yoghurt from the dairy shelf, and then watch myself walk past the tills out of the store, not even attempting to conceal my actions. Surely the people behind the cameras want me to eat, to sustain myself so that I'm able to carry on their show. As I'm crossing the parking lot a large hand closes around my arm. I don't resist in the slightest as he drags me across the parking lot, back inside, past disturbed shoppers and stockers, up the stairs to his office. He slams shut the door and cuffs me to an office chair.

He snaps his fingers in front of my face. "Go on then! Explain yourself!"

Numbly, I reply, "It's not my choice"

"Should I call the police?"

Must be a cop show they're shooting lately.

His question hangs in the air. A fly buzzes into the room and lands on his desk. He slams his hand down and lifts it away to reveal a smudge of reddish-brown, with the other half of the fly crawling away in slow agony. I start to sob. I'm crying for the fly.

"Look at what you're doing! Look at the fly!" He doesn't even clue in that he should finish the job and put the helpless creature out of its misery. I can't do it myself, with my hands cuffed. He lays into me, telling me I'm the monster. I can't peel my eyes away from the half-dead animal before me. Tears stream faster down my cheeks. Overwhelmed by the insect's pain, and my own hatred for the man responsible and indifferent to its suffering, I call him an oaf, a pathetic bully. He calls the cops.

Still, I'm crying, begging him to finish killing the fly. The police arrive.

Seventy-Four

Sitting in the dark backseat of a cop car, I'm told that I'm being brought to jail. If I wasn't so exhausted, maybe I'd care. I hear a voice in my head, Yeah, we roboted you...

"Chi's" and "Yogi-hurt."

It's a riddle, weave your way out!

I'm pushed up a set of stairs into a sterile building. Two brutes in uniform demand fingerprints. In crooked French, I refuse, believing that they want to graph my palm and it's destiny, to make a robot clone of me. A clone that could impersonate the prism in my palm, along with the destiny it marks, while the original me is kept hidden and locked away. Therefore, my destiny to better the world, won't be realized. The window for salvation will pass. Earth and her children will remain in a realm of suffering for much longer, possibly eternity.

They press the ink pad towards me. I pull away, backing into the corner of the room. One of the creepy cops towers over me, sneers, then laughs as he grabs my wrist. With force that brinks on bone-breaking, he stabs each of my fingers from the ink pad to the film sheet to collect my hand's data. World Eudaimonia is now in peril. Because of my resistance to comply, the police become more severe. I am handcuffed, then ankle cuffed, then pushed into a cage in the back of a truck. They take me to a real prison.

This is definitely a movie. They're exaggerating. There's

no way prison is this bad. Rusting metal toilets and sinks, thumb-sized rations of recycled soap with hairs congealed into them, miniscule rations of toilet paper that disintegrates at the slightest drop of liquid. One toothless, tiny woman here is covered in scabs. She must be going through withdrawal. She incessantly itches at her wounds, tossing the pieces onto the ground, and throws fits of screaming rage at the slightest provocation. Obviously, this is all being played up for entertainment in the film that I'm starring in.

I inform the guards I'm vegetarian. One replies that I need to talk to the pastor about my religious diet. Every time she makes the rounds, she repeats that exact same sentence: "You need to talk to the pastor about your religious diet." She's doing takes for a scene in the movie, and it's taking forever to get the shot right. She says it again.

I reply with the same answer I've given each time: "Everyone needs clean water." I was only thinking small, within the context of the prison, but I have been misunderstood, because, suddenly, I hear the voices of several well-wishers in my head.

Literal well-wishers, the millions of people that don't have access to clean water and need wells dug.

"Thank you, Maya. We commend your protest of self-sacrifice, of staying in prison as long as it takes for clean water to be brought to us."

Deep down inside, I don't have faith that my refusal to leave prison would have enough impact to solve the problem. I cry shameful tears of apology and voice that I'm not prepared to embark on the martyr's mission of remaining in prison until all of the people of Earth have clean water.

We're not allowed to bring stuff in from the outside world. Instead, we order stuff off flimsy yellow forms.

Detainees that have money can mark the items they want on the sheet and hand it to the prison staff. Once a week, the guards come around with the crap that the prisoners purchased. I scan the list of what's being sold. It's mostly junk food and toiletries, along with some cheap stuff like stationery supplies. It's all slave labour, inorganic, and violently sourced. The hypocrisy is infuriating. If one wants something, their only option here is to support sociopathic companies that commit worse crimes than what some people in here are locked up for. The prison owner is getting rich on selling cheap wares made in China, supporting Tibetan genocide. Chocolate bars made with sugar and cocoa harvested by slaves under sponsored dictators. Shampoo made of chemicals that pollute the rivers and murder ecosystems. I am not insane, the system is. Okay, well, on second thought, maybe we both are. Could it be society's influence that, at least in part, has made me crazy?

I am charged with theft. My court hearing is in five days. The lawyer assigned to meet with me asks a few questions, and then, "Are you mentally ill?" I tell her I was diagnosed as schizoaffective type bipolar, some time ago. Her face is impossible to read.

After speaking with the lawyer, I'm assigned to a bunk with another girl. I'm raking the cheap plastic comb I was given through the dreads that have formed on my head, wanting to look clean cut for my court case. The teeth of the comb just snap off into my ropes of hair as I try to brush through them. Then, from the corner of my eye, I see my cellmate quietly reach beneath her mattress, producing a tiny steel razor blade, and bring it straight toward my head. Dreadlocks thick and long like tarantula legs plop to my feet as she saws them off. Her kindness leaves me deeply uneasy. I'm locked in a cell with a mysterious inmate who has hidden weapons. I better bite my tongue, or risk getting cut.

Day Two. I'm alone in the cell. Razor Blade is in the common area that's unlocked for a few hours of each day. I completely lose control, again. It's the wind, or the spirits, voodoo, possession, being a robot... I don't know why; I just know it's definitely not a choice that I have any say in. I eat most of my cellmate's food, all the good stuff that she has hoarded from the order sheets at jailhouse premium prices. Chips, chocolate bars, two boxes of cereal, and half a tub of peanut butter vanish down my throat. I try meekly to sweep up the evidence and return to lying in bed just before Razor Blade returns to her emptied shelf. She snaps. She rages. Gets right up in my face and screams things I dare not hear. My ears ring as her spit splatters onto my face. I can't handle it. I'm hovering above as a witness, watching all the other inmates as they watch us, unsure if her and her crew are going to beat the shit out of me.

The guards come and separate us. I'm moved to a different cell, this time with a huge, also toothless, old woman. It's hard to look at her, but it's even harder not to. Whenever she catches me staring, she shoots her piercing, dead-eyed gaze straight through me, barking violent insults and threats. I can't decipher if I'm more depressed or frightened by her deeply distilled anger.

Day three. One hour of each day is designated as outdoor time. For us, "the outdoors" is a small, concrete court enclosed by a twenty-foot barbed-wire fence, with a corner watch post towering above. I sit alone on the ground. A group of five women walk to the only picnic table, at the far edge of the square. The oldest woman among them stumbles and falls and does not get up. She lays still, completely disregarded by the others. I can't help but observe the scene. The bravest part of me stands and makes my way over to her. Blood is dripping through her cropped white hair. I put my sweater under her head, take her hand in mine, and tell her that everything is going to be okay, not believing the words coming out of my mouth. The others remain unperturbed. At least they ignore instead of attack. I'd ask for their help if I wasn't terrified of them. This can't be real. This has to be a movie. These people are far too hateful, too soulless, too dead inside to be real. This *has* to be an act. But she's actually bleeding from her skull...

I wave the guards over. They roll their eyes, and slowly walk towards us, brandishing their big, black batons, as if looking for an excuse to strike someone. They hover, sneering over the injured woman as if pleased to see her in pain. An old wheelchair is procured. The two biggest guards callously grab her under her armpits and slam her into the chair. Where are they taking her? Will she be safe, alone with the guards? I shiver and, with all my might, hold back my tears. I mustn't show any weakness.

Day four. I have a shower, without soap, because I might be a political prisoner, protesting for clean water rights for all those in need of it. In bed, I can feel invisible little bugs hop all over me. The guards that do the evening rounds are all men. They can tell we're afraid of them. We can tell they like scaring us. I spend the night wide awake, finding comfort in my cellmate's roaring snores. I'm safe from her while she's asleep.

Day five. I'm delivered to court, cuffed at my hands and ankles. My lawyer coolly announces I am not in my right mind. I don't need to say anything. The judge promptly orders me to a psychiatric hospital for a two-week evaluation.

Seventy-Five

That same evening, I am taken to an enormous psychiatric hospital. This time it isn't a cosy psych ward with patients briefly passing through. It's a full-blown, horror-movie insane asylum. The old, grey bricked building lords over the rundown neighbourhood surrounding it. It's even spookier on the inside. Three men escort me down cold, lifeless corridors, up an ancient elevator, then up to the legal ward. The patients here are prisoners, like me, all awaiting their fate. After our stay, we will either be sent to prison, kept indefinitely in psychiatric care, or released if we are deemed innocent and newly sane. The ward consists of one hallway with eight bedrooms and one bathroom. At the entrance there is a common area that hosts a TV with stiff, decrepit seats in front of it. Next to it there's a dining area with plastic tables and chairs bolted to the floor. Adjacent is the observation post, where the nurses watch and assess us twenty-four seven from behind plastic windows. We are denied the simplest of things. I'm not allowed to use my markers, we aren't allowed to have cups or bottles of water. There's no computer, we aren't allowed to wear hoodies or shoelaces. But, much worse than the strict rules, are the disturbed people trapped in here with me. Some of them clearly belong in prison.

After a sleepless night of listening to the radio and the snores of a roommate, in a hard, starchy bed, a nurse comes bursting into the room and announces it's time to make our beds and have breakfast. I hermit at the corner table, ignoring my toast, unable to resist staring at the others. Some people smile, and some scowl. I'm afraid. But it's a much milder kind of fear than in prison. Sometime mid-morning, I meet with a psychiatrist in a tiny, bland office, table and chairs also bolted to the floor. I'm explaining myself more to the invisible viewers than the psychiatrist...

"If you want to help people have mental stability, working in a place like this is not how one brings people into wellness. This place causes humanity more harm than healing. There's no compost, there's barely any recycling. The food is imported from ridiculously far places and grown with pesticides and poisons. This hospital is fuelling climate change — thus creating famine and drought for other parts of the world and sustaining mass sickness. If you look at the big picture, you can't deny that this hospital is a source of more sickness than health." He's not open to discussing my sentiments. I'm not open to taking the antipsychotics he prescribes.

I meet with the psychiatrist several times. Each time he urges me to take medication, I continue to refuse, insisting that he has to stop perpetuating mass global illness before I take him seriously as a doctor, or, in other words, a healer.

In another attempt to be understood, I show him my right palm, explain that in other places and times, palmistry was as much a respected science as western medicine is today. I show him how my heart and headline are one, I explain that, for my mind to be at peace, my heart must also be at peace. And that my heart is in turmoil about living here...

"Do you really believe that medicine that causes illness will be respected in the future? Yes, western medicine has some truly helpful aspects. But it's greatly flawed in many areas. Do you really think you can bring people into the trinity of mental, physical, and spiritual health by sustaining them on Wonder Bread, processed meats, and Jello? Health and medicine should be synonymous. I'm sorry you dedicated years of schooling, and then years of work, to this profession, but you still have a lot to learn if you sincerely want to bring people into health. *You* actually have the power and karma to make positive impact!" He cuts me off and informs me that at, my court case, he's requesting me an ordinance of compliance to follow his recommendations of me taking medicine. My eyes bulge in terror at this.

"I'm trying to help you," he insists.

Two weeks of killing time, lying in bed in the legal ward, slowly pass. I'm cuffed at the hands and ankles again, brought to a tiny cell, where I wait alone for most of the day. My court case is over in less than three minutes. My lawyer convinces the judge to have me sent back to psychiatric care, but, this time, as my doctor requested, I must comply with all the treatments he prescribes. I thought my lawyer was supposed to help me! She just turned me into a legal lab-rat! That evening, a student nurse sits at my bedside and listens to me as I explain why I don't feel that this is a place of healing. Instead of rolling her eyes and walking away, she just listens then tries to comfort me by saying she truly believes I'll improve here, and that I can trust their care. She's different. She cares. Maybe it's because she's young and new at her job. Her heart and spirit aren't numb yet. Instead of sitting in the observation area all day, she comes out from behind the plastic windows and listens to the prisoner-patients about what they're struggling with.

As I talk with her, I notice how fast my mind is moving,

grabbing out in all directions. I have so many things I want to express, things that feel like imminent epiphanies that must be acted upon, prophecies and conspiracies and cosmic wisdom, all the radio stations playing at once. They're all racing through my brain simultaneously as I stumble to articulate myself well, in French.

One evening, perched in my room's window, I stare out at the intangible autumn, hoping it could help calm my mind and breath. I start to experience frequent anxiety attacks. Breathing becomes difficult, shallow and panicked. I'm unable to quell my terror about being a locked-up science experiment. In those moments, I make collect calls to lost friends, tearful and desperate to inform the outside world that I'm a lab rat. No one accepts the charges. No one wants me in their life. No one loves me anymore. I'm too crazy. I'm under constant surveillance, yet utterly alone.

About once a week, the nurses force me to shower. The suspected potential reality of being a political prisoner, staying locked up until all of the world has clean drinking water, makes me resist. I explain to my nurse that the shampoo they supply hurts the rivers, the creatures and the plants living in them. "If I shower, I make the Earth dirty. So, you see, it's not actually cleaning myself, because we are not separate entities from the Earth." They don't care. I'm made to shower in front of a nurse. She watches me the whole time, forcing sickly-sweet-smelling soaps and shampoos into my hands and hair.

My fellow in-patients confuse me, some even frighten me. I see dark shadows flailing and lunging in efforts to leap out of one guy's body. My friends, the ones who won't pick up my collect calls, teleport into another patient's body, though they are trying to help me when doing so, giving me telepathic information on how to get released. Another patient is a pervert, his eyes, his words are disgusting; so far, I've managed not to be alone with him. There's an elderly woman filled with energy and enthusiasm that shares her cigarettes while she showers me with her life stories and wisdom. Still another is catastrophically depressed. The lifeless two glued to the TV are either extremely grumpy or half-friendly in a sedated kind of way, never know what you're gonna get with those two.

Slowly, the hissing ghosts, the voices, and the telepathy start to diminish. My psychiatrist asks me if I'm open to believing that I'm mentally ill. I tell him that anything is possible, that coining down reality is naive. I confide that, in this moment, I'm more convinced that I have an electronic implant that can control my thoughts and actions, and that the controllers continue to watch and manipulate me via satellite. That just rings truer with everything I've been through than any other explanation. The medical staff ask me how I explain the lessening of symptoms as I take medication. "The robot controllers are just temporarily decreasing my symptoms for now so that they can fool me and torture me longer, once I'm released."

It nearly breaks me when I hear a nurse respond, "If you're released." My emotional state worsens from that grim conclusion. Staying positive is impossible.

They look deeper into my skull and find an eight-millimetre growth on my brain. They're guessing it's a tumour but need to consult a specialist to be sure. So that's that, I have a tumour and my life might be nearing its end. More than anything, this comes as a relief. Life isn't something I'm very fond of any more. Its leaves have passed their beautiful bloom, fallen, and gone to maggot filled muck. It has no more gifts to give me. I get a tad sentimental. I realize that if my life is, in fact, going to be short, I'm grateful that I got to travel, instead of spending my youth at school or at some mediocre job. At least I got to experience some good times.

After days in limbo, the specialist finally comes to speak with me. He informs me that the growth in my brain is benign. The medication I'm currently on is affecting my hormone levels and might be what's causing the cyst to grow. *No!* The mix of new antipsychotics might have actually started helping, if not for this. Again, hope is stripped.

I snap back into sheer bleakness. I don't want to live a long life if I'm going to have to spend it in crippling sickness, unable to control my mind, body, and choose my whereabouts. My doctor tells me there are still some medications that haven't been tried on me yet. He says that there is hope. I'm so tired of this.

Two months pass. I return to court for the judge to determine my mental-aptitude to bear innocence or guilt for stealing the chi and yogi-hurt. I spend another day waiting in a holding cell. Even though it's only a day, being cooped up like this is horrible. I imagine myself as a chicken in a filthy cage, surrounded by countless other cages in all directions, with no room to move. I decide to go vegan again. I've been too numb to care lately. But now I feel for myself similar living conditions to a factory farm. No amount of cheap meat is worth this.

Last time, court was a movie. This time, it's mortifyingly real. Strangers silently judge me from the pews, while the two lawyers battle to determine whether I'm a dangerous thief or a straight up lunatic. It becomes so humiliating that I leave my body again, hover invisibly above the trial.

The judge concludes that, two months from now, I will be mentally apt to stand trial for the charge of shoplifting.

I'm granted disability money. With it I chain-smoke my way through the long days. Nothing happens in the tiny, isolated, legal ward. And never am I allowed to leave. The boredom is excruciating. I try to stay positive, to be grateful that I have shelter, food, water, a bed, and a handful of kind people around me. I try to stay optimistic about how I might actually be recovering from illness — all this opposed to being alone, homeless, and totally insane. When I can muster it, I try to focus on the bright side. Millions of my brothers and sisters are trapped in illness, poverty, filth, war, violence… I just feel like an entitled western asshole when I get all negative about my circumstances. Medicine was given to me for free. The medicine wasn't ideal, but it might actually be working…

Slowly I become better than I have been in years, now potentially diverted from a whole array of possible futures in poisonous places. Why must it be a privilege to have access to such a thing? Healthcare shouldn't be a luxury — healthcare should be a human right.

My symptoms improve with each passing day. Hours go by where I am uninterrupted by voices pillaging my brain. My thoughts are mostly mine, or at least I'm willing to believe that they are. The controllers, the voices, the night-time spirits, the extreme moods, the gorging on food… this was all mental illness? The weeks and months of sleeplessness were mania? The bizarre sights were hallucinations? All this time I was just sick? The desire to intoxicate myself just a by-product of it all?

It is difficult to accept that there were no persons behind those years of cruel influence, that it was all from inside me.

I was not wrong to criticize western medicine. But I might be right in accepting it, now. Just the impression of what I pray is a full recovery baffles me. The gratitude I feel is profound, yet at the same time fragile and terrifying. If I were to become broken again, I don't know if I'd have the strength to cope with more loss.

Slowly I start to spend less time curled up in bed in the foetal position. The panic attacks stop. There's a few art supplies, so I use them to make the days go by, instead of just chain smoking. The graphite pencils in here are encased in rubber instead of wood or plastic. We're not allowed normal pencils because they could be used as weapons or suicide tools. The narrow bendy grips are tricky to use but I'm trying to practice patience and positivity. It's better than nothing. All we have is broken crayons to add colour to our pictures. I like the Mandalas that I've created. Watching empty white sheets absorb colour from the stubby crayon-tips is uplifting in this gloom-ridden corridor.

More and more, I peek out from my bomb shelter. I've become good friends with one of the other patients. The days are much more pleasant and flow by faster, now that I have someone that I can share good conversations with. We talk about our lives while we pace the hallway. His birthday is my half-birthday. Being zodiac opposites supposedly means we're the perfect balance for each other. After a week or two he tells me he's fallen in love with me. All I have to respond with is "thank you." Our friendship becomes awkward. He doesn't let up. I retreat to hermiting in my room again.

Back in court, I squirm in shame as I stand in front of a room of people arguing over my actions in third person, like I'm not even here. But there is a happy ending; I am declared criminally non-responsible due to my mental state.

Seventy-Six

Now that my trial is over, I am allowed to leave the legal ward. It is dizzying and surreal to step beyond the hallway that I had been confined to for the past four months. I follow the painted stripes on the floor, one colour at a time, zigzagging through the sprawling building like a life-sized subway map.

There's a small art gallery in the building that exclusively exhibits work from the patients. I get lost in the maze of hallways to find it. The art on display leaves something to be desired, just some meek, paint-by-numbers landscapes. The next day I bring my best rubber-pencil and crayon drawings to the gallery and show them to the curator behind the desk. He commends my work and tells me to come back with more creations, now that I am able to use more than crayons. Typically, the gallery requires at least five years of practice before admitting the work of new artists to its walls. But he's willing to make an exception for me, due to the calibre of what I've shown him. His simple encouragement restores a little bit of the self-esteem I once carried.

Life continues to improve. I am now allowed to go outdoors. Spring is in bloom. Clear skies are returning to the bloodied battlefield of my brain. But I'm not fully receptive to this happy truth. I'm often groggy and detached, unprepared to fully accept and embrace my recovery. My psychiatrist tells me I'm experiencing Post-Psychotic Depression, caused from the trauma, shock, and lost time of what I'm emerging out of.

He says this is normal and will pass with time.

My medications continue to take effect, this time without inducing growths in my brain. The side-effects of fatigue and increased appetite are strong, but I'm told that they will also subside with time. My brain is mine; my thoughts are mine. My body is mine; my movements are my decision. These mantras are realized again and again by experience.

I come to accept that I was, in fact, mentally ill. This breakthrough is stunning. I truly thought there was no escape from the nightmare my life had become.

After another idle month, there is finally room for me in the unit they want me transferred to. Here in the youth ward, I belong. I am welcome. The others are nice and friendly. There're artists, musicians, kind people that I can easily relate to. People with hope for life, for recovery. Hope, to become healthy and beautiful, and to do good things in the world again. Not creepy and mean, like the many dark occupants of the legal ward. Being here starts to revive my fragile soul. I am finally among friends.

Weeks go by where I hang out with the other young folk that I genuinely like. I start doing yoga again. I do inspired art, this time with the privilege of pens, markers, and paint! My psychiatrist tells me that, if all stays well, I am to be discharged from the hospital in three weeks.

Hardly believing my circumstances, I start to look for apartments online. I fall in love with the first one I visit. It's a yellow walled studio in the historic part of downtown Quebec. The apartment's old, its wooden floor warped and weathered, but I don't mind. It's five hundred dollars a month. I can actually afford it with my social assistance. There are cheaper places in this city, generic ones in bland neighbourhoods. But

I have become aware of the influence that my environment has on my emotional wellbeing. It would be a waste not to live in the most special part of this special city.

"I'll take it!" I say. The current tenant beams with astonished relief. He gives me the contact info of the landlords to finalise the arrangement, and I return to my temporary home at the hospital.

Contentment cautiously wriggles its way into my cells. Letting myself feel nice emotions doesn't come easily. My faith is frail, now that I know what it feels like to break and mend and break again, be blasted into shards, time after time.

Seventy-Seven

This story ends with a beginning.

I move into the downtown studio apartment. Being a writer was a childhood dream of mine. I loved playing with words and floating to the faraway places they took me when I'd read. My first night in the tiny apartment, I lay on my small thrift store mattress, springs poking into my back. I stare at the ceiling, and it occurs to me: I now have something to write about. *Psychonaut* was born. The title idea at the time was *Pieces of What Peace Is,* and I began to work on bringing the book to life the day after moving into my new space.

Fin.

Author's Note

I thought writing a novel would take a few months. The process began with notes on paper of all the things I wanted to include. Next, I typed them out in chronological order. Half a year later, it was almost starting to resemble a true book. But the result was messy and poorly articulated. So, I revised it. Then I revised it again, and again. I've lost count on how many times I've gone over the manuscript. Adequately expressing my experiences was no easy task. It was often overwhelming, and I struggled to persevere. Will the prose ever be good enough? Will this even be interesting or helpful to anyone? What are the chances of getting published? If it does get read, will the stigma that surrounds mental illness just bring more ostracization into my life? Why bother? I kept at it though.

Three years later, I was satisfied enough with the prose to finally print out the manuscript. Two days after that, I started a new job, painting a house. As I was making small talk with my new co-worker, I asked him what his dream job would be. "An editor," he replied. The Universe delivered me to an aspiring editor that had travelled and studied psychology, and I to him. He was delighted to help. So, with him, I went over the book, again. A little over a year later, we finished the initial revisions.

I have remained on medication and have gradually returned to my whole self. I have stayed well for the past seven years and am confident that I will stay well. When I look back on those years of sickness, I can barely relate to the person ravaged by schizoaffective bipolar disorder. It feels like a nightmare that I am very lucky to have woken up from. In the last seven years, I've had meaningful jobs, travelled to other exotic lands, and gone to college. I am in love, in a happy relationship, with a wonderful man. His name is Lynx — yes, the same Lynx from early on in the story. I apologize for the fairy-tale ending.

The chapter of my life where I was ill is still bewildering and traumatic to look back on. I can hardly believe how sick I was. But it's made me stronger and given me deep appreciation for the simple things in life. As challenging as it was to stay optimistic while writing Psychonaut, it was also profoundly cathartic and healing. I am proud of myself for seeing it through. Composing this memoir was my attempt at alchemy.

I hope you enjoyed the read.

CPSIA information can be obtained
at www.ICGtesting.com
Printed in the USA
BVHW070715171221
623984BV00001B/3